Praise for *Spells for Tough Times*

"A Goddess and God-send during these rough and troubling times. Whether you want to rid yourself of an abusive relationship, avoid legal entanglements, or deal with fire, flood, or famine, *Spells for Tough Times* is a potent change element that can help you do just that! Hats off to Kerri Connor for seizing the moment and giving us a terrific hands-on spellbook that is both insightful and valuable!"

—Sirona Knight, author of *Runes* and *Enchantress Awaken!*

"This extensive magical compendium should be a basic text for any householder. It covers the problems and mishaps that we all face, in a practical and useful way. Every reader will find something of value in this book."

—Ellen Evert Hopman, Druid Priestess
and author of the *Priestess of the Forest* trilogy

"Kerri Connor shares active spells that blend the magical with the mundane. *Spells for Tough Times* is steeped in ethical considerations, acknowledges financial and logistical limitations, and remembers that we have to take practical steps to get our magic to work. Connor shows us how to bring a spiritual approach to our down-to-earth daily lives, and I think her book is going to be a favorite for years to come."

—Ashleen O'Gaea, author of *The Portable Spell Book*

"If you have issues and haven't been able to find a spellbook that deals with them, look no further. *Spells for Tough Times* is chock-full of practical, sensible, and easy-to-use magical help for whatever is dragging you down. Kerri Connor speaks from the heart and writes from the soul. Everyone will want a copy of this book for their magical tool kit."

—Deborah Blake, author of *Everyday Witch A to Z Spellbook*
and *Witchcraft on a Shoestring*

Spells for TOUGH TIMES

About the Author

Kerri Connor is the author of *The Pocket Spell Creator: Magickal References at Your Fingertips* (a New Page Books bestseller), *The Pocket Guide to Rituals: Magickal References at Your Fingertips* (New Page Books), *The Pocket Idiot's Guide to Potions* (Alpha Books), and *Goodbye Grandmother* (Wyrdwood Publications).

Kerri is the High Priestess of The Gathering Grove and has been practicing her craft for twenty-five years. She has been published in several magazines and newsletters including *The Blessed Bee, Sage Woman, PanGaia,* and *New Witch.* She is the former editor of *The Circle of Stones Journal.* Currently she runs the website *The Pagan Review* (www.facebook.com/pages/The-Pagan-Review/100387167714) on behalf of The Gathering Grove as well as the Witch Hat Society, Northeast Illinois chapter. A graduate of the University of Wisconsin, Kerri holds a B.A. in Communications. Kerri lives with her husband, children, cats, and chickens in rural Illinois. She loves reading, writing, gardening, and the Chicago Bears.

Spells for

TOUGH TIMES

Crafting Hope When Faced with Life's Thorniest Challenges

KERRI CONNOR

Llewellyn Publications
Woodbury, Minneosta

Book design by Bob Gaul
Cover art: Tree © iStockphoto.com/Stanislav Pobytov
      Rose © iStockphoto.com/nicoolay
      Pentagram © Llewellyn Art Department
Cover design by Kevin R. Brown
Editing by Laura Graves

Llewellyn is a registered trademark of Llewellyn Worldwide Ltd.

  ISBN 978-0-7387-2728-8

Llewellyn Publications
A Division of Llewellyn Worldwide Ltd.
2143 Wooddale Drive
Woodbury, MN 55125-2989

Printed in the United States of America

For the Earth Elements family
and The Gathering Grove

Contents

Part Three: Relationships

Part Four: Pets

Part Five: Health

Part Six: House and Home

Part Seven: Career and Work Life

Part Eight: Finances

Part Nine: Legal Problems

Part Ten: World

Part Eleven: Death

Introduction

*L*ove and money.

You can always easily find a spell for these two topics. They are everywhere—just try an Internet search and there will be hundreds of spells to choose from. But these two things are all these spells are good for, drawing them to you. They don't help you deal with specific situations, and that just isn't good enough.

Other topics aren't as easy to find. Try looking for a spell to help you deal with the angst of your child bringing home F's on a report card, or housebreaking the new puppy. What about a spell designed to help you get along with your mother-in-law?

What if you are going through an extremely difficult time? What spells or rituals are out there to help you with the specifics of life-altering crises such as the death of a loved one, loss of a job, or the loss of your home—whether it be through fire, flood, or foreclosure?

These are the very specific occurrences people often need the most help with, yet they are also the events for which very few spells can be found.

You can find general spells to boost your happiness, but sometimes you need something far more specific, personal, and powerful. We are often told the most powerful spells are the most specific spells, yet these types of spells are also the most difficult to find. If you've just lost your job and house, is a spell to draw happiness going to do you much good? Probably not.

Often when things start to bother us, or worse, go terribly wrong, we don't think to include our spirituality as part of the answer. I know, because I've done the same thing myself. I had gone to the Goddess and God for so many things in my life, so many wants, yet when it came down to it, I realized that when it came to my actual *needs*, I was ignoring all of them. For years I did not think to consult with my deities on things I was taught I should be able to deal with on my own. Asking for help meant I was weak.

Through some of the biggest challenges in life, I never thought to include Her or Him in them. I never thought to use my magic in a way that would truly help me.

I realized that by only dealing with these problems in the mundane world, I was missing out. I was limiting the spirituality and magic in my life at the times when I needed them the most. I began looking around to see what was already out there. I couldn't find what I needed, though; the specifics weren't there. Yes, I could find spells for patience, or help getting a job, but I wanted more. I felt that without specifics, I was putting a pinky finger bandage on a knife wound. It just wasn't nearly enough to get the job done.

I spoke with friends, asking them what they needed spells for—what problems they have in their lives that weren't being addressed by spell books or through websites they visited for answers. The result of these conversations, combined with my own experiences, brought about this book. In here are specific spells to help you deal with crises in your life. No matter their size, we all have problems, and we all have to learn how to ask for—and accept—the help the universe has floating around for us.

The spells in this book are classified into categories such as self, family, work, etc. In each section you will find several spells dealing with very specific situations you may find yourself in. Perform the spell that most closely relates to your situation and feel free to personalize it further if you need to: add names when necessary, begin the spell by stating your specific problem out loud, and add pictures or items to represent the problem. Make these spells your own.

While not every problem is completely fixable, every problem can be effectively dealt with—sometimes we just need help dealing with the things we can't control. However, many problems can be fixed; where we can fix those problems, we will!

Some people have the same problem I did—dealing with problems only in the mundane and not in the magical, while others did the opposite: dealing with matters only in the magical realm and leaving the mundane to fend for itself. Spells and rituals should be the starting point when working on your problems, not the ending point. What this means is: don't do a spell once and expect your problems to disappear. We know the best way to help a spell along its way is to back up whatever we do magically with work in the mundane world as well. You can't do one without the other and expect the best possible results. If you are working on something in the magical world, you need to be working on it in the mundane world as well. I can't emphasize this enough, and though it may sound like common sense to some, to others the idea is foreign.

A few years ago, I met a woman whose coven met once a month to celebrate the full moon. During their rituals they would do some spell work and each month one member performed a spell to win the lottery. However, as the saying goes, you have to play to win. This person was expending energy on working spells on a monthly basis to win a lottery, but had *never even purchased a ticket!* She firmly believed the universe would find a way to provide her not only with a ticket, but a winning ticket, at that. Perhaps the universe was *trying* to provide her with a winning ticket. Perhaps the universe wanted her to stop at the convenience store to pick up a gallon of milk on her way home from work, and at the same time actually buy a lottery ticket. But no, she refused to buy a ticket, saying the universe would provide. Unfortunately, this just isn't how magic works. Again, in order to get the best results from our magical work, we must back it up with work in the mundane world. These workings help the magic do its thing. If we don't do this work in the mundane world, we are only sabotaging the work we did with our magic. Mundane and magical need to go hand in hand in order to achieve the best results.

If you aren't sure where to start working on a problem in the mundane world, don't be afraid to ask! Use the Internet to do searches and find resources to help you out. If it is a serious matter, check with your local crisis center or United Way agency. There is help out there—you just have to learn how to find it and apply it to your particular situation.

I also want to add that you will notice some of these spells have a long list of ingredients. All the items should be available at your local metaphysical store or health food stores and I focus on using ingredients that can be used in several different kinds of spells. Once you fill up your witch's cupboard, you will be good to go for quite some time. Stones and candles can be picked up on an as-needed basis, and I recommend using the "chime" candle size candles; you can usually find them very cheaply. Also be sure to check stores for post-holiday sales to find votives and tapers at clearance prices.

If you can't find every single listed ingredient, don't fret! Work with what you have, because the most important tool in your workings is you. You and your mind.

Quite unfortunately, I have experienced many of the problems in this book. Those I have not personally experienced, I have helped friends deal with when they encountered their obstacles. While writing this book, several crises came up in my life that I had not thought to include here. After they occurred, I realized they needed to be included. I feel I encountered these problems just when I did so I would be able to include them and therefore help others who end up experiencing the same problems.

Needless to say, my hard times ended up stretching out the time it took to actually write this book—far longer than I had expected. While writing this book, my oldest cat got a bladder infection, I found a job, injured my knee so badly I had to quit that job, my son attempted suicide, my daughter's friend committed suicide, my sister and an aunt died, and literally days after writing the spell for "My best friend passed away," my own did—just to name a few. It was a difficult time, in fact the most difficult months of my life. But time goes on and we have to adjust to our new settings.

With all the problems in the world these days, we could use all the help we can get. People know this is true and so now, more than ever, people who never would have imagined they would ever cast a spell are trying it out. Therefore, this book is written for experienced practitioners and neophytes alike.

If you feel the need, you can add to these spells to really personalize them. Different traditions do things differently, so it is ultimately up to you what you feel works best. While most of the correspondences I use have come from my own experience over the past twenty-five years, your experiences may be different. If you want to substitute herbs, stones, colors, or whatever, check the bibliography at the end of this book for more resources to help you in your spell work.

Certain affirmations, meditations, and spells can be done in the shower for a few reasons. For starters, there's the peace and quiet—people aren't usually harping on you while you are in the shower. It gives you a chance to be relaxed and at one with yourself. There's nothing to distract you…unless you take too long and the water turns cold! Other than that, it's a very quiet, personal place. Also, consider the aspect of what the shower represents—it is a place of cleansing. The old is washed away. You leave a shower feeling fresh and renewed. I highly recommend many of the spells (especially in the Self section) be done while in the shower. Give yourself a fresh start. If you would like to use candles in any shower spell, be sure it's in some kind of container. I use votives and keep the candles on the shower shelves out of the way of the water.

Some of the spells in this book require doing a banishing. The directions I give tell you to go clockwise, but if you and/or your tradition prefers for you to perform banishing counterclockwise, feel free to reverse the direction.

Other spells you may notice call for moon water. If you are not familiar: moon water is simply made by filling a clear glass bottle with fresh spring water and placing it outside under the full moon to allow the moon to charge the water. You can make extra-special moon water under a blue moon, or even during a lunar eclipse.

While some of these spells give you an optimal day, moon phase, etc. for performing the spell, the most important aspect is that you perform the spell when it is needed the most.

It is also extremely important to remember that when you are in a dire emergency, your crisis needs to be dealt with in the mundane world first—whether this is through local authorities, medical help, crisis centers, interventions, etc. This book is *not* a substitute for the actions you take in the mundane world; it is magical work you do *in addition* to the mundane work you must undertake to deal with these problems.

If you have questions, don't hesitate to ask. My contact information is in the About the Author page of this book. I truly believe the best way to help ourselves is to help each other.

Part One

★ ★ ★ ★

SELF

I always have too much to do
and not enough time to do it

This really is the story of my life: I have too much to do, all the time. The house and kids alone end up taking up a lot of it, but I also work part-time as an assistant manager in a retail store. I write, run the Gathering Grove, which requires a bit of prep work for group rituals, volunteer for different nonprofits, run *The Pagan Review*, run my own charity called Nurturing Necessities to help families with things like clothing and other items (especially for babies), and I'm sure there are a ton of other things I can't think of off the top of my head right now!

I always have so much to get done and often a limited amount of time in which to do them. Sometimes things end up falling to the side while I work on something that in one moment may be far more important. There just isn't enough time in the day for me to get everything done that I need to on a daily basis, no matter how well I budget my time.

Sure, sometimes things are easier and there just isn't much to get done, but most of the time, I have to admit, my life is so terribly hectic I often wonder what I was thinking when I got involved with everything in the first place. I crave, action though, and like to be kept busy. I suffer physically and emotionally when I don't have a lot going on. How do I manage to get it all done? Where do I find the energy and time? Some days, I don't. Some days I just don't want to think about all that I have to do and I push it all aside. Those are the bad days because delaying always leads to having twice as much to do the next day.

To give myself the extra edge I needed in order to get everything done, I came up with this quick mini-meditation spell to do in the morning. I admit, I don't always do it myself, and when I don't, I suffer the whole day always with that nagging feeling that I'll never finish everything I should. I do this meditation in the shower—because it's seriously the only time I have some days! I'm all about multi-tasking, so while I'm washing my hair in the shower, I can also use that time to do this meditation. As a result, it helps keep me on track in getting my work done for the rest of the day.

Don't expect changes to be instantaneous—like everything worth having in life, you will have to work at this problem and remember to do the given affirmation throughout the day to help you along your way. Once you get into the habit of doing this every day, you will notice a difference in how much you can accomplish in just a day's time.

For this spell you will need:

• rose oil

• your shower

Take your shower as you normally would. Before you get out, find a comfortable spot under the running water. You may stand, sit, use a shower chair, or whatever will help make you comfortable. Take your rose oil and sprinkle just a couple of drops in an area near you where the water does not hit directly so it isn't immediately washed away. You may want to sprinkle it on the shower wall opposite the shower head. The fragrance will be released into the air, but won't quickly wash away.

Let the scent wash over you and relax you. Close your eyes (this may be easier done sitting so you don't sway or get dizzy). Feel the water wash over you.

Say the following to yourself, or even quietly out loud:

Today I have enough time.
Today I will get done the things
that need to be accomplished today.
If there is something I do not finish today,
it was not yet meant to be done.
Today I have enough time
to finish what I need.

Repeat this at least three times. As you inhale the scent of the rose oil, feel the water wash away any negativity or stress—especially if these feelings are associated with your plans for the day. Know that these feelings are being washed away and carried down the drain. You are taking everything in stride. You are counting on the universe to let everything fall into place as it should.

Once you feel comfortable, relaxed, and ready to start your day, leave the shower to start your day on a fresh foot.

I'm having problems concentrating lately

This is one of those problems that seems to pop in and out of my life with really no rhyme, reason, or explanation. One day I'm fine, and the next I'm a complete scatter-brain. Whether it's related to hormones or the fact that dementia runs in my family, I don't know. I just know that some days I wake up and can't focus on anything. On those days, I feel like life is spinning around me and if I could only reach out and grab on to something, I would be fine, but my arms seem to be tied down at my sides. My brain tries to focus, concentrate, and recover, but it's not working.

When I have this feeling, nine times out of ten it begins first thing in the morning. I can climb out of bed and forget to have my coffee. Yes, it's that bad at times, but it also lets me know right away when I am going to be having one of those difficult days where forming a complete thought—and actually retaining it for more than fifteen seconds—is going to be just out of reach. When I feel those kinds of days have begun, I do what any sane person would do—hop in the shower, of course.

I like to multi-task, and this particular problem is well suited to be solved with a spell in the shower. I can wash away both the confusion and the brain cloud that seems to have invaded my head.

For this spell you will need:
- azurite
- a brown candle (optional)
- your shower

You are going to charge the azurite while in the shower and keep it with you the rest of the day. If you have the right kind of shelving in your shower, you may even be able to bring in a brown candle to help increase your concentration.

Once you have everything you need, go ahead and shower normally. When you are done and ready to move on, light the candle (if you are able to include one) and grab hold of your azurite. Stand underneath the shower with the water running over your head. Clasp the azurite in both of your hands. As you stand there, say:

Let the water wash away
the clutter in my mind.
Charge this stone
with the power to
help me to focus
and concentrate on what is at hand.

Repeat this as many times as needed until you feel the stone is charged and your mind feels steady and ready to go. Finish your shower. For the rest of the day, keep the azurite with you. If you start having problems concentrating, take a quick break. Hold the azurite again and imagine yourself back in the shower with the water washing away the clutter and confusion. Feel the azurite filling you with clarity and giving you the power to concentrate.

You may have to perform this spell daily for a while so the azurite can be continually charged. The more focus and concentration you take from it during the day, the more often you will need to recharge it.

I find myself daydreaming more and more often

I will be the first to admit that life just sucks sometimes. We get bogged down with work, the house, the spouse, the kids, the bills; suddenly it seems like everything is going wrong. Sometimes you just want to escape, but a real vacation would take money and/or other resources that you likely don't have lying around. If you did, chances are you wouldn't be so stressed out thinking life sucks in the first place.

You might daydream about being another person or being in another place. Maybe you fantasize about being rich. Maybe you fantasize that you have a dream job—you are an actress, a best-selling writer, or the director of a blockbuster movie. Maybe you dream you are romantically involved with a hot actor who plays a crime-solving best-selling writer.

Daydreams or fantasies every now and then are normal. But if you notice yourself slipping into a pattern where you are daydreaming more and more, there may be something else going on in your life. Perhaps you are getting sidetracked and need the relief of a little fantasy indulgence. If you need some help focusing on your life back in the real world, this spell is for you. However, if you find that this spell doesn't help you out, you may need to speak with a counselor or therapist about what might be going on.

For this spell you will need:
- a brown candle for grounding and concentration
- a bowl of grapes for grounding and focusing mentally
- a bowl of celery, cut into snack-sized pieces

Place the items on your altar and cast your circle.

Begin by saying:

Fantasy and reality
sometimes become blurred.
My mind tends to wander,
not wanting to deal with the here and now.
Instead, I find comfort in a world of make-believe.
I need to refocus, re-center.

Light the brown candle and say:

The flame of this candle
captures my attention.

Staring into the flame,
I find I am able to concentrate.
I ground my energies,
bringing them back into me
instead of sending them outward
into the world of make-believe.

Spend some time meditating while staring into the candle flame. Focus simply on focusing. Do not allow your mind to wander. To focus on focusing is your goal. This is harder than it sounds. Don't let other thoughts enter your mind. Stay in the here and now. Feel yourself in the present moment, know that all you are doing is staring into the flame of the candle. When you feel you are successfully able to stay in the here and now without your mind wandering, you may stop.

Take the bowl of grapes. Hold them out in front of you above the altar. Say:

Charge these grapes with the power
to help ground me;
to help focus my mental abilities
on the task I will have at hand.

See the power of focus traveling through you into the bowl of grapes. Feel the grapes filling with the power to help you focus.

Take the bowl of celery. Hold it out in front of you above the altar. Say:

Charge this celery with the power
to help ground me;
to help focus my mental abilities
on the task I will have at hand.

Again, see the power of focus traveling through you into the bowl of celery. Feel the celery filling with the power to help you focus. When you are finished, extinguish your candle and close your circle.

In the future, when you catch yourself drifting off into your imagination too much, you may pick from the three items you have just charged. You may want to eat some grapes while focusing into the flame of the brown candle. At work, you may be unable to use the candle, but you can snack on the grapes and celery at your desk.

When using the candle again, say the following to help you focus:

> *Staring into the flame,*
> *I find I am able to concentrate.*
> *I ground my energies,*
> *bringing them back into me*
> *instead of sending them outward*
> *into the world of make-believe.*

When eating either the grapes or the celery, chant to yourself:

> *Ground and focus.*

to help bring you back to the present.

I am overly sensitive and I know it, but I can't seem to stop it

Whether it's due to a woman's time of month or some other cause, every now and then it seems like every little thing gets to us far more than it should. If you have this problem frequently, you should see a medical professional. Sometimes, though, we have bad days and it seems like the world is out to get us, or it feels like everything is bugging us more than it should.

Even if you are under the care of a medical professional for something of this nature, this spell can help you relax and build a "thicker skin" so things won't bother you as much.

This spell is perfect for performing in the shower.

For this spell you will need:
- your shower
- amber oil for self-confidence, stability, and peace

Begin the spell by sprinkling a few drops of amber oil into an area of the shower where the water will not hit it directly and wash it away.

Inhale the scent of the amber oil, feel it relaxing you, becoming a part of you. The scent encircles you, shrouding you in a protective barrier. "See" this barrier forming in your mind's eye. Only the water can pass through. Nothing else can dent or even scratch this barrier. The water of the shower washes away any discomfort you are having. Any feelings that are bothering you are washed away, swirling down the drain.

As you envision this happening, chant to yourself:

I am cleansed.
I am protected.
I am at peace.

Feel yourself growing stronger and braver. Continue chanting until you feel your barrier is completely built and solid. Though you will still notice what goes on around you, the little things will no longer be able to break through the barrier.

This spell may take some practice to get right. You have to learn to focus on creating the barrier in your mind and seeing it all around you. You also have to focus on letting the water wash away all that you want to lose. Allow the scent of the amber to surround and guide you, and this will help you greatly in successfully performing this spell.

Any time you wake up feeling like you're going to have one of "those days," go ahead and perform this spell. To give it an added boost throughout the day, carry a small bottle of amber oil with you. Inhale the scent when needed or put a dab onto your pulse points. If you feel you need it, add in a chant of:

I am cleansed.

I am protected.

I am at peace.

I need to stop procrastinating

I am truly a great procrastinator and have had many, many years of practice. In high school and college, I often waited until the night before papers or other projects were due to even start on them. I always told myself that I work best under pressure, which is often true, but at the same time, I was creating a whole lot of stress for myself I really didn't need. Part of the time I was attending college, I had three young children—all under the age of five—and was trying to make ends meet besides. The last thing I really needed was to add more stress, yet for some reason I kept on doing it.

This spell will help you drop the barrier that makes you procrastinate, for that's exactly what procrastination is—a barrier between you and what needs to be done. When looking at it this way, procrastination is something that can be destroyed. This spell is going to help us blow the barrier away so nothing stands between us and our final goal.

This is another shower spell. Why? Water can be a very destructive force—just look at the Grand Canyon! If it can carve out a gorge that size, well, a little bit of procrastination is simple child's play.

For this spell you will also need:
- some lemon oil for mental and physical energy
- dried columbine for willpower
- cheesecloth or another thin material through which water
  will easily pass, but not the columbine

Tie the columbine in the cheesecloth or other material, let it run under the water for about a minute to get it good and wet. Add a few drops of lemon oil to it. Place it in an area of your shower where the water will not hit it directly.

As you stand in the shower, visualize the water washing away at the barrier. As the water beats down on it, the barrier breaks apart. Bits and pieces fall off, some small, some large chunks. They dissolve in the very presence of the water. Inhale the scent of the columbine and lemon. Feel it working its way through you. The lemon is clearing your mind, attacking the barrier too. It builds up your energy, charging and revitalizing you. The columbine boost your willpower. As you stand in the shower visualizing all of this, chant:

The barrier breaks down.
My mind and body are fully charged,
ready to take on my task at hand.

Feel yourself growing stronger and more anxious to get started on your project. The barrier is washed away, leaving nothing between you and your goal, only the steps needed to get there.

When you are ready, finish your shower and get moving right away on the project you need to do. This spell may take some practice before it is completely successful. You may need to practice the visualizations until you have them down pat so this spell will become easier for you to perform. Once you get the hang of it, use it any time you feel that barrier of procrastination going up again.

I'm always sad

As the parent of a child who suffers from depression, I know firsthand how serious the problem is. I cannot emphasize enough how essential it is for anyone suffering from depression to seek the help of a mental health professional. I almost lost my son. The tragedy depression can create is life-altering and earth-shattering.

Life is a precious gift, but depression can make people forget that. It can make people forget all the good things that have ever happened to them, and make them feel as if nothing good will ever happen to them again. Though this isn't true, if you are suffering from depression, it surely feels like it is true.

I have found that depression is contagious, in a way. When my son is having a particularly hard time, it affects me too. In fact, as I write this, he is currently back in the hospital. This time, however, he realized he needed help and went on his own. While I am very happy and proud that he has come far enough to realize when things are getting too overwhelming for him and that he needs some help, it saddens me greatly that he is again in the hospital because of how bad he feels. When I know he is *that* sad, it makes me sad too. Getting out of that funk, no matter how temporary it may be, is difficult.

Often people don't notice when they are slipping into a depression, and many times, people who are in deep depression don't seem to know it at all. The key is to try to catch it before it worsens, to realize what exactly is happening. Then we can take the steps needed to counteract the sadness.

Chances are your mental health professional will want you to undertake counseling and probably take a prescription besides. There is nothing wrong with that whatsoever. Sometimes we need a little help to help us get through the day. It's not a sign of weakness. It's a sign of illness, and like most illnesses, it can be successfully treated if you give it a chance.

However, you can do more than counseling and medication. You can work spells to help you feel better. Spells to help you realize when you are getting too depressed. Spells to help you see things in a better, more clear light—a light that doesn't cast shades of gray everywhere you turn.

This is another spell that will take place in the shower—you are going to want to wash the blues away. At the end of your daily shower, you will spend a couple of minutes rinsing your slate clean and recharging yourself for the day ahead of you.

For this spell you will need:
· amber oil for stability
· hyacinth oil for happiness
· your shower

Begin this spell when you have finished your normal shower routine. Take the amber and hyacinth oil and sprinkle a few drops in the shower in an area that will not be in the shower's spray directly. You will want about six or seven drops of each to build a good, potent scent in your shower.

Stand under the running water and chant:

> *Cleanse me.*
> *Wash away the sadness,*
> *wash away the pain.*
> *Cleanse me.*
> *Wash away the blueness*
> *like ever-loving rain.*

Because of the little rhyme in this chant, you may feel a rhythm and beat start—let it take you. Feel the rhythm, feel the rhyme. These are tools that will help uplift you.

Visualize the clear water running over you and washing a blue sadness away. Watch as the water swirls around the drain and then disappears. See the blueness of the water. How blue is it? Is it a deep, dark blue? This color represents an extremely profound sadness. Lighter blue is still sadness, but the pain isn't as severe. Continue chanting, feel the pain wash away. Watch as the water becomes lighter and lighter blue.

Inhale the scent of the amber and hyacinth. Let them bind to help cleanse you and build you back up. Feel yourself becoming more stable, happier. Your emotions begin to level off as the blue water turns clear once again.

You may want to make a tape or CD to play while you are performing this spell in the shower. You can add uplifting music or simply talk yourself through the process. Tell yourself that the water is running clearer. Tell yourself that you are feeling better, and that you feel the sadness leaving your body. Replace the sadness with happiness. Continue the chant until the water runs clear.

This is a spell you will probably need to repeat daily when you are having a rough time. Sometimes these bursts of sadness go away quickly, other times they can hang on for a while. Just remember to keep doing what your doctor recommends and work this spell every morning for as long as needed. The first few times, you may feel like you felt better only while in the shower, but then the sadness rushes back as soon as you get out. This is normal and doesn't mean you performed the spell incorrectly, it just means that the sadness right now is stronger. You can turn that around by continuing to perform the spell every day. The power of positivity will eventually overtake negativity; the effects of your spell will be longer lasting.

I feel like everything I do turns out wrong

Just the other day my son said these words to me. They are painful to hear, but even more painful to say.

Do you ever have one of those days when nothing seems to be going right? Does it seem like these days are coming more frequently with fewer and fewer good days in between? This can be a sign of depression, and if it isn't depression yet, it can easily develop into it. If it seems everything you try to do either fails or backfires almost every day, it can very quickly build up into a case of depression that may need a mental health professional's help to overcome. I too have these days on occasion, and when I get into the "everything I touch turns to crap" mood, what I really want to do is crawl into bed, pull the covers up over my head, and just hide until I feel better. Doing so, however, isn't going to get me to work to pay the bills, feed the kids, or cuddle the kitties, and it's certainly not going to get the laundry done. Hiding under the covers just means when I do come back out, I'll have all my regular work to get done, plus everything I missed while I was attempting to escape into the oblivion of my comforter.

Sometimes these feelings get to be a bit much. They can overwhelm you sometimes and you may need some help getting rid of them and giving yourself the opportunity to start over, fresh from scratch. This spell is going to help you wash the slate clean and get that fresh start you so desperately long for.

Since we want to wash away our bad feelings, it will take place in the shower.

For this spell you will need:
- your shower
- lemon oil to stimulate the cleansing process for a
  "mind scrub"
- amber oil to help boost your self-confidence

Finish your normal shower routine and then add a few drops of the lemon oil to an area of your shower out of the spray.

Stand underneath the running water and visualize the water washing away all your negative feelings. Inhale the lemon scent and feel it cleansing the inner you. Imagine the negative feelings being pulled out of you and washed away down the drain. Your mind, body, and soul are all being thoroughly cleansed. Any and all mistakes you made in the past are disappearing. Their existence is being completely washed away. They are no longer. As you visualize this, say:

The slate is washed clean,
my mind is new and pure.
My mistakes in the past are gone,
washed away,
with the water down the drain.

Continue this chant for a minute or two. Feel yourself becoming revitalized and refreshed. The old mistakes are gone. The path ahead is clear for you to begin again. Pour a few drops of the amber oil, again into an area of your shower not directly hit by water.

Inhale the scent of the amber oil. Feel it filling your body, mind, and soul. The amber brings self-confidence. You are being renewed and refilled with self-confidence. You have the ability to do what must be done and to do it right. You will excel and succeed at whatever you try.

As you inhale the scent of the amber, say:

Fill me with light,
fill me with strength.
My confidence has returned.
Success is at hand.

Again, continue this chant for a minute or two. When you fully feel your new potential, go ahead and leave the shower. Start your day on a fresh foot.

I keep having nightmares

Unfortunately for some of us, the only dreams we remember are the nightmares. I had this problem for years before I realized I could do something about it.

In this spell you will create a dream bag to keep under your pillow to help keep nightmares at bay.

For this spell you will need:

• a small drawstring bag—organza bags work well— one in lavender, white, or black would be best

About a teaspoon of each of the following herbs (you can also use a couple of drops of the essential oil in place of some of the herbs):

• amber for peace

• apple blossom for peace

• bergamot for peace and restful sleep

• celery seeds for restful sleep

• chamomile for peace and restful sleep

• freesia for peace

• gardenia for peace

• hyacinth for protection and peaceful sleep

• jasmine for peaceful dreams and good sleep

• lavender for peace and sleep

• magnolia for peace

• mugwort for peaceful dreams

• narcissus for peace

• sweet pea for courage and strength

• tulip for dreams

• valerian for sleep, protection, and peace

• vervain for peace and protection

• violet for peace and sleep

Set up your altar and cast your circle. Prop the bag open on your altar. You may need to place the first herb in it to get it to sit upright. Add each herb as you say the following:

The dreams that come to me are unpleasant
and frightening.
I combine together these herbs,
their magic and scent,
to chase the nightmares away,
to bring me peace, protection, and a good night's sleep,
as I lay my head upon them.

Say this three times as you add all of the herbs. When you are done, tie it off and say:

Let my dreams
and myself be at peace.
I charge this magic with this task.
So mote it be.

Close your circle and place the bag under your pillow. Eventually the herbs will get old; you will need to replace them once their scent becomes too weak. Until then, not only will this bag help protect against nightmares, it will help relax you into peaceful sleep with its wonderful scent.

Part Two

★★★★

FAMILY AND
CHILDREN

My child is suffering from separation anxiety and it's tough on both of us

Separation anxiety often takes place when a child first goes off to school, but it can happen in other situations too, such as when a child is first going to sleepovers at friends' houses or if the parents have divorced and the child has to go back and forth between two homes. Some children will never have a problem with separation, and others may wait until they are headed off to college before that nervousness of not constantly being with mom and/or dad settles in.

My youngest child hated leaving his mommy to go on a visitation at his dad's. At two years old, he would throw tantrums and kick and scream, but court orders are court orders and they have to be followed. To this day (he is now seventeen), if I am gone for too long, he calls my cell phone to make sure everything is okay. It's quite a difference from my oldest son, who couldn't wait to be out on his own, away from his parents!

No matter their age, children sometimes take their cues from their parents—if the parent is nervous when the child is going to go away, the child may be too. Therefore, as parents we need to make sure none of the parties involved are nervous about the upcoming separation in order to make as smooth a transition as possible.

This spell combines protection, courage, and love, for both you and your child to carry when you are apart. If your child is willing, perform this spell together. If you do this spell on your own, you will give a pouch to your child when you are done—a figurative piece of your heart he or she can carry.

For this spell you will need:
- 2 square pieces of black material, about 6 inches
  (black for protection and absorbing negative energies)
- 2 pieces of black cording (12 inches each)
- teaspoon of blessed thistle (for protection)
- teaspoon of carnation petals (for protection, strength, and healing)
- 4 whole cloves (for protection, healing, and courage)
- ½ teaspoon whole cumin (for protection)
- ½ teaspoon dill seeds (for protection)
- ½ teaspoon mugwort (for protection and strength)
- a few drops of patchouli oil (for protection)
- large mortar and pestle

What you will do:

If you are doing this spell with your child, you will take turns adding each ingredient to the mortar and grinding it with the pestle, saying the given lines.

Add the blessed thistle to the mortar and grind it with the pestle (does not have to be finely ground) and say:

> *Blessed thistle, while we are apart*
> *protect the one I love, deep within my heart.*

When it is ground, pour it into the middle of each black square.

Add the carnation petals to the mortar and grind them with the pestle while saying:

> *Carnation petals, while we are apart*
> *give strength to the one I love, deep within my heart.*

Add this to the black squares.

Add the cloves to the mortar and grind them with the pestle while saying:

> *Spicy cloves so bold and strong, while we are apart*
> *give courage to the one I love, deep within my heart.*

Add this to the black squares.

Add the cumin to the mortar and grind it with the pestle while saying:

> *Spirited cumin, while we are apart*
> *protect the one I love, deep within my heart.*

Add this to the black squares.

Add the dill seed to the mortar and grind it with the pestle while saying:

> *Fragrant dill, while we are apart*
> *protect the one I love, deep within my heart.*

Add this to the black squares.

Add the mugwort to the mortar and grind it with the pestle while saying:

> *Mugwort of strength so bold,*
> *connect us together in a psychic hold.*

Add this to the black squares.

Take the patchouli and drip a few drops into each pile of ground herbs while saying:

As your scent surrounds,
so shall it protect.

Gather up all the sides and hold them together. Using the black cords, tie each pouch shut tightly. If you are doing this spell with your child, do these one at a time—one holding the pouch while the other wraps the cord and ties it off. Then switch, so the other person holds the pouch and the other person ties it off.

Together, hold a pouch close to your hearts and say:

My intentions are wrapped deep inside.
Safe you will be when you are away,
as you always carry my love with thee.

Exchange pouches and carry them when you are apart.

If you are doing this spell by yourself, give one pouch to your child and keep the other for yourself.

My child is doing poorly in school

One of the most difficult things for parents to do is watch their children struggle, and with school this can often be the case. While some kids seem to have everything come to them easily, other children can have a very difficult time grasping certain concepts.

Some children may grasp math instantly, while others (myself included) struggle day after day, semester after semester. Those same students who can't grasp mathematical equations may love history and be able to memorize facts and details as if they have a photographic memory. While some students never struggle at all, others struggle in all areas. No matter what subject or how many your child is behind in, this spell will help get him or her back up to speed again.

My youngest child had problems in school for many years. He needed extra help, attended summer school many years, but he just wasn't getting the hang of things. He wouldn't bring his homework home, and if he did, he would forget to do it, or even worse, do it…but then forget to turn it in! He was unorganized and unmotivated. It took a lot of work for us to help him; this spell came about to help him.

This spell is designed to help open your child's mind to being receptive to new concepts—including organization!—and to help him or her grasp and retain what's being taught.

This is a spell your child should know you are doing, and you should have his or her permission to cast it.

For this spell you will need:
- a yellow candle to represent intelligence, studying, communication, and examinations and tests
- a yellow ribbon
- a fireproof container, self-lighting charcoal tablets, and a lighter
- a piece of azurite for concentration
- 1 teaspoon black pepper
- 2 teaspoons celery seeds
- 4 teaspoons rosemary
- 4 teaspoons dried peppermint leaves
- 4 teaspoons dried lemon zest
- 1 teaspoon vanilla extract

- 3 drops tangerine oil
- 3 drops lily of the valley oil
- 3 drops honeysuckle oil

This spell should be done weekly on Wednesdays, the day best suited for spell work related to communication and intellectual pursuits. Combine the herbs and oils listed above. You may either grind them or simply blend everything together. The ingredients listed here will make a large supply you can keep in an airtight container, so you'll have all you need for future workings of this spell.

Set up your altar. Light the charcoal tablet and the yellow candle. Place the yellow ribbon and the azurite on your altar.

Cast your circle as you normally would. Sprinkle some of the incense onto the charcoal tablet. Take several deep breaths and visualize your child studying. If your child is joining you in this spell, have him or her do the same. Visualize your child studying and actually *absorbing* the material. See words float off of a text book page and swirl into the air above your child's head where it is then soaked in. Watch as equations lift off of paper and float into your child.

Take a pinch of the incense and drop it onto the lit charcoal tab. Say:

> *We call upon the spirits*
> *to guide my child in his/her*
> *intellectual pursuits.*
> *To open his/her mind*
> *in order to absorb, digest, and comprehend*
> *the materials he/she needs to learn.*

Sprinkle another pinch of incense onto the charcoal and say the following:

> *With each day,*
> *each learning experience,*
> *may more and more be retained.*

Hold the azurite in the smoke of the incense and say:

> *Charge this stone*
> *with the ability to increase mental acuity.*

Hold the yellow ribbon in the smoke of the incense and say:

Charge this ribbon
with the ability to increase mental acuity.

Spend some more time visualizing your child studying and bringing home good grades. Imagine what the report card looks like. See the happiness in your child's eyes for doing a good job in school.

When you are done visualizing, extinguish the candle and close the circle.

When your child is studying or doing homework, let him or her hold on to the ribbon in the hand not used for writing. That ribbon is there as a reminder. You can also burn some of the incense during study time. (This is why we made so much of it—to keep and use at later dates when studying.) Let your child carry the azurite to school in a pocket.

Remind your child that the spell is there to help, but ultimately he or she must also put the work in to be successful.

My child acts like she/he is scared of everything

We all have fears, and while some are generally considered reasonable, some become overwhelming and debilitating. When we see these type of behaviors in our own children, not only does it hurt them and ourselves, it can be incredibly difficult to help them get over those fears—especially if their fears happen to be reasonable ones. When a child takes fear to the extreme and becomes scared of just about everything, it is time to do some serious damage reversal.

This spell is designed to help give your child confidence and overcome his or her fears. You will need your child's permission in doing this spell, and your child should also participate as much as possible.

When my kids were young, not much really scared them—of course now that they are older they have fears I never imagined they would have. I have a 19 year-old who refuses to drive because she is afraid of getting into an accident. She took driver's ed and passed it, but needs fifty hours of driving practice and only has six because she simply refuses to drive. This has led to many problems within our family: trying to arrange rides for her, and becoming upset when we tell her to find her own ride. She has severe anxiety about cars in general. Why? About a month after her sixteenth birthday, a friend of hers (a new driver himself) was in an accident, and one of the passengers in his car was killed. So while her fear was based on a real, scary situation, it has taken over her life and made her totally dependent on others.

These types of fears are truly debilitating, making life a chore and miserable instead of being something to experience to the fullest. This spell is going to help you help your child overcome his or her fears. It is best performed as soon as you begin to notice consistent fear in your child. Breaking the hold the fear has on your child as soon as possible makes it far easier; don't give it time to fester, grow, and strengthen.

For this spell you will need:
· ribbons of black, gold (look for metallic gold ribbon,
  not yellow), and red

These ribbons are going to be braided into a bracelet (or necklace or anklet if you prefer) so you will need to figure out just how much you will need. Obviously if your child is young or doesn't know how to braid, you will do the braiding part instead.

Tie one end of the three ribbons together. As you braid, you and your child should chant together the following:

Black to protect me,
gold to make me strong,
red to give me courage
all the day long.

Continue this chant until the braid is long enough for whatever purpose you choose—be it bracelet, anklet, or necklace. Tie the other ends together and cut off any extra ribbon. You can then tie both ends together to form one continuous loop.

This spell is best completed on a Sunday to help bring about swift change, power, strength, and success for your child.

When doing this spell, keep the atmosphere upbeat. Explain to your child the two of you are making a special talisman of sorts that will help him/her be braver and less afraid. Let your child know that this new piece of jewelry is very special, but is also easily replaced if it gets too dirty from being worn, or if it is lost. You can always quickly make up a new one with the same chant that will hold the same special powers for your little one.

My child doesn't do his/her chores
and blows up when reminded

Chores can often be a struggle with children, no matter their age. Though we as parents may believe our kids are old enough to understand the importance of helping out around the house and learning responsibility, that doesn't mean *they* think the same thing!

The issues around chores can create a lot of tension and stress in a home for everyone. Kids often don't understand the reasons for chores and instead see them as a power or servitude issue—not an issue of learning responsibility, pride in doing a job well, or even about taking care of possessions so they will last a long time. Nope, not at all. They simply believe parents are using them as indentured servants. It could be "take out the garbage," "wash the car," or "pick up the fork off the floor." It's all the same—being a servant.

This spell will help you to explain to your child the importance of chores while also bringing peace to your home. As this spell involves your child, try to include him or her when doing it. It will not work nearly as well if you can't do this spell with your child. The key is to do this spell when no one is upset. Do not have an argument with your child and in the middle of the tensions demand you do this spell together or it won't work. In fact, you will likely make the situation worse.

Instead, when things are calm, tell your child you would like to work a spell together that will help the two of you get along better and understand one another in the future. If possible this spell should be done a Saturday, the best day for spells relating to peace in the home. Since weekends are often the time when a lot of chores do get done, it may be best to plan to do this spell early in the morning before chores or arguments have had chance to get started. The key to this spell being successful is that everyone gets their a chance to speak without being interrupted or corrected. It is *vital* you and your child both agree to this beforehand.

For this spell you will need:

Several different colored candles:

- black for defining boundaries
- green for neutralizing difficult situations
- brown for help with family issues
- pink for household peace
- sky blue for patience and understanding

You will also need one of each of the following stones:
· carnelian to stop apathy, fear, and rage
· obsidian to prevent negativity

Place the items on your altar. The candles should form a circle. Place the two stones inside. (Check the order of lighting the candles so that you can place them in the most convenient way as to avoid burning yourself.)

Cast your circle as you normally would. Begin lighting candles (you may take turns with your child or just have him or her help you say the following).

Light the black candle and say:

> *We light this candle to help us define boundaries.*

Light the green candle and say:

> *We light this candle to help neutralize our difficult times.*

Light the brown candle and say:

> *We light this candle to help us deal with family issues.*

Light the pink candle and say:

> *We light this candle to help us maintain*
> *peace in our home.*

Light the sky blue candle and say:

> *We light this candle to aid us in our patience and ability to*
> *understand one another.*

After all of the candles are lit, you and your child should hold hands and say together:

> *These stones we charge with our intent,*
> *to prevent negativity for and from one another*
> *and to dispel and disperse anger and apathy.*

At this time, you and your child may either remain standing, or get comfortable sitting on the floor. Just remember to continue facing one another, and continue holding hands. Each person will take turns and say to the other how they feel about the situation and why it is important to them.

For example, you may tell your child that it is important to you that chores be done without arguing because you want him or her to learn to be responsible and to learn respect. You might also point out things like such as your work schedule. Explain that while you understand your child has school to deal with, he or she may have more free time than you; you need some help.

Your child may mention independence and free time are important to him or her, a feeling of too much pressure to be responsible, or that he or she has too many chores to do. Remember that anything said in the circle is sacred and is not to be corrected. The circle gives you both a safe place in which to express your feelings.

That being said, this spell is not an excuse for a child to get out of doing chores! It is designed to help the two of you communicate better and to help eliminate arguing when chores need to be done.

When the spell is completed for the day, close your circle, extinguish the candles, and place the two stones in a central location in the house where they can be seen often and have the opportunity to disperse their energy into the environment.

You may have to repeated this spell several times—perhaps every Saturday morning before chores begin for a while. Soon you will both find you are far more understanding of each other's points of view.

My child's behavior is changing in a negative way (i.e., lying, disrespect, etc.)

Just about every parent will go through this at some point in their child-rearing lives, unless of course they really are raising perfect angels. The reasons for behavior changes and the extent to which a child's behavior changes, however, may be different. While some children are just trying to be their own person and assert their own independence and individuality, other kids may be facing more serious problems, such as drugs, drinking, or getting in with the "wrong" crowd. There may also be a chemical imbalance or mental illness involved, so it is important to also make sure you talk with professionals to make sure you are covering all the bases. It can be hard to know which situation you are dealing with, and it can be even more difficult figuring out exactly *how* to deal with that situation.

I have a son with severe mental illnesses, which has made my parenting life rather challenging at times. When he began acting out more than normal, things got scary. I couldn't trust him and he was very impulsive and unpredictable. It is a sad and tragic way for any family to have to live. We were dealing with mental illness topped with teenage rebellion, and a side order of lack of authoritative respect besides. Life was downright hard. As a parent, you may not be able to eat or sleep, or you might end up crying yourself to sleep at night wondering what on earth to do. How do you fix something that doesn't seem fixable? We went to doctors, counselors, therapists, behavior therapists, all kinds of specialists, and every one of them gave us the same answer—"I've done what I can, I can't do any more." It was frustrating to say the least; the people trained to deal with the extremely difficult cases lowered their heads, shrugged their shoulders, and mumbled "sorry," as they headed out the door.

Unfortunately, even without any sort of mental illness involved, in today's times, many kids are growing up without any respect for their parents or other authority figures. The easiest way to avoid problems such as this one in the future is to ensure your child is brought up to respect you from day one. Sometimes, though, even the best intentions and the best possible planning don't always work. Sometimes it seems as though you have the most absolutely perfect child one day, and the next, things seem to go suddenly, terribly wrong.

This is a difficult situation for both you and your child. To get things back on track is going to take some serious work, both magical and mundane. The magical work will help you through the mundane aspects you will need to put effort into.

This spell is best performed on a Saturday, the day for setting limitations and boundaries, and for a peaceful home. Since this is a very serious matter, you will want to plan to do it on several Saturdays.

You may notice there are quite a few ingredients needed for this spell; the reason is that we want to conjure up as much power and energy as possible.

For this spell you will need:

- dragon's blood incense to amplify the power of all the other ingredients

Several different colored candles:
- black for defining boundaries and absorbing negative energy
- blue for peace, healing, truth, honor, change, unity, and wisdom
- brown for stability, integrity, strength, and dealing with family issues
- green for its calming abilities, healing, growth, and neutralizing difficult situations
- orange for communication
- pink for harmony and household peace
- purple for growth, insight, and inner strength
- red for willpower, courage, and strength
- silver for balance, stability, and intuition
- sky blue for calmness, patience, and understanding
- white for cleansing, peace, healing, and truth

Several different stones. You will need two of each, separated into two glass, ceramic, or earthenware bowls to create two complete sets:
- agate for courage, strength, love, and protection
- carnelian for peace, courage, and to stop apathy, fear, and rage
- calcite for centering, grounding, peace, and to calm fears
- chrysocolla for wisdom, peace, love, and to aid communication
- hematite for its grounding and calming abilities

- kunzite to aid in communication and for peace, balance, and grounding
- moonstone for grounding, love, protection, harmony, and peace
- obsidian for grounding and preventing negativity
- onyx for emotional balance, self-control, and strength
- rhodochrosite for peace, calmness, love, and emotional balance

As you read over this list, you probably noticed the energies we will be working with and may have thought to yourself, "Oh yeah, I really need that!" about one thing or another, which is why they have been included. On another note, this type of problem brings out many kinds of emotions—the grounding and centering qualities are very important here.

Ideally, it would be great if your child wanted to do this spell with you, but considering its nature, there's a very good chance your child already doesn't want to spend any time with you and your spell, and will have no problem telling you that. Though it would be nice to be able to snap your fingers and make everything all better, or at least have your child understand what it means to you, that just isn't going to happen. Being able to deal with the changes your child is going through, deciding how you are going to react, and what actions you are going to take are essential components to how you deal with this problem. This spell will focus on those aspects.

Begin this spell by setting up the candles on your altar with one bowl of stones behind the line and one bowl of stones in front of that line. Line them up in the following order, left to right: green, sky blue, brown, black, blue, orange, pink, red, purple, silver, and white.

Open your circle as you normally would. Say the following:

> *Great Goddess and Great Father,*
> *I come to you as both your child and a parent myself.*
> *I seek your assistance, your strength, your help,*
> *in dealing with my own child who has gone off track.*
> *I know that people change, and though*
> *change can often be good,*
> *I feel the changes in my son/*
> *daughter to be negative in nature.*

I come to you for guidance, strength, and help in dealing
with the matters placed before me.

Light the green candle and say:

To bring calmness to my family and my home,
I light this candle.
As the flame burns, let it burn away negativity
and bring healing energies and growth
to myself and my family.

Light the sky blue candle and say:

To bring calmness to my family and my home,
I light this candle.
As the flame burns, let it bring patience and
understanding to myself and my family.

Light the brown candle and say:

To bring stability to my family and home,
I light this candle.
As the flame burns, let it bring integrity and strength to
myself and my family while dealing with our issues.

Light the black candle and say:

To absorb negative energies,
I light this candle.
As the flame burns, let it bring me the strength and wisdom
to set defined boundaries for myself and mine.

Light the blue candle and say:

To bring peace, wisdom, and honor,
I light this candle.
As the flame burns, let it bring healing energies,

> *change, unity, and truth*
> *to my family and myself.*

Light the orange candle and say:

> *To bring successful communication to my family,*
> *I light this candle.*
> *As the flame burns, let it bring the openness and*
> *honesty needed for members of my family to communicate*
> *effectively with one another.*

Light the pink candle and say:

> *To bring harmony to my family,*
> *I light this candle.*
> *As the flame burns, let it bring peace to our household.*

Light the red candle and say:

> *To instill me with strength and courage,*
> *I light this candle.*
> *As the flame burns, let it instill me with willpower, courage,*
> *and strength to meet the stressful and difficult days*
> *yet to come.*

Light the purple candle and say:

> *To bring me inner strength,*
> *I light this candle.*
> *As the flame burns, let it bring growth*
> *and insight to my problems at hand.*

Light the silver candle and say:

> *To bring me stability,*
> *I light this candle.*
> *As the flame burns, let it bring balance and*
> *the intuition needed to handle my problems at hand.*

Light the white candle and say:

> *To bring my family peace and truth,*
> *I light this candle.*
> *As the flame burns, let it be cleansing and healing.*

Allow yourself a few moments to meditate over what was said with the lighting of each candle.

Carefully pick up the bowl behind the line of candles and run it left to right through the candle smoke. Use a circular motion and go back to the left and then run through the smoke again, left to right. Do this a total of three times.

As you do this, say (three times):

> *My intents, as expressed through the lighted candles,*
> *I instill into these stones:*
> *bring us strength, harmony, peace,*
> *and comfort in our times of need.*

Place the bowl back in its location and do the same with the second bowl. When done spend a few more minutes meditating on what you have performed. Take a few more additional moments and vision your home as being peaceful: everyone is getting along and communicating, and everyone is happy.

When you have finished meditating on this, go ahead and close your circle.

Place one of the bowls of stones in a central location in your home, a place people either spend a lot of time in or travel through frequently. A living room is generally ideal, but if your child has taken to spending more time in his or her room than with the rest of the family, the kitchen may be the most ideal location. Keep the other bowl for yourself. When you need an extra boost, take out a stone that corresponds to the area you need the boost in, and carry it with you.

Remember that this spell won't necessarily change the way your child acts, however, it is going to help you have the strength and peace to deal with your child in a more positive light. Back up your work in the mundane world in whatever way you think is necessary, whether it means having your child taken in for a drug test or a psychiatric evaluation. You should now have the strength to follow through.

I'm happy to say that with this spell and a lot of hard work, my son and I have a much better relationship now.

My family refuses to accept my religious/spiritual choices

It can be very discouraging and depressing when our own family refuses to accept us for who we are. Whether it be an adult with siblings and parents who don't agree with our religious choices, or even a spouse or children, it can put quite a strain on family relations if they oppose the choices you have made.

My own parents are devoutly Christian and raised me as such for many years. Though I discovered my path while still living with them, I hid it from them for quite a while. My "coming out" to them didn't happen until I was thirty-three years old and had just sold my first book. Since it was a spell book, I had a bit of explaining to do. After explaining things to them and the rest of my family, they insisted I speak with their pastor too—which I did for their sake. None of them were going to change my beliefs nor change my mind about my beliefs so I saw no harm in it. In the long run, it made my parents feel better about my choice.

I won't say my parents are happy with my religion; they aren't, but they have learned that I am the same person I was before they knew what choices I had made. They don't wholeheartedly accept my choice, but they don't harp on me about it anymore either.

A brother of mine told other relatives not to come to my home for a graduation party for two of my boys—one from high school and one from eighth grade—because he claimed I was lying and that the party was really to celebrate my graduation from a witch school! Of course we were indeed celebrating the double graduation of my sons, but some people actually believed him that I would lie and lure people to my home under false pretenses. According to him "that's what witches do."

Needless to say, that brother doesn't accept my choices at all, and instead was openly hostile about them. We now keep the peace by simply having no contact that isn't necessary. If my dad wants me to call that brother and tell him something I will. I end up leaving messages on his answering machine anyway, since he won't pick up the phone when he sees it is me calling. In the long run, all this brother has done is cast (no pun intended) a more unfavorable impression on himself for his unwillingness to cooperate and attempt to be a family.

This spell isn't going to make your family members jump around with excitement because you are a witch (not unless they were already doing that), but it will help you to feel at ease with your choice and may help them see that you are who you are. The labels "Witch," "Pagan," "Druid," or whatever do not change who you are, they are only a part of who you are. You are a person of many facets, and this spell will help both you and your family accept that.

This spell is best performed on a Sunday as it relates to strength, healing, and spirituality. You will be doing some writing in this spell, so make sure you can get comfortable.

For this spell you will need:
- black paper (you may need more than one sheet)
- a white crayon
- lavender oil
- a fireproof container and lighter (you may also perform this
  spell in front of an outdoor fire)

Cast your circle. Using the black paper and white crayon, write a letter to your family. Tell them how you feel about their reactions to your spiritual choices. Explain to them why you made the choices you have. Explain to them why these choices are important to you. Explain that while their acceptance of your choices would be nice and make it easier for everyone to get along, their acceptance is not a necessity. Explain that you are your own person with your own thoughts, ideas, and beliefs. Let them know you understand their concerns, but that you are happy with the choices you have made. Let them know you appreciate them worrying about you, but *your* choices are *your* decisions. Write down everything you would like to be able to their faces if you knew they would truly listen and appreciate what you have to say.

When you are finished writing, shake, dab, or sprinkle lavender oil onto each page of your letter. Crumple each page and place into the fireproof container and light it on fire (or throw the pages into the bonfire). As the papers burn, your thoughts and ideas are released into the air. When you feel ready, close your circle.

Back up your work in the mundane world by not flaunting your choices in the face of your family. You don't have to hide, but don't be outrageously flamboyant either. Give them time to adjust and time to realize you are still the same person you were before you made your religious choices. Let them discover that you're still "you"—only better.

Often in these situations you have to make a "don't ask, don't tell"-type of agreement to keep the peace for a while. Eventually you may find your family has some questions and are more interested in learning than in condemning. When and if this time comes, be open and honest with your beliefs. While your beliefs may not always be accepted, chances are your family will learn to distinguish between you and your beliefs. They may not always be happy with your choices, but hopefully they will come around to being able to accept you.

My spouse is cheating on me

You've just found out your spouse is cheating. Most likely, you are either heartbroken and devastated, or seething with anger and wanting revenge. Though both of these reactions are quite normal, it is important to remember to not do anything rash at this point. Sure, you could look up on the Internet how to hex your spouse, but this probably isn't the safest route—especially if you are a believer in the threefold law or karma.

It won't be long before you will find yourself flip-flopping back and forth between numerous different feelings, not just the few listed here. You may feel it was your fault, your spouse's fault, your fault again, and back to the spouse's. You may first want a divorce, then counseling, then back to divorce, then again want counseling. You may want to know who the person was, and why, and in the next moment, want to totally forget it even happened. At the very least, you will feel massively confused.

Before you can decide what you want out of your spouse in this matter (Do you want him or her to leave? Do you want to be asked for forgiveness?) you must first figure out what you want from yourself—do you want to forgive? Do you want to be alone and start over? No matter how you look at it, cheating is damaging. It damages trust and it can also damage your self-esteem and your nerves.

My husband and I have been married for just over eleven years. He is my third husband. My first marriage lasted barely six months, and ended when he cheated. My second marriage lasted exactly three years—yes, our divorce was finalized on our anniversary. He too cheated. I know how it feels: the hurt, rage, and pain are awful, but you can overcome it and get your own life back on track. Your spouse has already stolen part of your past and your present by cheating on you. You need to take control of your life so your future won't be stolen too!

This spell is designed to heal some of that damage and give you back control over your own feelings, to give you back your self-esteem and confidence to make the right decisions.

For this spell you will need:
- one black candle
- one white candle
- ribbons about 18 inches long in sky blue, pink, and purple—
  make sure they are all the same width
- one piece of agate

- one piece of bloodstone
- one piece of carnelian

A pinch of each of the following herbs:

- allspice, amber resin, cedar, cloves, gota kola, hyacinth, lily, rue,
  witch hazel, juniper, and myrrh (you may substitute oils
  for dried where possible)
- moon water (see p. 4)
- large pot and stove (or a cauldron and outdoor fire,
  if possible)
- shovel and an area of ground where you can dig, or a large
  flower pot (at least 18 inches tall) filled with dirt

Cast the circle in your kitchen or outside, as appropriate. Add the moon water to the pot/cauldron and turn on the stove or light the fire.

Say the following:

> *Sacred water, blessed by the Goddess and the moon,*
> *this magic I do will infuse you*
> *with the power to quiet my mind and heart,*
> *to enable me to be at ease,*
> *while contemplating my wants and needs.*

Take a pinch (or few drops if using oil) of each of the following and recite the phrases that go along with them, as you add them to the water.

Allspice:

> *Heal my heart and my soul*
> *so I may move forward instead of dwelling in the past.*

Amber resin:

> *Grant me peace and stability as my*
> *confidence begins to grow again.*

Cedar:

> *Heal my heart and soul,*
> *give me courage and strength to see this through.*

Clove:

> *Heal my heart and soul,*
> *and bring courage back into my heart.*

Gota kola:

> *Quiet my mind so I will be able to meditate*
> *on my problems before coming to a solution.*

Hyacinth:

> *Ease the pain of my grief, as I turn it over to you.*

Lily:

> *Whether my marriage ends or not,*
> *this relationship as it once was, already has.*
> *Ease my pain as I deal with this loss*
> *and transition to the next step.*

Rue:

> *Calm my emotions so I am not ruled by them.*

Witch hazel:

> *No matter the future, my heart is broken.*
> *Help me to heal it so it can become whole again.*

Juniper:

> *Heal my heart and soul,*
> *and calm me in my meditations and communications.*

Myrrh:

> *Heal my heart and soul,*
> *and quiet my soul for meditations.*

Drop in the three stones, one at a time. Say the following:
Agate:

> *Instill in me the courage and strength*
> *to face my fears and problems head on.*

Bloodstone:

> *Instill in me the courage, strength, and self-confidence*
> *to face my fears and problems head on,*
> *particularly if my path leads me into legal matters.*

Carnelian:

> *Instill in me courage to face and control my fear and rage,*
> *to stop my jealousy, and to give me the*
> *verbal skills necessary to*
> *communicate my wishes, desires, and needs.*

Drop in the three ribbons, one at a time, and repeat the following:
Pink:

> *Restore my honor and virtue, let it be taken by no one.*
> *My morality stays in good standing.*

Purple:

> *Restore my self-esteem, inner strength, and insight*
> *to see which is the right path in front of me.*

White:

> *Restore my peace and tranquility. Cleanse me in truth.*

Light the black candle and allow some of the wax to drip into the water while saying:

Banish my negative feelings.
Protect me from the loss and confusion I feel.

Light the white candle and allow some of the wax to drip into the water while saying:

Bless me with calmness, tranquility,
patience, and understanding.

Take time now to meditate. Let your mind open to the calmness and serenity around you. Do not focus on the betrayal you feel. Instead, focus on being open and at peace. Spend plenty of time in this meditation. Don't go looking for answers as to what your next step should be—that will come to you in time. Simply focus on the here and now. The peace. The tranquility. You, whole again.

When you are done with the meditation, close your circle and carefully remove the pot/cauldron from the fire. Take it to either the flower pot or the area of your yard where you can dig. Dig a hole nine inches deep. Silently pour the entire contents of the pot/cauldron into the hole and cover it up.

Continue to meditate daily. If after a week you still feel you are unable to look at the situation objectively, perform the spell one last time. If after another week you still feel the same way, you already know what you need to do, you just aren't ready yet to see it. Don't worry, answers will come to you when you are ready.

I feel like my spouse and I are drifting apart due to our schedules

Sometimes when we are trying to make ends meet, it means we have to take work shifts that are opposite to those of our loved ones. One partner may have to work the second shift, the other the third. Though this eliminates the cost of child care, the pressure it puts on a marriage can be quite taxing.

You see less and less of each other, and often the only time you do get to spend with one another is while at least one of you is asleep, or dealing with things that have to be discussed such as which bills to pay at what time, issues with the kids, or even health problems. There often isn't time to spend just talking to one another, much less anything romantic. You may feel rushed in the time you do have together, or even come to resent that the other person never seems to be around anymore. You may feel guilty that you aren't doing enough yourself to be able to spend time with your spouse. Feelings of guilt and resentment end up getting in the way, and generally instead of trying to spend more time together, you could end up avoiding each other even more.

You might not even work different shifts; something else may be keeping you apart. Perhaps your spouse comes home from work and is so tired that instead of spending time with you, he or she falls asleep, wakes up for dinner, and then goes right back to sleep until the next morning when it starts all over again. Maybe one of you is spending too much time on the computer, watching television, or playing video games to notice the other one, who is starting to feel left out and neglected.

This spell will help you and your spouse reconnect. It will help you relax and put away negative feelings and energies so you can focus instead on positive feelings and energy. It will help you both spend time together in a supportive and loving atmosphere. Therefore, it *needs* to be done together. Schedule the time to make this spell happen. It may mean one of you has to go to sleep a half an hour later, or wake up a half an hour earlier than usual. This is a small sacrifice to make; sometimes we seem to forget that these small sacrifices can make all the difference in the world.

If you can arrange it, perform this spell on a Friday, the day for love, friendships, and reconciliation.

For this spell you will need:

- Specific-colored items of clothing: one pink (for compassion, tenderness, harmony, affection, love, romance, contentment, and household peace) and the other light blue (for calmness, tranquility, patience, and understanding)
- green candle, preferably pillar-type (for healing, growth, security, and calmness)

Let me emphasize that this spell is not about sex. It may have been a while since you've been able to experience intimacy with your spouse, but this spell is about reconnecting on emotional and mental levels.

Begin by casting your circle. Sit on the floor or ground facing one another. Set the green candle between you and light it. (Be careful!) Take turns holding the candle and say something you miss about the other person. For example, "I miss seeing your smile," "I miss talking to you about my day," etc. Each time the speaker changes, the candle changes hands. Continue to go back and forth telling each other what you miss. Look each other in the eye as you speak. Feel the connection between you. It is okay to cry if you feel like it—this is an emotional working and may bring out some strong feelings! You may feel some anger and resentment and sadness too. That is just fine. You are going to get everything out into the open now and will get to know how your absence has affected your spouse and hopefully the reverse as well.

Getting these feelings out into the open allows you to purge yourself of them. No more negative feelings, no more blame, no more resentment. Just let it all go.

When you can no longer think of anything else you miss, continue passing the candle back and forth, this time telling each other what you love about the other. Remember back to when you first met, what first attracted you two? What were some of your favorite things to do together? What are the qualities your spouse has that you really appreciate. How do those qualities complement your own qualities?

Continue taking turns, passing the candle back and forth as you do. You should be able to feel the connection between you grow. Words have power, whether they are in a pretty rhyme like a greeting card or spoken plainly. The words you are giving to each other now are positive and purposeful. They are strong and sentimental. They are building each of you and your relationship back up. You should feel a surge of energy. Things are going to get better.

After you have finished sharing the positives, pass the candle back and forth as you take turns reciting each of the following lines:

My love for you is strong.
I know that we are stronger together than apart.
I promise to always do my best to remember
the love and set aside the distance.
When I am away, I will forever keep you in my heart.

Extinguish the candle and end your spell with a passionate kiss. Close your circle.

Whenever one (or both) of you start to feel as if you are becoming distant again, repeat this spell.

I provide care for my elderly parent, and I just don't want to do it anymore

Providing care for an elderly parent can be taxing on a person for many reasons. For starters is the mental anguish and stress of watching your parent's mental and physical health decline. The care can be physically demanding, financially demanding, and of course it can be incredibly time consuming. At the same time, we feel obligated to take care of our folks. After all, they took care of us once upon a time!

The reasons as to how someone ends up being the party responsible for parental care are just as varied. There might not be any other family members to help out, there might be a lack of funds for housing, and my favorite—the parents might just be too darn stubborn to want to go to a facility like an assisted living community, or a retirement or nursing home.

What about when the struggle becomes too much? What if the person doing the caring is losing his or her home and simply cannot do this anymore? What if your own health is in jeopardy? Perhaps there are alternatives, just ones that haven't been explored because you have simply gone ahead and done what your parents expected of you.

Very few parents want to be a burden to their children. Believe it or not, they do know when they have actually become a burden. When they figure out that you are suffering because of them be it physically, mentally, emotionally, or financially, they will not be happy. While you are feeling guilty about not wanting to care for them anymore, they feel guilty for having made your life more difficult. Maybe you are trapped in a situation where even though you don't want to take care of your parents anymore, you know you don't really have a choice. You assume you will be continuing to care for them until they leave this world behind.

While writing this book, I was also spending a great deal of time looking into assisted living facilities for my parents. For over a decade they had been living in another state where my sister was taking care of them. However, she passed away and in addition to losing my sister, my siblings and I then had to convince my parents that the only way we could help take care of them was for them to move back to where all the other kids already lived. My parents weren't happy about it, and Dad made finding a place very difficult—nothing was good enough for him and he found some wrong with every place we showed him. If it wasn't size, it was money, or that he couldn't keep his dog. Then he wanted to leave all the furniture behind, but Mom wanted to bring some things and more arguments ensued.

In the meantime, my siblings and I were just hoping to find a place where our parents would be close by and would be happy to live out their days. During this time my father's oldest sister also died, which sent him into a complete tailspin as he wanted to blame the facility (and by association *all* facilities) she had been living in, instead of accepting the fact that she was ninety-three years old when she died and had lived a good, long life. We siblings couldn't agree on places and none of us were in a position to take our parents into our own homes and care for them because they required specialized care we weren't capable of providing. It was an extremely stress-filled ordeal for everyone involved.

This spell will help you cope with the negative emotions and stress associated with this situation. It will also help enable you to step back and look at things more objectively to find ways to help you manage the circumstances in your life.

This spell takes place in water. You can do this spell in any sort of water—a pool, bathtub, hot tub, shower, lake, river, even a stream as long as you can sit and relax in it. Because the element of water is associated with emotions (and this is a very emotional situation) we are going to use the concept of water washing those emotions away. We want to leave a clean slate so you can start over feeling fresh and renewed.

For this spell you will also need:

- dried lavender buds
- cheesecloth and some string
- lavender incense
- a lemon cut into slices, not wedges
- three pieces of paper and a writing utensil

Light the lavender incense and place it near the water you will be submerging yourself into. Tie the lavender buds into the piece of cheesecloth. Step in to your water source and get yourself fully wet.

As you do so, say the following:

> *Gentle Goddess of fairest beauty,*
> *cleanse my heart and soul.*
> *Wash away the pain, guilt, anger, and confusion.*
> *Let me start anew.*

Using the lavender buds in the cheesecloth like a sponge, "wash" your body, chanting the above over and over again.

Visualize the pain, guilt, anger, confusion, and any other negative feelings you have being washed down the drain, stream, or out into the lake. The negative energies are leaving you. Continue to chant and visualize until you feel yourself become clean and renewed. Set the lavender buds aside.

If you are in a place where the lemons won't float away, simply lay the slices on the water and one by one, squeeze the juice over your body. Use one to drip juice across each arm and leg, your torso, down your back, and through your hair.

As you do this, imagine a bright light shining upon you, cleansing and recharging you. Chant the following:

> *Gentle Goddess of fairest beauty,*
> *recharge my heart and soul.*
> *Refresh me with love, peace, and vitality.*
> *Let me start anew.*

When you are done, dry off and find a comfortable place to sit and write.

On one piece of paper, write down all the things your parents did for you while you were growing up and into your own adulthood. Feel the gratitude for their assistance. On the second piece of paper, write down all of the things you can do for your parents now that they need your care. On the third piece of paper, write down things that would help you help your parents. This would probably include things like more money, maybe someone who could fill in for a couple of hours so you can have a break, more space—whatever it is you need to make the care easier for you.

Refer to these three pieces of paper when you need to back up your spell work in the mundane world. Look into finding ways to make your third list come true.

Above all, remember that when you are down and negative, your parents will know— you won't be able to hide these feelings from them. Your negativity will not only reflect in their mood, it may also affect the care you give.

My child has a mental illness

As mentioned elsewhere, I have a son who suffers from several mental illnesses, and it has been the greatest challenge I have ever faced. Having a mentally ill child is probably one of the most stressful situations one could possibly imagine. Mental illness doesn't go away. Sometimes, in some cases, it can be controlled with medication, therapy, and/or behavior programs, but often it is something you will have to deal with every day. Even if you finally get to a point where the illness is controlled, you will have had a long, tough road to get there.

As with most problems, there are varying degrees of severity. You may have a child with a mild case of ADHD or a child who suffers from several different severe illnesses rolled into one. No matter what the degree of illness your child suffers, there are common emotions and feelings you may be experiencing while attempting to cope. Often parents become depressed, guilt-ridden, inpatient, frustrated, and can end up feeling completely helpless. Your child will most likely pick up on these negative feelings and act out more, which can cause more frustration…which leads to anger, which leads to the child acting out more. It is a vicious cycle, and one of the best ways to help the situation is to break it.

Often in these cases, children may not even know there is something different about them. On the other hand, they may know and they may not be happy about it as they don't understand why they ended up being the different one in the family instead of someone else. They might harbor anger and resentment against their parents, blaming them for their illness. They might not be able to control their actions. They might not *want* to control their actions. Some may never speak a word and others may scream non-stop. Some may be loving and quiet, others may be violent and volatile. You will have to work on being patient with your child and not let guilt or frustration get hold of you. Chances are, however, it already has.

My son is now nineteen years old and has had a very difficult life. He seldom had friends, and was very impulsive and disruptive throughout his school years, which first led to disciplinary issues. Those were followed by specialized school settings, which resulted in more disciplinary issues, including suspensions and arrests. At the age of seventeen, he became violent against me and his younger brother; he was removed from our home and placed as a ward of the state. He went from foster home to foster home because he was violent toward his foster siblings and parents. Eventually he ended up in intensive care after an extremely serious suicide attempt.

Though he is doing better at the moment, after getting his first job and being able to return to our home for extended visits, I always have to keep in mind that his illness could turn on us at any time, and things could become difficult once again.

This is a tough way to live; my heart truly goes out to any parent who has to live through similar circumstances. It is heartbreaking to see your child go through the pain and frustration that comes with being mentally ill. It is stressful, and the emotions you have on any given day are varied, intense, and often overwhelming.

This spell will help you let go of any guilt you may harbor. It will help you relax, become more patient with your child, and lower your frustration level. This is a spell that should be done as often as is needed.

Since we want to bring about a feeling of peace, this spell is going to use different soothing components.

This spell is best performed in a dim location—perform it at night if you can. Obviously if you are very stressed out, you may not want to wait until it gets dark outside!

For this spell you will need:

Several different colored candles:
- 1 blue candle
- 1 sky blue candle
- 1 pink candle
- 1 black candle
- 1 brown candle
- 1 gold candle
- a fireproof container, charcoal tablet, and lighter
- lavender essential oil

Begin by opening your circle. Light the charcoal tablet in the fireproof container and allow the whole tablet to light up. Once it begins "graying" add a few drops of the lavender oil. As the oil smokes, take the container and walk your circle with it saying the following:

Here in my circle I am safe.
The world is shut outside.
Inside it is only me and my Gods
(you may use a specific name if you wish)
Outside is the stress, frustration, anger.

> *Inside is peace, love, compassion.*
> *I come to this circle to renew, refresh,*
> *to leave my bad feelings behind.*

Set the container down on your altar. Light each one of the candles. As you light each one, say the following:

> *My child is not to blame for his/her illness.*
> *I am not to blame for his/her illness.*

Repeat this for each candle you light.

After they are all lit, take a seat and get comfortable. Do some deep breathing. Inhale for a count of four, then exhale for a count of four. Do this several times. Feel the new, good, clean, energy come in, and the old, bad, dirty energy go out. You will soon begin to feel yourself relax more deeply. (Any time you begin to feel to anxious or frustrated dealing with your child, this is a quick, easy way to help relax yourself and gain a new perspective.) Once you find yourself more relaxed, more at ease, and less stressed, you will be able to think more clearly.

Say the following out loud and really *feel* the words as you say them:

> *Grant me the tranquility, patience, and understanding*
> *to separate my child from his/her illness.*
> *He/She is not the illness, though it is a part of him/her.*
> *My child is not to blame for his/her illness.*
> *I am not to blame for his/her illness.*
> *When I become impatient, my child becomes impatient.*
> *When I become depressed, my child becomes depressed.*
> *When I become frustrated, my child becomes frustrated.*
> *When I become angry, my child becomes angry.*
> *I will not encourage these feelings,*
> *I will fight them instead.*
> *I will be patient with my child*
> *and teach him/her patience.*
> *I will be happy my child is alive and a part of my family,*
> *and teach my child love and kindness.*

I will be accepting of my child,
and teach my child how to be accepting of others.
I will be proud of my child,
and teach my child to have pride in himself/herself.
Grant me the tranquility, patience, and understanding
to separate my child from his/her illness.

If you feel the need to meditate or do some more deep breathing exercises, do so now. Otherwise, close your circle and go give your child a hug.

My child is physically handicapped

Physical handicaps take many different forms—from asthma to paralysis, heart problems to blindness. There is a wide variety and different levels of severity. There are also many different causes. Some physical handicaps may have been present since birth, others may be due to traumatic accidents. How a child becomes handicapped can greatly affect how he or she deals with having it. It can be very difficult for someone who is in an accident and loses a limb, for example to learn how to adjust, and not only physically. There are mental and emotional adjustments that must also be made.

As sad as it may be, being born with a handicap means the adjustment starts for the child before they are conscious of the handicap. In fact a baby doesn't really have to do any adjusting—the parents do. This child will grow up not knowing anything different than what he or she is presented with. A child who loses an arm, by contrast, knows what it was like to have that arm in the first place. Parents in this situation may often experience many of the same feelings parents with a child who suffers from a mental illness feel. These parents may become impatient, feel guilty, or become frustrated and angry about their situation.

We don't know why the Fates decide to give us what they do, but perhaps some theories on reincarnation can give us some insight. Some traditions believe that each time we come back and are reincarnated, it is to work on lessons from our previous lives. Perhaps we were very impatient and always rushing, not giving people in our lives the time they needed. Maybe we didn't take time to be with others. What better way to learn patience than to be put into a life that absolutely demands it? Maybe it's just a fluke that things work out how they do. It is really impossible to say, but things happen for one reason or another and we have to learn how to live with it.

Some friends of mine have both types of handicapped children; some have had their afflictions since birth and another was the result of a traumatic car accident. All these friends have gone through the same range of emotions about their child's handicap—just at different times.

It can take a long time to come to terms with either of these situations, and learning to cope on a daily basis can be painful and extremely difficult. This spell will help get you to the point of acceptance and learning how to incorporate this handicap into your and your child's daily lives.

In this spell you are going to make a type of mojo bag. This bag will consist of ingredients that will bring you energy and revitalize you when you are feeling down, and help you relax when you are wound too tight.

This spell is most easily done by setting up all your ingredients and then casting your circle. You may need to do it in your kitchen for the counter space.

For this spell you will need:

- A small drawstring bag, made of a breathable material, no larger than 3 x 4 inches. I recommend a soothing color, such as purple or blue, though you can use any color you want.
- one silver and one gold candle
- lighter

Choose ten to fifteen of the following ingredients in dried, powdered, or oil form:

- amber—stability, confidence, peace
- apple blossoms—love, peace
- balm of Gilead—emotional healing
- bayberry—peace, harmony, well-being
- bergamot—peace, happiness
- black pepper—mental alertness, physical energy, courage
- camphor—physical energy
- caraway—physical energy, love
- carnation—strength, healing, vitality, physical energy, love, health
- cedar—healing, courage, self-control
- cinnamon—physical energy
- coltsfoot—peace, tranquility
- columbine—courage, willpower
- costmary—stills emotions
- cypress—comfort, solace, eases feelings of loss, healing
- dragon's blood—power amplifier, love
- freesia—love, peace
- gardenia—love, peace, healing
- geranium—health, love, happiness

- hyacinth—love, happiness, overcoming grief
- jasmine—love, peace
- lavender—happiness, healing, peace, love
- lemon—health, healing, physical energy
- lily of the valley—happiness, peace
- meadowsweet—peace, love
- mullein—courage, love
- narcissus—peace, harmony, love
- pennyroyal—peace, strength, physical energy
- peppermint—love, mental stimulation, energy
- pine—healing, physical energy
- plumeria—love, peace
- rhododendron—peace, strength
- rue—healing, mental powers, love, calming emotions
- spider lily—love, peace
- sweet pea—courage, strength, happiness
- water lily—peace, happiness, love

Set up the ingredients you need and have your bag ready. Cast your circle and light the silver candle for the Goddess and the gold candle for the God. Ask them to join your working as you normally would.

As you take a pinch of each herb, say the following:

> *God and Goddess*
> *instill these herbs*
> *with your power and grace—*
> *to mend my soul*
> *and infuse my faith.*

Then drop the pinch into the bag. Repeat for each ingredient you have. If you are using oil, simply change the language to "instill this oil." Remember that if you are using any oils, you will only need *one* drop of each since they are so strong. You probably don't want to always smell like your mojo bag!

Once you have all of the ingredients in the bag, tie the drawstring as tightly as you can. Go ahead and knot it if you like.

This bag provides you with many kinds of healing—emotional, mental, physical for your child—we want you to be in all over good health!

Take the bag and hold it high above your head. Visualize the God and Goddess are there with you, shining their brilliant light down upon you.

Say the following:

> God and Goddess,
> I stand here in your guardian light,
> empower this working with your might.
> The gift of healing is what I ask,
> please accept this as your task.

Thank the God and Goddess for their presence and blessings. Close your circle.

Carry your mojo bag around with you. If you begin to feel too stressed, overwhelmed, or you need an extra boost of positive energy, take it out and hold it in your hands while doing some deep breathing exercises. Inhale the bag's scents. Let them fill you, relax you, and recharge you.

My teenager is pregnant

Teenage pregnancy isn't easy for anybody: the teen, parents, or the baby. With teen pregnancies come heart-wrenching decisions—to have the baby or not, to put the baby up for adoption or to keep it. These decisions will affect you and your child for the rest of your lives. The parents of a pregnant teen must also make the choice as to whether or not to support the teen, be it financially or emotionally, for example. These are, or course, decisions that need to be made calmly and rationally. During this time, emotions will most likely be running quite high; serenity, clarity, compassion, empathy, and understanding will all be needed.

When I first wrote this spell, I only had friends who have had to deal with this situation. However, by the time the editing process began, my own nineteen-year-old daughter had moved out and announced she was pregnant and getting married. I suddenly found myself in the same boat as those friends of mine.

Different people react to this situation in different ways. Some parents are excited to become grandparents, others are embarrassed and angry that this is how they discover their child has been sexually active.

Pregnant teenage girls have to deal with a lot of problems that teenage boys—or any male of any age—often do not. I realize there is a huge difference between having your daughter tell you she is pregnant and having your son tell you his girlfriend is pregnant. No matter which situation you find yourself in, it is difficult and decisions must be made.

These decisions need to be made when everyone has a clear, calm head. Quick-tempered reactions don't have any place in this situation and this spell will help you keep your calm while you work out in your mind what decisions you would like to see being made. While it's important for you to experience your own feelings, it's even more important to realize that final decisions do not reside with you, except for the decision on how you decide to act or react. You cannot force your child into any situation he or she doesn't want. If your son's girlfriend is pregnant, you will most likely have even less control or influence over the situation.

This spell should be performed before any decisions are made about anything.

For this spell you will need:

· two pictures of your teen—one as a baby themselves,
  and one recent photograph

Candles (pillar style would be best):

· one black—to absorb negative energies
· one sky blue—for calmness, tranquility, patience,
  and understanding

You will also need:

· a blank piece of white paper
· a brown thin-tip marker
· a piece of brown yarn about twelve inches in length
· a candle snuffer
· fireproof container such as a small cauldron and a lighter

If possible, and if the weather cooperates, do this spell outside. The outdoors and connection with nature should help relax you and put you into a better state of mind. Set the above components on your altar and cast your circle. Take the black candle and sit comfortably. Light it, and hold it in front of you with both hands.

Stare into the flame and project any negative feelings into the black candle. Give those feelings up. Watch them be absorbed first by the candle wax and then burned in the flame so they disappear. Rid yourself of feelings of anger, resentment, and disappointment. Any negative feelings you have regarding your teen's pregnancy need to be released into this candle. This may take awhile. Feel free to take as much time as is needed. When you are done projecting those feelings and watching them burn away, use a snuffer to extinguish the candle, choking any remnants of negativity left behind.

Next, take the sky blue candle and again sit comfortably. Light the candle and hold it in front of you with both hands. Stare into the flame and feel the positive feelings of tranquility, patience, calmness, and understanding flow from the flame into you. Imagine these feelings drifting down upon you and soaking into your skin. Feel the calmness coming over you. Take deep breaths and relax. Continue this as long as you need to in order to get yourself relaxed and into an open and understanding frame of mind. When you feel you are ready, place the lit candle on your altar.

Pick up the pictures of your child and again sit comfortably. Meditate over these pictures. What is it you want to say to your child right now? Have a one-sided conversation with your child at this point. When you have said what you want to, pick up the paper and brown marker.

Write down what decisions you would like to see made and what your role would be. For example, you may write down:

"I want my daughter to have the baby and put it up for adoption."

"We are not ready to deal with bringing a new life into the world right now."

When you are done writing, roll the paper up and tie it closed with the brown yarn. Say the following:

> *These decisions which are so hard*
> *to make must be made.*
> *I have contemplated my role in this manner*
> *and wish my desires be known to the universe.*

Using the flame of the blue candle, carefully light the paper and drop it into the fireproof container. As the paper roll burns, say:

> *I release my choice into the universe.*
> *I ask for guidance and understanding*
> *while my child makes hers,*
> *the final decision,*
> *in this matter.*

If you find yourself becoming too upset to remain calm and rational, repeat the spell as needed.

Remember that the final decision rests with your child—her decision may differ from yours. This does not mean your spell did not work. This spell is to help *you* be understanding of and compassionate toward your child's wishes during this difficult time. It is not designed to control your child and have her make the decision you would like.

My child keeps running away from home

Having a child who runs away is nothing but downright scary. In today's world, it's hard enough to keep our children safe when we *do* know where they are. When they take off and we can't find them, it's one of the scariest feelings in the world.

This spell is not something you do when your child first splits and runs out the door. The first thing you should do is try to stop them. If you can't or if the child left without your knowing it, **call the police** immediately and report him or her as missing. First things first: find your child *any* way you must to get him or her home safe and sound.

That being said, this spell is one of the few spells you will ever hear me discuss that makes use of interfering with another person's free will. Why? I believe when it comes to the safety of a child who probably does not fully comprehend the possible consequences of actions like this, interfering with his or her free will is needed for safety and to keep him or her out of harm's way. It is not only your right to do so, it is your parental responsibility to do everything within your power to keep your child alive and free from harm.

As mentioned elsewhere, I have a son who is mentally ill. One of the problems we experienced due to his impulsiveness is that he would take off and run away when he got upset about something. Some days we could tell him to clean up his room, and he would run out the door—sometimes without shoes even—and he would just run. We live in a rural area very close to a forest preserve so the area is rather wooded in some places. In other places it is farmland, mainly corn. These types of environments make it very easy for a child who doesn't want to be found to quickly disappear. My son is also an asthmatic, so running and corn fields would also bring on an asthma attack, putting his health in danger. I eventually came up with this spell to stop him from running.

It should go without saying that this spell is going to need backing up in the mundane world. If you have a child who habitually runs away, you should seek professional help. A child who runs may do so for many reasons, including perceiving a threat from something. Their "fight or flight" response is programmed to "flight" only. Your child needs to be able to learn how to face situations that may be uncomfortable or that he or she might not like without always fleeing. Obviously if the fleeing is a result of being physically harmed, then your child and the person doing the harming also need professional assistance.

Because of the circumstances, this spell will be a binding spell—it is designed to bind your child from running away and therefore provide protection and safekeeping.

For this spell you will need:

· a black cord about 18 inches long

· a black candle

· small piece of black paper—¼ sheet is plenty large enough

· black pen, crayon, marker, or ink and quill

· fireproof container/cauldron, charcoal tablet, and lighter

Herbs to make protection incense (you may substitute oils for
some dry ingredients; use only one or two drops of each):

· angelica

· black pepper

· blessed thistle

· burdock

· cedar

· clove

Black paper and ink? Yes, we *are* going to write black on black. It's okay—you don't
have to go back later and reread anything so you don't have to be able to actually see
what you've written. On the piece of paper write your child's full name, top and center.
Underneath that write:

> *Running, fleeing, hiding,*
> *do not keep you safe.*
> *Flying, eluding, evading*
> *put you in harm's way.*
> *It is for me to protect you*
> *however that I may.*

Roll the paper into a scroll. Wrap the black cording around the scroll and leave a few
inches of cording hanging. Say:

> *I bind thee once.*
> *I bind thee twice.*
> *I bind thee thrice.*
> *You shall not run and put yourself in harm's way.*

Knot the cording at this point and then wrap it again while saying the above. Again knot the cording and then wrap it again while reciting the above. After doing this three complete times, knot off the cording one final time.

Light the black candle and use it to light the charcoal tablet. Sprinkle the incense you've made onto the charcoal tablet. Waft the bound scroll through the smoke of the incense while repeating the above three times.

When you have completed the above chant, extinguish the black candle. Store your scroll in a safe location such as a locked box. If you do not have a place where you feel safe storing it, find a safe location to bury it.

My child was sexually assaulted

There aren't many things that could be more traumatic to anyone than to be sexually assaulted, but when it involves a child, this heinous crime is even more tragic. Catching and punishing the perpetrator may help with the healing process, but that doesn't *always* help.

I consider myself lucky not to have experienced this trauma with my own children, but a close friend, Miranda, had to experience this when she found out her current husband was molesting her daughter. Needless to say, as soon as she realized what was happening, she called the police. The man was found guilty of his crimes and locked up. Though he could no longer harm this little girl, damage had been done and it was time for the healing to begin—a road that is often long and bumpy. In Miranda's case, one of the people the girl was to love and trust harmed and damaged her. An event like this can conjure feelings of betrayal and often guilt—for the child. It can take children a long time to understand that what happened wasn't their fault. Miranda's daughter had an extremely difficult time dealing with this—she had loved her "daddy" and when he was taken away, her siblings blamed her.

Your child will desperately need emotional, physical, mental, spiritual, *and* legal help in this matter. Make sure you cover all the bases. Use every resource available to you to help your child cope with this life-altering tragedy.

This spell will help boost the effectiveness of the work done in the above listed areas. Since it is best performed on a Sunday for healing purposes, you may want to consider doing this spell on a weekly basis for a while. You can actually perform this spell right in the child's bedroom as long he or she has said it's okay. Before doing this spell, it might also help to explain to the child what exactly you are going to do, in case he or she feels nervous around adults. Have your child get ready for bed and lay down in the bed while you perform the spell around them. It would help if you can walk all the way around the bed but if that isn't possible, that's just fine.

You will need:

- a black robe for your child to wear over clothes (this can be a simple bathrobe)
- a portable TV tray to set up a small altar and the candles at the foot of the bed
- a sage smudge bundle for its healing, purifying, and protective qualities

- frankincense stick incense for protection, to banish negative entities and consecration
- myrrh stick incense for healing, protection, and consecration (or a blend of frankincense and myrrh)
- lavender incense (optional, see below)
- fireproof container and lighter

Three candles:

- brown for justice
- green for healing
- white for cleansing, peace, protection, healing, tranquility, purification, and innocence

Although this is a serious spell for a very serious matter, we want to keep it brief so as to not add any additional stress to your child. Your child's age will also play an important role in how well he or she is able to cope with things, so you need to make sure you are using your best judgment on what is too much or too little.

Begin by setting up the TV tray at the foot of the bed and arrange the items needed on your altar. You will also place the candles here. If your child has been having a hard time relaxing and sleeping, you can also add lavender incense. Because we will be smudging and using so many different kinds of incense, you may want to crack a window while you perform the spell. If there's a ceiling fan in the child's room, put it on its lowest setting.

Have your child put the black robe on and lay down in bed. Cast your circle as you normally would, keeping the bed in the circle. If you are unable to walk around the bed, use your finger or a wand to cast the circle around the bed.

Light the brown candle and say:

For justice to be found, and to be swift.

Light the green candle and say:

To heal you—body, mind, and soul.

Light the white candle and say:

To cleanse you, protect you, heal you, purify you.
To bring you peace, tranquility, and innocence.

Light the sage and waft the smoke over your child. Begin at his or her head and work your way back and forth across the body, all the way down to the toes.

As you do this, visualize your child being cleansed and healed. Visualize him or her returning to the child he or she was before this terrible crime was committed. Finally, visualize the sage creating a protective, impenetrable barrier, a shield, around him or her.

It is not necessary to say anything at this time, however as mentioned earlier, you may want to explain to your child what you are doing. You will need to use your best judgment to know how much (or how little) to say. Your child may also want to say something during this point of the spell.

If you do want to say something keep it simple, such as:

> *We ask of the Lord and Lady*
> *to use this sage*
> *to cleanse, protect, and purify.*

Next, light the sticks of frankincense and myrrh. Again begin at your child's head (be careful not to drop any ash!) and move it back and forth, from head to toe.

Again visualize your child being cleansed body, mind, and soul. Imagine the negativity being washed away, and a protective barrier being formed in its place. It is not necessary to say anything at this time, but if you would like to, use the following:

> *We ask the Lord and Lady*
> *to use this frankincense and myrrh*
> *to heal, consecrate, banish negativity,*
> *and protect from any further harm.*

When you are done, close your circle.

You may wonder why words aren't as necessary with this spell. It is because you are going directly to the Lord and Lady, God and Goddess, or whatever specific deity you want to go to. You and your child have both been through a traumatic experience and our higher powers understand this. Sometimes words simply aren't necessary to know what is in our hearts. Also, because this matter is so upsetting, just speaking about it tends to bring on very strong, painful feelings. Keeping the spoken part of the spell generic will not prevent the magic and energy from knowing where it needs to go and what it needs to do.

Finally, because this matter is very upsetting, and because our children often take their cues from us on how to act and react in a situation, if you become visibly disturbed while performing this spell, chances are your child will too. The chances of this multiply if your child is an empath. Though it seems difficult, try to remain as calm and collected as you possibly can while working this spell.

My child has a drug/alcohol problem

If your child is suffering from substance abuse, you will definitely need to seek professional help. Some drug and alcohol problems aren't actually addictions, but you will probably want professional help to assist you anyway. Your child might be "just experimenting" but understand that there are underlying causes as to why they feel the need to experiment. Talking to a counselor or therapist may help your child deal with his or her issues in a more positive manner and environment.

Many parents claim their children have never done any kind of drugs, but statistics show that probably isn't true. When I've asked people how they know their children haven't done any kind of drugs, they respond with the same answer—"I asked them." Truly, it would be nice if children were completely and utterly 100 percent honest, but I don't personally know a single child who would answer that question with, "Yup, I sure am!"

Random drug testing takes place in my home. Kits are available at your local drugstore, and most can give immediate results for some illegal drugs, which can then be mailed in for a more complete report. Plenty of people think this is an invasion of privacy. If it is, so be it. I firmly believe my child's life is more important than his or her privacy. It bears remembering too that in this day and age just about every job requires a drug test as part of the application process. Some workplaces also perform random drug testing, so privacy becomes less and less relevant. Your children might as well get used to tests now, because as adults it may very well become a part of their lives.

If your child is involved with drugs in any way, you are going to need to get him or her help. During that time, both you and your child will need some extra support—who better equipped to give you that support than your deities and the magical world around you? Call upon the universe to help hold you both together during this difficult time.

This spell can be done on any one of three days: Sunday, for healing, strength, and protection; Monday for healing; or Saturday for setting limitations and boundaries. Pick whatever day works best for you.

For this spell you will need:
Two colors of ribbon, each about 18 inches long:
- black for protection, binding, to set limitations,
  to deal with confusion, to absorb negative energy,
  and to define boundaries

- green for healing, calmness, and to neutralize
difficult situations

You will also need:

- one white piece of paper for cleansing, protection, healing,
tranquility, and purification
- an agate stone for courage, strength, love, and protection
- a hematite stone for grounding, calmness, and healing
- fireproof container such as a cauldron, charcoal tablet, long-
handled lighter, and small tongs

Combine the following to make incense:

- balm of Gilead for emotional healing
- blessed thistle for purification, protection, and to break hexes
(just in case!)
- carnation for protection, strength, healing, and energy
- cedar for healing, courage, purification, protection,
and self-control
- clove for protection, courage, and healing
- columbine for courage and willpower
- eucalyptus for healing, protection, and purification

If your child is indeed addicted, the detox process is not a whole lot of fun. The body must rid itself of poisons which can have some nasty side effects. Having good energy, physical strength, and wellness can go a long way in making detox less painful, which is why we are asking for these energies in this spell.

It would be best to do this spell with your child present, but it is okay to do it solo, too.

Begin by casting your circle as you normally would with all the listed components laid out on your altar. Light the charcoal tablet. Once it is ready, sprinkle a pinch of the incense you made onto it while you say the following:

Lord and Lady,
(or name specific deity you work with)
I/we come to you with our burden and our request.
(Child's name) *needs your help*
and blessings to fight his/her battle.

Lay the white piece of paper on the altar and place both stones next to each other at the center near one of the short ends. Fold the paper over the stones and proceed to roll the paper all the way to the opposite end with the stones wrapped up inside of it. Take the ends and fold them up on each side of the stones so the paper is making a "U" shape. Using the two ribbons, tie these two ends together. Hold this bundle out in front of you and say:

> *I/We ask for your blessings upon these stones.*
> *I/We ask for the blessings of healing and good health.*
> *I/We ask for the blessings of courage and strength.*
> *I/We ask for the blessings of love and protection.*
> *I/We ask for the blessings of grounding and calmness.*
> *I/We ask for the blessings of purification and energy.*
> *I/We ask for the blessings of self-control and willpower.*

Add another pinch of incense to the charcoal tablet. Hold the bundle in the smoke for about half a minute and then set it in the cauldron. If the charcoal tablet does not ignite it, go ahead and use the long-handled lighter.

As it burns say the following:

> *As the fire burns,*
> *Lord and Lady,*
> *instill these stones with your power and blessings.*

After the paper burns away, use the tongs to remove the stones from the cauldron. Set them on your altar. Be careful, they may still be hot. Say the following:

> *Lord and Lady,*
> *thank you for your blessings.*

Close your circle.

After the stones have cooled, your child may carry them in a pocket and hold them whenever he or she feels the need for a power or energy boost.

My child is violent

Having a child who acts violently can be cause for confusion. If your child is young, it is important to stop this type of behavior as soon as possible. He or she needs to understand that it is not acceptable behavior and can lead to severe problems later in life if it continues. Violent behavior can lead to criminal damage to property, assault and battery, domestic battery, or even worse charges.

If your child is older, you also need to decide whether or not to involve the law. At the very least, your child needs professional help, though how well he or she responds to therapy will be entirely up to him or her.

Unfortunately, I have had a great deal of experience with this problem. Originally, I didn't think it was right to try to use magic in this situation, but perhaps things would never have gotten as bad as they did if I had tried sooner. My son who is mentally ill became extremely violent against me and his youngest brother as well. It is because of that violence that he no longer lives with us and until recently he had to be supervised during visits. Now the judge allows him to come see us as long as I am comfortable with having him here. Once I *did* finally perform this spell, he has not become violent with me or anyone else in our household. I wish I had thought of it years earlier!

This spell is a binding type with a bit of banishing thrown in. The idea is that you will bind your child from behaving violently and you will banish the inclination to have these behaviors as well. Try to do this spell under a new moon both for its banishing aspect and because your child obviously needs some healing as well.

Set up your altar to face north, the direction related to physical matters.

For this spell you will need:
- a black candle
- black cord, about 18 inches in length
- black paper and black writing utensil
- fireproof container such as a cauldron, charcoal tablet, and long-handled lighter
- dragon's blood oil

Cast your circle as you normally would. Light the charcoal tablet and put one drop of dragon's blood oil onto the charcoal tablet while saying:

(Name of deity),
I come to you tonight
with a special request.

Dress the black candle with the dragon's blood oil and light it. Say:

I call upon you for
your help and aid.

Set the paper on your altar and with the black writing utensil, write "VIOLENCE" in large letters across the paper. Say:

My child, (child's name),
has yet to learn self-control,
not lashing out,
and that violence is wrong
and not the answer.
He/She needs to learn and understand
these behaviors are wrong and not allowed.
They do have consequences.

Roll the paper up like a scroll. Wrap the cord around it three times and knot it. Say:

With your blessing,
I bind my child from using violence to harm others.

Do the above a total of three times. Sprinkle a few more drops of dragon's blood oil onto the charcoal tablet and pass the scroll through the smoke. Say:

With the blessing of (deity's name),
and the power within me.
I bind (child's name) from using violence to harm others.
I banish the desire for violence from him/her.

Drop the scroll into your fireproof container. If the scroll does not light from the charcoal tablet, go ahead and use your lighter. Allow the paper to burn away completely while you chant the following:

I bind (child's name) *from using violence to harm others.*
I banish the desire for violence from him/her.

Close your circle as normal.

My parent is suffering from dementia/Alzheimer's

Dementia and Alzheimer's are terrible diseases that end up taking away the person we love, leaving an empty shell. It is devastating for both the afflicted person and his or her loved ones. Perhaps the only saving grace is after these diseases have progressed to a certain state, the afflicted eventually doesn't know he or she is afflicted. Though this doesn't sound like much, it can be comforting if you really think about it.

At ninety-six years of age, my grandmother thought she was six years old living on her daddy's farm in Wisconsin. Her best friend was there with her. In reality, her best friend had drowned eighty-three years earlier. Grandma was actually confined to a hospital bed with a broken hip in Arizona. Which world would you choose to spend your last days in?

When I began writing this book, my aunt was still alive, but recently she too passed away at ninety-three. She also had full-blown dementia: she didn't recognize her own family when they visited her in the special locked-down facility for dementia and Alzheimer's patients and believed herself to be in her early twenties…and just about every man at the nursing home had asked her to marry him, she said. She was having the time of her life, almost right up to the very end. She eventually became bedridden, and her decline after that was rapid. While she was still up and about, however, she was happy—very happy! She didn't know that she was in what the rest of us considered bad shape. She had men swooning over her and telling her how beautiful she was over and over all day long.

This aunt's daughter had an extremely difficult time accepting the fact that her mother didn't know who she was. She was angry and very bothered by the fact that her mother was "engaged" to at least twenty different men. Why? She was scared something similar would someday happen to her. It's true, it might. But if the end result is happiness, can we begrudge them that?

I realize that the above story is not representative of all people who suffer from Alzheimer's or other types of dementia. Some have an extremely difficult time dealing with the symptoms and the toll it can take. In the end, however, the result is always the same: we end up losing our loved one to the Otherworld. For some people, this is what they're *really* fighting against, not the illness. Though every single one of us will die someday, it is still something we constantly try to stop. Death is just another fact of life and we can't stop it. It will happen to all of us, and we must learn to accept when it happens to those we love. Very seldom do people say to their loved ones, "It's okay. We will be okay, you go ahead and move on."

Dementia is a disease that takes our loved ones away from us mentally before taking them away from us for good. This spell is designed to help the family of a dementia or Alzheimer's parent cope with the changes that parent is going through. It is to help us deal with being left behind—even before our loved one crosses over.

This spell is best performed on a Monday, the day best suited for bringing out compassion.

For this spell you will need:

Two candles:
- one pink for compassion and tenderness
- one sky blue for calmness, tranquility, patience, and understanding

Three herbs for incense:
- balm of Gilead for emotional healing
- bayberry for peace, harmony, and well-being
- cypress for comfort, solace, healing, and to ease feelings of loss
- a fireproof container such as your cauldron, charcoal tablet, and long-handled lighter

Open your circle as you normally would with the candles and cauldron (or other fireproof container) on your altar. Light the charcoal tablet.

Begin by calling your patron deity/ies or the Lord and Lady to the circle with you. Say the following:

(Your patron deity's name),
I call upon you today
to help me find my way
through the loss, pain, and confusion
I suffer from while my (mom/dad/other loved one)
slowly slips away.
Though I know death comes to us all
in our own time,

I have not yet come to terms with
the suffering that befalls me.

Light the pink candle. Say:

Grant me the compassion and tenderness
I need to help my (loved one)
along his/her way.
Let me be aware of his/her needs and happiness,
and not centered on my own.

Light the sky blue candle. Say:

As he/she becomes more confused, muddled, and forgetful,
allow me to be his/her strength.
Help me to remain calm and patient.
Help me understand this is not a punishment
for him/her or for me.

Sprinkle a pinch of balm of Gilead onto the lit charcoal tablet. Say:

Allow my heart and emotions to heal
so I may focus on his/her needs and set mine aside.

Sprinkle a pinch of bayberry onto the lit charcoal tablet. Say:

Please grant both me and my mother/father/loved one
peace, harmony, and well-being
as we go down this tumultuous path

Sprinkle a pinch of cypress onto the lit charcoal tablet. Say:

Allow me to remain tranquil
in the comfort and solace that someday
soon he/she will pass into the Otherworld,
into your loving embrace.

> *This world will end for him/her,*
> *but another will go on,*
> *where he/she will be free and whole, once again.*

You may take a few minutes to meditate if you would like, or simply thank your deity or deities for their presence and close your circle.

My parents just don't understand me

Whether they're children, teenagers, or adults, people often feel their parents don't understand them. Sometimes this may be attributed to a generation gap, but other times it may go deeper than that. Perhaps you and your parents hold extremely different ideals. Politically, you may be a die-hard liberal and they may be extremely conservative. You are Pagan, and they are Christian. There are many, many areas of thought where you and your parents may have extreme differences of opinion. This isn't always a bad thing. What makes it "bad" or uncomfortable (or worse) is when you or your parents can't accept that having different opinions is okay.

Perhaps you are fine with them having different viewpoints, but your parents aren't okay with *you* having viewpoints different from their own, which is often the case. We tend to try to raise our children to believe what we ourselves believe and to hold the same things sacred we do. Life doesn't always work out this way, and some parents have a hard time accepting this, thinking it means they failed somewhere along the way. Different thinking doesn't mean failure, though. It simply means they were able to raise someone who is capable of independent thought. In today's society of "sheeple," individuality is a *good* thing!

However, having your parents harp on you because they don't understand you and your choices can be … aggravating, annoying, and mind numbing. My own father loves to say to me, "I don't know why it surprises me, you've been doing what you want since you were six years old." Now I simply reply, "Well, you've had thirty-five years to get used to it. You'll adjust." It took him a long time to get to the point where he doesn't constantly bring up our differences—though election time is a completely different story. We tend to avoid calling until an election is over. Sometimes he calls to gloat, other times (when his candidate didn't win) he just lets it pass by quietly, but for the most part he has learned to put our differences behind him. I believe I have this spell to thank for that.

This spell will help open the lines of communication. It's not meant to change anyone's mind or beliefs, but it is designed to help you express yourself more freely, and to better understand your parents' point of view.

You can get a boost in this spell if it happens to be the right time of the year. February is a good time for spells about life's challenges; November is good for family-related spells. Obviously you don't have to wait for either one of those months, but if it's convenient, you know you can get an extra boost if needed.

This spell is best done on a Wednesday, the day best suited for spells relating to communication. If you can, perform this spell outside with a small bonfire.

For this spell you will need:
- basil oil for peace and happiness
- a green candle for neutralizing difficult situations
- an orange candle for communication
- a sky blue piece of paper for calmness, tranquility, patience, and understanding and a writing utensil
- a fireproof container such as a cauldron and a lighter

Open your circle as you normally would. Using the sky blue paper, write a letter to your parents and tell them exactly what you would like to say. Explain how you feel. Let them know you do not feel they are understanding or accepting of you and your choices and opinions. Tell them how it makes you feel when they point out differences and how they feel about them. Be as detailed as possible. When you finish, say:

> *These words I know I cannot say*
> *I write to you anyway,*
> *to open my heart and speak the truth.*

Light the green candle and hold it at an angle so the wax will drip. Hold it over the letter you have just written and allow the green wax to drip all over it. Green neutralizes difficult situations, so you are going to neutralize the difficulties you just wrote about. Let the wax continue to drip until the entire letter is covered in it. As it drips say:

> *The arguments we always have*
> *about the ways we feel*
> *will be overridden*
> *with this waxy seal.*

Extinguish the candle.

Carefully roll the paper up into a scroll, with the wax on the inside. Set it into your fireproof container. Gently sprinkle several drops of basil oil onto it and say:

> *I cover our problems with happiness and peace*
> *and hope that it soaks through.*

Using the orange candle, ignite the paper, wax, and oil inside your cauldron or throw it in your bonfire. In a cauldron, the scroll may sputter quite a bit so take safety precautions. As it burns say:

With communication, our problems can be burned away.
Open us up to a better way to say
what we truly need to say.

Allow the paper to burn up completely and close your circle.

I haven't spoken to my siblings in years and want to reestablish contact

Some people simply lose touch with others because they are too busy with their own lives. By the time these people realize how much time has passed, they feel like it's too late to reconnect, given how much time has passed. This is often true particularly in cases where there is a large age gap between siblings. A period of ten to twenty years with no contact is often possible especially when siblings are old enough to be one's parents. Sometimes the older siblings may already be out of the house by the time the younger ones come along. They may be away at college or simply too busy with high school life to pay much attention to the little one at home.

As we grow older, many people want to feel a stronger connection with their siblings but don't know how to go about it because so much time has already passed. They want to call, but really—what do you say to someone you haven't talked to in months…or years?

I have performed this spell to reestablish contact with siblings and cousins, family members I had lost touch with whom I wanted to reconnect. Keep in mind that this spell is only for the people you truly want back in your life. Sometimes reconnecting can happen in strange and unusual ways, so make sure you are receptive to finding them again.

This spell will help draw your family closer to you again and to help you reconnect. Set your altar up facing east, the direction related to social, intellectual, communication, and relationship aspects.

This spell is great to perform in November, the month related to family issues, but obviously if you can't wait that long, you can't wait! If it happens to be the end of October when you decide to reach out to your estranged siblings, hold off just a little bit longer to have the aspects lined up as best as possible. Perform this spell under a waxing moon to help you invoke things you want, on a Wednesday for its communication correspondence, or a Friday for reconciliation. If you could find a Wednesday or Friday in November during a waxing moon—that would be the best bet!

For this spell you will need:

Three candles:
- orange and yellow, both for communication
- brown for family issues and neutrality

You will also need:
- incense made by crushing together cypress (for comfort, solace, healing, and to ease feelings of loss), frankincense (to banish negative energies), and rue (to calm emotions)
- a fireproof container, charcoal tablet, and lighter

This is probably quite an unnerving time for you; you may feel anxious about attempting to make contact. Just remember that even with the best intentions, a lot of the outcome of your efforts will be based on the person you are attempting to reach. You are neither responsible for nor in control of the person's response.

Open your circle as you normally would and light your charcoal tablet. Begin with the orange candle. Hold it in both hands in a prayer-like position. Recite the following:

> *Great God and Great Goddess,*
> *aid me in my quest to reach out to my family.*
> (you may add names)

Set the candle on your altar, light it, and repeat with the yellow candle. Repeat a third time with the brown candle. When all candles are lit, take a pinch of the incense and sprinkle it onto the lit charcoal tablet. Again hold your hands in the prayer position and recite the above.

Sit for a moment, and reflect on times you had with your sibling/s when you were younger. Think about vacations, holidays, or even everyday occurrences. What do you remember? Try to pinpoint how and when you went your separate ways and drifted apart.

Imagine what you would like to say now to your sibling/s. Do you have a message? Is there a question you have always wanted to ask but never did? Think about what you want to say and how you want to say it. Do you want to call? Write a letter? Organize these thoughts in your mind.

After you have spent plenty of time considering what you want to do, place another pinch of the incense on the tablet. Hold your hands again in the prayer position and blow out each candle individually, saying the following as you blow each candle out:

Great God and Great Goddess,
aid me in my quest to reach out to my family.
I send my request into the universe.

When finished, close your circle. Either sit down and write your letter, or make your phone call.

My child is constantly teased at school

Teasing and bullying have become huge problems in our schools. It's not terribly uncommon to turn on the news these days to hear that a child has committed suicide due to incessant taunting and harassment. This problem has become more and more serious, and sometimes a matter of life and death.

For starters, if your child is having this problem, make sure you do everything humanly possible in the mundane world to stop it. You need to talk to the teachers and administration, the parents of the other children involved, and if necessary, the police. Hire a lawyer if you need to. Move if you need. Consider homeschooling. These seem like extreme measures, but this sort of problem deserves serious attention. Many states and schools are currently re-evaluating and rewriting laws about bullying, but legislation takes time. Some children simply can't afford the wait. Again, I cannot stress enough the importance of ensuring your child's safety.

When I first began writing this book, one of my daughter's friends had committed suicide three months before he graduated high school. It was a terrible, awful, and traumatic situation. The student was bullied for years on end and his parents couldn't get any help from the schools. For their part, the schools turned a blind eye and claimed there wasn't a bullying problem. They said this to many parents, myself included. It wasn't until parents started talking to each other that they realized the problem was much larger than they had feared. Not only were many students getting bullied, the school was covering it all up.

Since her friend's death, my daughter has taken an active part in the fight against bullying, going as far as speaking out on the news about what happened in our small town. Needless to say, I am extremely proud of her for standing up for the rights of those who are being told they don't matter by the very school system that is supposed to be educating them.

The boy's mother and other friends have started support groups, both local and on Facebook to help students who are dealing with bullying issues. The help is out there, though it may be difficult to find. Find out what your school's rules are and what your state requires them to be—many schools are behind the times and are not meeting the state mandates. Do everything in your power to protect your child. Their very life may depend on it.

This spell has many aspects to it: we want it to boost your child's self-esteem and heal him or her from damage already done, offer protection, and give the child courage to face any future attacks. We also want to include aspects of binding to try to eliminate future attacks before they happen.

For this spell you will need:

Candles, one of each color:
- black for banishing, absorption of negative energies, protection, binding, and defining boundaries
- brown for justice, endurance, strength, and grace
- green for healing and to neutralize difficult situations

The following herbs for incense, half a cup of each:
- slippery elm to stop gossip
- yarrow for courage and protection
- pine for healing, protection, and banishing negative energies
- passionflower for friendship
- mugwort for protection and strength

You will also need:
- a glass bowl for holding the above incense mixture
- agate for courage, strength, love, and protection
- sodalite for healing, wisdom, calmness, grounding energies, and to reduce stress
- a piece of paper, writing utensil, and black cord (about 18 inches in length)
- a fireproof container, charcoal tablet, and lighter
- a place to bury things when you are finished (either outside or in a deep flower-pot type container)

Make sure your child is not allergic to any of the above ingredients. Use an electric chopper/grinder to combine the herbal ingredients together and grind into a powder.

Set up your altar with the candles on it. Pour the powder you made into the glass bowl and set the agate and sodalite in it. Cast your circle as normal.

If you know the names of the people harassing your child, write them down on the paper. If you don't know the names, write down a description that includes something like "the kids causing my child pain." Write it so there is no mistake you are focusing on the children (or adults) who have done harm to your child.

After writing names down, roll the paper up like a scroll and wrap the cord around it three times before knotting it off. As you wrap the cord around the scroll say:

> *I bind you once,*
> *I bind you twice,*
> *I bind you thrice.*
> *You shall not harm my child.*

Again wrap the cord around the scroll three times and say the above. Do this a total of three times. Set the bound scroll on your altar.

Light the black candle. One at a time, pick up each stone and pass it through the candle's smoke and say:

> *Through the smoke and the flame*
> *you are instilled with the power to protect.*
> *No harm shall come to the person*
> *who carries this stone.*

Light the brown candle. One at a time, pick up each stone and pass it through the candle's smoke and say:

> *Through the smoke and the flame*
> *you are instilled with the power of justice.*
> *No harm shall come to the person*
> *who carries this stone.*

Light the green candle. One at a time, pick up each stone and pass it through the candle's smoke and say:

> *Through the smoke and the flame*
> *you are instilled with the power to heal.*
> *No harm shall come to the person*
> *who carries this stone.*

Pick up the glass bowl filled with the powder. Pass it through the smoke of the black candle and say:

> *Through the smoke and the flame*
> *you are instilled with the power to protect.*

Pass it through the smoke of the brown candle and say:

> *Through the smoke and the flame*
> *you are instilled with the power of justice.*

Pass it through the smoke of the green candle and say:

> *Through the smoke and the flame*
> *you are instilled with the power to heal.*

Hold the bowl up toward the sky, high above your head. Say:

> *Great Goddess and Great God,*
> *your love and blessings*
> *are requested.*
> *Bless this powder,*
> *instill in it the power to protect,*
> *to banish ill will,*
> *to bind those who would harm.*
> *Instill in it the power to heal,*
> *the power to draw friends near in support.*
> *The power to close the mouths of*
> *those who only speak harm.*
> *The power to open the hearts of*
> *those who support and love.*
> *The power of your blessings and love*
> *strengthen my child.*

Thank the deities for their presence and close your circle.

Bury the scroll in a deep hole and cover it with as much earth as possible. Remove the stones from the powder. These you can give to your child to carry. If you know how, use wire to wrap the stones to make into a necklace. When you wash your child's clothes, add a tablespoon of the powder to the wash.

Remember, it is extremely important to back up this working in the mundane world. You must fight for the right for your child to be educated in a safe environment.

My in-laws drive me insane

I myself have been blessed with a wonderful mother-in-law…this time around. In my first marriage was a mother-in-law who, um, was a bit trying at times. Most of the time. Really, all the time. For her, no one was going to be good enough for her son (which is odd because in the long run, I realized *he* was nowhere close to good enough for me!), and she didn't have a problem letting me know she didn't think I was good enough.

It's hard to get close to people and start a relationship with them when all they do is point out that you either aren't who they expected their child to marry, or that you do things differently—where "differently" means "WRONG." Often these are complaints against mother-in-laws, but any in-law can be guilty of the same thing.

This spell will help keep you in a peaceful state when dealing with your problematic in-laws. We can't control the behaviors of others, but we can control our own, so we are going to make sure that nit-picking, sarcasm, and other snide remarks don't have their intended effect. There really is no sense in getting yourself worked up over their behavior. Simply work on taking the high road and be responsible for your own behavior; let them deal with their own.

This spell has different ideal times for performing it. It can be performed during a waxing moon to help you get along better with your in-laws. It can be done on a Wednesday if you want to improve your communication skills, or it can be done on a Monday if there is already much communication going on (most of it negative) and you just want some peace and quiet.

For this spell you will need:

Two stones
- amethyst for courage, peace, and happiness
- chrysocolla for wisdom, peace, love, and communication

Essential oils:
- narcissus for peace and harmony
- magnolia for peace
- gardenia oil for peace and happiness

- a bathtub or a foot-soaking tub
- a small glass bowl
- moon water (see page 4 for an explanation)

If possible, it would be great to wire-wrap these stones and incorporate them into a necklace or bracelet you can wear all the time, or at the very least when you will be spending time with your in-laws.

Cast your circle at your tub (or foot soak container) and fill it with water. Add three drops of each oil to the water. Take the small glass bowl and add moon water to it along with a drop of each oil.

Immerse yourself in the tub and add your stones to the glass bowl of oil with water. Relax and let yourself breathe in the soothing scents. Let calmness, peace, and serenity wash over and flow through you. Take as much time as you need to unwind and relax. Imagine being able to feel this same way when you are interacting with your in-laws. Imagine that your dealings with them are serene and pleasant. Calm and collected. Loving and joyful.

This spell is all about visualizing how you want your relationship with them to be, how you want to act with them, how you want them to act with you. Continue to hold these thoughts in your head until you are ready to get out of the tub. Ask your patron deity to bless your visualization and finish with "So mote it be."

Drain the tub and get out. Take the stones from the bowl and dry them off. Either use them in jewelry or carry them on you when you know you will be visiting with your in-laws.

Remember, some spells take time and patience. You will get out of it what you put into it. Remember when you see your in-law to not just expect them to act the way you visualized them acting. Begin by acting the way you visualized yourself acting.

My stepchildren don't like me

For many years, some of my stepchildren didn't care for me much. Their mother had lied to them, saying I was the reason she and their father had gotten divorced—which couldn't have been true as we didn't even meet for nearly two years after they divorced. However, the kids were young and couldn't comprehend the possibility that their mother may have lied. In fact, this woman had several affairs, a fact the children all learned when they were older. She also suffered greatly from different mental illnesses and was frequently hospitalized. She would go into the hospital for long stays, not seeing her children for months at a time; when she was out, she refused to have anything to do with them, but would make up for it by buying the kids whatever they wanted (not needed, mind you, but wanted). The kids believed her behavior was normal. When I came along and actually provided for them and also expected them to follow rules, it was just downright intolerable for them for many years.

Knowing I couldn't "give in," I had to hold my ground and continue to parent them the same way I parented my own children. It did take a while before the kids were able to understand that what they had been used to was not the normal way children are raised. All those years were quite difficult on me—always being treated like I was the villain. It was stressful and sometimes absolutely excruciating.

Though this spell isn't going to make your stepchildren instantly like you (that isn't the goal), it is going to help you deal with their negative feelings and your feelings. It will give you the strength to continue being the parent you know you need to be.

For this spell you will need:

- a brown candle for stability, strength, grace, endurance, integrity, and family issues
- a turquoise stone for courage, protection, happiness, and emotional balance

Set up your altar and cast your circle. Light the brown candle and hold the turquoise in your hand. Get in a comfortable position and say:

Though I know I am doing as I should,
I sometimes feel the drain,
the stretch,
the strain.
I come today for strength,
for the courage to go on,
for the stability and grace
to continue dealing with these issues
placed before me and my family.
I ask the Goddess and God
to grant me this in all I ask.

Continue holding the turquoise, feeling your energy pass into and through it, charging it for later use. See yourself happy, relaxed, and at ease. You are strong and capable. You are a good parent, a good person.

Meditate for a little while on your situation. Remember to see yourself as strong. Don't let the difficult times get you down. Use this spell to build yourself up.

When finished, extinguish the candle and close your circle. Keep the stone with you and hold on to it when you feel the need for a quick recharge. Let the energy from the stone wash over you and recharge you when you need it.

Part Three

★ ★ ★ ★

RELATIONSHIPS

My roommates are very inconsiderate: they don't clean up after themselves, they blast music all hours of the night, and let's not even talk about the overnight guests

Living with roommates can be both a joy and a burden. In my experience, at least, most of the time it falls on the side of burden! Though it is generally less expensive to share living quarters it can also be stressful. And when you live with people who believe the public/shared areas of the home (such as living room, kitchen, and bathrooms) are their own personal space, disregarding the others who also use that same space, it's downright frustrating! You will have to discuss this problem with your roommates. You might not make a lot of headway, but you must discuss it and see if you can set some rules everyone can agree to follow that will benefit everyone. You may find yourself being taken advantage of and if that happens, you need to have a much more serious conversation than if you are dealing with rudeness. Either way, this discussion is not a fun one, but is something that needs to be addressed as soon as possible. Don't let these type of problems prolong, it only makes them worse.

In the past I have lived with roommates in many different capacities; I've even taken in family in their time of need. Now, however, I don't know that I would do it again!

I would suggest doing this spell before you have the discussion with your roommates and then again right afterwards. It's a way to clear the air before and after—a fresh, new starting point.

For this spell you will need:

- a black candle to absorb negative energy and define boundaries
- a sage smudge for purification
- several lemons (one for each public/shared room in your home) to purify, absorb negativity, and add joy and positive energy
- a knife and cutting board
- small dessert-sized paper plates (not foam)

This spell is going to involve a lot of walking around, so an altar and circle are not necessary.

Begin at your front door and light the black candle. Turn to the left (or as soon as you can) and walk all along the edges of the rooms as close to the walls as possible. Go through any room that is a public room—or a private room if you have permission to do so. Always turn to the left—you are going clockwise throughout your home. Be careful not to spill or drip wax.

As you walk throughout your home, chant the following:

Banish the bad,
take it away.
Set the boundaries,
here to stay.

As you chant and walk your home, keep in mind that the "boundaries" you are setting here are boundaries that negativity should not cross. Continue the chant until you reach the front door again. Extinguish the candle.

Light the sage smudge and follow the same path as you did with the candle. As you walk, chant the following:

Refresh, renew,
purify, protect

Continue the chant until you reach the front door again. Extinguish the smudge.

Cut each lemon in half and place them cut side up on paper plates. They will roll a bit, take care to not drop them as you walk. In each public room (and any private room you have been given permission to do this in) place a lemon in one corner and also in the corner diagonal from it. As you deliver these lemons to their locations, chant:

Energize and renew,
affirm and enliven.

Set up a time for a house meeting to discuss how you feel about the situation. If you do not feel the meeting went well, perform the spell again immediately. As the lemons soak up bad energy, they may begin to blacken. Replace the lemons as needed by repeating the entire spell. After you have replaced all the lemons once, hold another house meeting.

In the meantime, remember to work on your differences in the mundane world as well.

I've discovered my significant
other has criminal tendencies

Some crimes are more serious than others and carry heavier sentences if someone is convicted of committing them. However, the law is the law, and if you believe in it firmly, any violation can also be seen as a violation of your own trust in the person who has committed it.

Being involved with someone who has criminal tendencies can be dangerous for several reasons. In addition to the possibility of ending up being a victim yourself, if you know someone has committed a crime or is going to commit a crime and you do nothing about it, that makes you an accessory. In most states, being an accomplice means you can be charged and punished similarly to the person who actually committed the crime. Deciding to turn your significant other in is far from easy; it can be a very painful experience even though it is the right choice to make.

An ex of mine was a very determined drunk driver. While it is a crime (and a rather deplorable one at that), it's not really easy to turn one in for doing it: the person breaking the law has to be caught in the act. Police don't show up at someone's house and say, "We heard you were driving drunk. How about a breathalyzer?"

I had tried to get my ex to stop at least driving after he had too much to drink but he didn't listen. I had some friends on the police force who explained what they could legally do, and were able to actually catch him in the act that way. Once he lost his license, he didn't drive anymore, so at least his endangering the lives of others had stopped. It was also followed quickly by our breakup, so it worked out for the best in many ways.

For some people, making that call to the police is a very difficult step and you might not have the courage yet to take it. This spell is designed to help you do the right thing and build up your own inner strength while doing so. You'll be doing a visualization with a scrying bowl.

You should also make sure your significant other doesn't know you are doing this spell if you believe it may lead to more dangerous problems. Do not put yourself in harm's way for any reason. If you feel you are in danger because of your significant other, skip the spell and go directly to the police!

For this spell you will need:

Three candles, one of each color:
- black for dealing with loss and confusion,
- sky blue for calmness, patience, and understanding
  (so *you* don't fly off the handle)
- "regular" blue for truth, honor, wisdom, and knowledge
- a black bowl with water
- cheesecloth and a bit of string

The following herbs:
- bluebell for strength and truth
- calendula for comfort
- coltsfoot for peace, tranquility, and visions
- columbine for courage and willpower
- honeysuckle for psychic awareness, healing, honesty,
  and mental powers

Place a pinch of each herb into the cheesecloth and tie it in a bunch. Allow it to soak in the water in the black bowl for fifteen minutes. Remove the herbs from the water.

Cast your circle. Light the candles, placing them in a triangle around the bowl, with the "point" at the back. Sit down in front of it and stare into it deeply.

Visualize yourself as a very strong person. This may take different forms, such as a super hero or even a wrestler. Whatever you imagine a strong person to look like on the outside, go ahead and visualize yourself in that role. After you find that image, imagine the strength you see on the outside inverting and moving to the inside of your visualized self. You are as strong on the inside as you are on the outside. Spend some time admiring this side of yourself. What types of feats would this version of yourself accomplish? What would you use that strength for?

Now you need to turn your visualization to what will probably be unpleasant thoughts. Visualize your significant other. Next, visualize that person committing the crimes they have committed. As hard as it may be, visualize them breaking the law and acting out their actual crimes. Next, visualize their victim/s. See their agony. Feel their pain and suffering. What can your strong self do to help them? Imagine yourself coming to their aid. Helping them out. How do they feel now? Can you feel their pain lessening? After helping them, say goodbye to the visualized victims. Wish them well.

When you have completed the visualization, you should feel empowered. You should feel you know the correct path to follow. Go ahead and follow the path that has been laid out before you.

I don't know if I should stay in my current relationship—it doesn't seem to be going anywhere

Have you been dating the same person for, oh, let's say—years, and feel like nothing has changed? Do you want more out of your relationship but feel that what you have now is all that your significant other is capable of giving? Have you talked with your S.O. only to be told, "I like how things are now, why do we have to change anything?"

If you answered yes to any of these questions, chances are you and your partner are not on the same path. The question is, do you want to stick around and hope that eventually your paths will merge together, or do you want to set off in search of a new partner and a new path?

I've watched friends stay with the same person for years even though they were completely unhappy with the situation; they always hoped things would change. Personally, I would think a few years of wishing would be more than plenty, but some people hold out for decades hoping something will someday be different. Maybe this kind of hope is less about people not wanting to be alone and more about realistically hoping the situation will change. Sometimes you just have to say, "Look—here is what I need out of this relationship," and if your partner isn't able to give that to you, it's time to move on.

This spell will help you decide which direction to take your own path in. It is best completed under a new moon for its contemplation aspect. It is also ideally done on a Saturday to shed light on hidden or obscured matters.

This is a spell/meditation that will take place in a tub. If a tub isn't available, simply soak your feet while you do the visioning.

For this spell you will need:

- an indigo candle for insight and vision
- a cup or two of chamomile tea for meditation
- myrrh incense for meditation
- some sandalwood oil to add to your bath or soaking
  water to aid in your meditation and psychic awareness

Fill your tub or foot soak container with warm water. Add a few drops of the oil. Light the incense and candle and place them nearby along with your chamomile tea. Immerse yourself in the tub or your feet into the footbath. Do some deep breathing and slowly sip your tea.

After you finish your tea, close your eyes and relax. Empty your mind of all thoughts.

Once your mind is clear, imagine what you want your future to be like. See yourself in five years. What are you doing with your life? Where do you live? What type of activities do you do? Imagine yourself in another five years. See what your life is like then. What do you envision yourself doing? Are you still at the same job? Do you live in the same house? Are you married? Do you have kids? Do you live alone? What is it you need to be happy?

As you visualize yourself in the future, you will begin to see the answer to your current problem. Is your current boyfriend or girlfriend in the future with you? If they are, are you happy? Are you still at the same standstill? If they aren't in the future with you, you already have your answer: you have no intentions of continuing this relationship and might as well end it now. If your partner is in your future and you are still in the same spot and the same sort of relationship, you have your answer there too—things simply aren't going to change and you need to move on. Perhaps you look into your future and things *do* seem to be different. Perhaps you are married or have children. If this vision shows itself, take some more time to reevaluate your relationship. Do some more talking with your significant other before making the decision to move on.

I just got a divorce and I'm not sure how to move on

No matter what anyone says, divorces are painful—whether you wanted the divorce or not. A life you have been living for possibly years has ended. Things are different. It is important to remember that different does not always mean "bad." Like the Death card in tarot, this is a time of new beginnings, not necessarily only endings. You may have had plenty of plans—things you wanted to do or accomplish, and somehow being married held you back. Well, now you are a brand new person, and can reinvent yourself any way you like. You can follow through on those plans you had made before. You can do whatever you want to make yourself happy.

After a divorce, people tend to go through a huge range of emotions—I've been there twice myself. While you may be happy that the relationship is over, there is also probably some pain, and the pain may be unrelated to your ex-spouse. Perhaps you've had to move or work more hours to make ends meet, therefore give up time with your kids or friends. Things change after a divorce, but moving on doesn't have to be difficult. Life is short, so don't let these emotions stand in your way. Use this spell to help get you on track to the new you.

This spell is best completed on a Wednesday for its association with communication, intellectual pursuits, the conscious mind, study, travel, and wisdom.

For this spell you will need:
- lavender incense for happiness, healing, peace,
  matters of the heart, and matters of the mind
- a journal and writing utensil

Find a nice comfy place to sit down where you will be able to do some extensive writing. Light the lavender incense and let the smoke waft over your journal.

Hold your journal close to your heart and say:

> *My heart will open,*
> *my mind shall too,*
> *I will share my secrets*
> *and dreams with you.*

You are going to write about several topics. Some of these may be more difficult than others. Some answers may be hard to remember but do the best you can. You can always come back later and add more if you would like.

Label the top of each page with the topics given here and write. Leave a couple of empty pages if you think you will want to come back to a topic later. When finished with one topic, move on to the next, labeling the top of a new page. You do not have to complete everything in one sitting, but use the opening (already given) and closing (to follow) each time.

When you are finished writing for the time being, again hold your journal close to your heart and say:

With blessings from the Goddess,
I share my dreams and wishes with you.
With work and luck, they will come true.
My goals and aspirations, that I hold dear,
will no longer be held back by fear.

As you write about the topics, know that you are helping to heal the pain associated with the loss of the dreams you set aside or gave up on. You are also internalizing new goals, giving life to them, or reviving old ones. Writing your goals down brings them one step closer to reality. You will end up with a real working plan of what to do with your life. You will know which way to turn to get your life back on track once you have completed these questions.

Your list of topics:

1. Think back to when you were younger, before your marriage. What were the things you wanted out of life? Did you want to go to college? Get married? Have kids? Travel? Own your own business? What did you want to do for a living? Make a list, trying to remember everything you wanted to do, be, or accomplish when you were younger.

2. When you met your former spouse, did anything in question 1 change? How? What goals did you do away with and what new goals (if any) did you set?

3. Which of the goals from question 1 did you achieve? Which did you give up on? Why did you give up on them?

4. What new goals do you want to set for yourself? Do you want to be able to marry again someday? Have you decided it simply isn't for you? Do you want children in the future? How about going back to school? Would you like to be able to move and start over someplace new? What about a new job? You

may want a new haircut, a makeover, a new wardrobe. There are no wrong answers. Think about everything you would change about your life right now if anything at all was possible.

5. Guess what? Anything *is* possible (okay, you might not actually learn how to teleport, but just about everything else is possible). Some goals just take far more work than others. Order your goals from question 4 from easiest to achieve to most difficult. Which goals can you accomplish right away? Which ones will take a lot of time and work to cross them off as completed?

6. Start with the easiest goal—it should be listed at the top. Now go do it. Just do it. No one is around to tell you no, and it wouldn't matter if someone was anyway. You are your own person restarting your own life. You were meant to enjoy it so go ahead. Keep working on those goals, dealing with the easier ones first while you contemplate how to go about those more difficult ones later on. Consider this your "bucket list." Over time, some of your desires will change—that is fine, add or delete from your list as you feel necessary, but don't give up on anything simply because someone says you should.

After ten years of being together, my significant other and I broke up

While the last spell was focused on how to get on with life after a breakup of a serious relationship, this spell deals with recovering from the pain. Maybe you didn't want to break up. Maybe the breakup was completely one-sided, and not your side at that. You are in pain. Your heart is broken and it feels like it will never be whole again.

Your heart *will* mend someday. It might not happen right away and in fact, it could take a while. This spell will help speed up that process and allow you to grieve in a healthy way while also lessening the pain you are feeling. It's normal to be hurt after a breakup and to feel sad. It's normal to be depressed. The key is to not let these feelings go on for too long or develop into a serious problem. We must learn to grieve, pick ourselves back up, and move on again.

For this spell you will need:

- cypress for solace, comfort, healing, and easing feelings of loss
- hyacinth for overcoming grief
- lily for easing the pain of ended relationships
- witch hazel for healing a broken heart
- clove to add spice back into your life
- a piece of cheesecloth and string

With this spell you aren't going to worry about the day of the week or the phases of the moon. You are hurting now and don't need to wait to start healing yourself—you need to start healing now! You also won't be using any candles due to how you're feeling now. You might feel a bit distracted and we don't want any fire accidents.

You will need a tub or footbath, though I really recommend using a tub for this one. If you happen to have an outdoor hot tub you could use, this would be great to do outside under a relaxing moon. Make sure you are not allergic to any of the above listed items. If you are, omit that ingredient. The rest you will add to the cheesecloth, tie it up, and toss it in the tub underneath the warm running water.

Before you step into the tub, say the following:

Oh Goddess, help me to see
the courage that resides deep within me.
Cleanse my heart, body, and soul—
help me to heal, to make myself whole.

Step into the tub and get comfortable. Close your eyes and just relax for a moment. In your mind, scan your body and find the points that are full of stress or sadness. Often your body will store these emotions and feelings in your body somewhere. This spell will help you begin to let those feelings out. Let them seep and weep from your body and wash away into the water you are soaking in. When you pull the plug or pour out the water, they will disappear with the water.

Focus on those areas. Imagine the hurt and stress breaking up on the inside and absorbing through your skin and then lifting off into the water. Go through each area of your body looking for these painful areas. You will probably find more in your lung and stomach area and in the top of your head. Your joints will most likely also be holding this pain, and your teeth may be stressed and sore from clenching your jaws. Let it all go—all the pain, hurt, anger. Feel free to cry. Cry as much as you need it. Let it out. Crying is often a great stress reliever. Let the built-up tension pour away. Allow your tears to cleanse the negative feelings from your body. Be conscious of the feelings leaving your body. Don't feel sorry for yourself; these tears let the bad out and make room for the good.

Pay close attention to these feelings leaving your body. When you begin to feel the difference and your body begins to feel as if a burden is being lifted, say the following:

Mother Goddess, as I begin to mend,
help me to feel refreshed and renewed.
Cleanse my heart, body and soul,
give me the strength to make myself whole.

Continue to focus on areas where you can still feel the stress and pain. Continue visioning the pain and stress breaking up and dissolving. This will make you tired, so before you feel exhausted, stop. Don't wear yourself out too much.

Before you step out of the tub or remove your feet from the foot bath, say the following:

As I leave behind my pain, my burden,
I look forward to the future,
to my new life,
whatever it may bring.

Step out of the tub before you empty it. Pull the plug, and then watch as your worries are washed down the drain. You will most likely need to repeat this spell several times. Use it when you are feeling overwhelmed, and know that things will get better. Life goes on even when we are hurting beyond our control. We just need some time and perspective to become realigned and refocused again.

I don't think I like my best friend anymore

Sometimes in our lives we may find that the people we've surrounded ourselves with aren't people we are really comfortable being around anymore. This often happens when one person has grown and the other hasn't, or the two have grown in different directions. Unfortunately, we could probably all name people we know who act pretty much the same (and about as maturely) as they did in high school.

When the time comes to end a friendship, it is best to just go ahead and end it. Drawing things out often leads to more problems, more hurt feelings, more heartbreak, more resentment.

If you've tried to work things out and nothing seems to be working, maybe it truly is time to call it quits. Even if you know your friend needs some serious help, but is unwilling to admit it, there's nothing more you can do. You cannot carry the burden of others, nor can you help those who refuse to help themselves.

Recently I finally said goodbye to someone I had been friends with for more than twenty years. Why? She had turned into someone I simply could not be around anymore. She became progressively more and more negative, wouldn't accept help, nor would she admit she needed any. She blamed everyone else for her problems and refused to admit any of her problems might actually have been caused by her own actions. Since I told her I was no longer able to be her friend, she's had more and more problems and her life has become filled with even more negativity. Though I hear about things that go on with her from time to time, I am no longer touched by her detrimental aura. I couldn't stop her problems, nor could I help her through them. Instead I had to make the choice that would save me from being dragged down with her. You always hope you can throw someone a life saver and they will grab on to it, but unfortunately things don't always happen that way. Sometimes you have to do what you have to do to save yourself.

Saying goodbye is usually hard, though. While you may feel you are making the right choice, you may also feel sad about saying goodbye. It is time for you to move on, however, and this spell is designed to help you do just that. This spell will help you put the past behind and move forward with your life.

This spell is best performed on a Saturday as it is best suited for endings.

For this spell you will need:

· an indigo candle for insight, vision, change, and flexibility
· a fireproof container, such as a cauldron, and a lighter
· a sheet of paper (one or more) and a writing utensil

Cast your circle, and light the indigo candle. Sit down and get comfortable. Close your eyes, and open your arms out to the sides with your hands up. Say the following:

> *My intent to be known, I call to Air*
> *to send this spell to the winds so fair;*
> *to ease my mind from choices made;*
> *to lessen the pain and let memories fade.*

Using the paper and pen, write about how your feelings for your friend have changed. Have you changed? Has the other person? Write about these changes and how they make you feel. Use more than one piece of paper if you have to. Get all of your feelings out and onto the paper.

When finished, say:

> *To ease my mind from choices made,*
> *to lessen the pain and let history fade;*
> *let memories be gone, I erase the past*
> *to end this now, finally at last.*

Tear the paper into shreds and put the pieces in the fireproof container. Use the candle to light the paper on fire and say:

> *Let memories be gone, I erase the past*
> *to end this now, finally at last.*
> *To pull me out of this quagmire,*
> *bless this decision and purify with Fire.*

When the paper has burned all up and the ash has cooled, either take the container outside or open a window (screen and all). Take the ashes in your hands and crumple them. Blow them out into the world. Say goodbye to your old friendship as it blows away in the breeze.

I have a serious crush on someone I shouldn't

Your boss. Your spouse's friend. Your friend's spouse. Your spouse's boss. None of these (or many other possibilities) are going to work out well romantically. They won't for you nor anyone else involved. The best course of action is to nip these feelings in the bud before *anything* has a chance to happen.

We truly can't help who we are attracted to; sometimes we have no idea even why we are attracted to a particular person and not another. It may be chemistry, that we just like the more risky behavior, or a combination of other things. We can, however, stop these feelings when we know it's the right thing to do.

Obviously this spell is going to need work in the mundane world. If every time you see this person you feel your heart go pitter-patter—then **don't look**! Put as much distance as possible between you and the object of your affection for as long as you can. Start acting like you aren't attracted to the person. The rest will follow. Don't flirt and don't spend more time with the person than you absolutely have to. Don't sabotage the success of your spell.

It is best to begin this spell on the night of a new moon for its association with endings and banishings. (You are in fact banishing your romantic feelings for this person.) If you have the benefit of being able to do the spell on a Saturday, it would help add power, as Saturdays are good for setting limitations and boundaries as well as endings. If the new moon doesn't fall on a Saturday, go ahead and do the initial working on the new moon and then subsequent workings on Saturdays.

For this spell you will need:

- a turquoise candle for discipline
- a red chunk of wax to represent passion and lust (you can use a red candle in the shape of a person if you want)
- a large bowl of cooked, mashed turnips to help end relationships
- a picture of the person if possible (and tack)
- wooden spoon
- towel
- a tiger's eye stone for courage, judgment, common sense, honesty, and to help ease depression

· something sharp to carve the wax (a nail will work)
· a place to bury things when the spell is complete

Place all the items on your altar and cast your circle. Light the turquoise candle. Take the hunk of red wax and carve the name of the object of your desire. If you have a picture of the person, tack it to the wax chunk. Say the following:

The name I give you
has been deep in my thoughts
and must now be freed from my heart and mind.

You may use a wooden spoon for this next part or your hands if you don't mind getting them dirty. Form a hole in the mashed turnips, insert the chunk of wax, and cover it back up. Say the following:

I remove you from my sight.
I remove you from my mind.
I remove you from my heart.

Pass the tiger's eye quickly through the flame of the candle, then circle it widdershins (counterclockwise) over the bowl three times and again through the candle flame. Say the following as you do so:

This stone shall remind me to be disciplined,
to keep you at bay,
to be courageous,
and to use my common sense.
I will be honest with myself and others.
I will not tread where it is not safe to tread.

Extinguish the candle, close your circle, and take the bowl of turnips to the place you can bury things. If you have to use a flower pot, only use a small amount of the turnips covering the wax and make sure the flower pot is LARGE. Too much turnip will smell bad. If you are able to do this outside, dig a large enough hole that once you dump the turnip and wax in you will still be able to cover it by several inches. As you bury the turnips, say:

> *I banish you from my heart.*
> *I do not hate you,*
> *but the passion felt for you*
> *has been extinguished.*
> *So mote it be.*

I've been unfaithful and don't know what to do

Chances are you *do* know what to do, you just haven't yet convinced yourself you really need to do it. Anything less than telling your partner the truth is a lie. It's a lie to your partner and to yourself.

You probably don't want to tell because you are afraid of how your partner will react. What you need to think about is this: are you afraid of hurting your partner, or that his or her reaction will end up hurting you? You've already committed one selfish act so it's probably not the best idea, for many reasons, to throw another selfish act on top of it.

Coming clean isn't always easy though. You had the guts to cheat, but now your backbone has turned to jelly. Though I myself have not cheated, I have been cheated on. It sucks. It sucks even more when you find out from someone other than the one person who should be telling you.

I've also had friends come to me with their confessions of infidelity, and I tell them the same thing: FESS UP. You did the crime, so get ready to do the time. Maybe you'll be able to work things out, maybe you won't. Either way, your partner deserves to know and deserves to be able to make a choice as to what he or she wants to do. It's time to be fair.

This spell will help you regain control of yourself and your emotions. It will help give you the backbone you need in order to follow through with the morally right steps to take in the very near future.

For this spell you will need:
- a purple candle for self-esteem, insight, spirituality, and inner strength
- a piece of onyx for emotional balance and self-control
- a piece of sodalite for healing, meditation, wisdom, calm, grounding, and reducing stress
- a fireproof container, charcoal tablet, and lighter
- thyme for courage (about a tablespoon)
- nutmeg for fidelity (about a teaspoon)

Cast your circle, light the charcoal tablet in your fireproof container and light the purple candle.

Mix the thyme and nutmeg. Set the onyx and sodalilte in the mixture, covering the stones as much as you can.

Begin by saying the following:

I know I was wrong.
I have hurt others and myself
even if those others do not yet know it.
I have made a terrible mistake
and must atone with honesty for my lack of judgment.
The truth is owed.

Take a pinch of the thyme/nutmeg mixture and place it on the lit charcoal tablet. Say the following:

I pledge my fidelity
to my partner and to myself.

Put another pinch on the charcoal tablet and say:

I pledge my courage
to my partner and to myself.

Take some time to visualize how you will approach your partner. Imagine where you will be when you tell him/her. Imagine the words you will use. Focus on your actions, not your partner's. Do not try to guess his or her reaction, simply focus on your part of the interaction.

Holding the purple candle in your hand, say the following:

I pledge to use the strength
inside of me to do what must be done.
I pledge to be honest
with my partner and myself.
Though it may not be possible
to right this wrong,
I shall try my best.

Set the candle back down and remove the onyx from what's left of the thyme and nutmeg mixture. Hold it in your hands and say:

I will keep a level head.
I will remember I chose to be unfaithful
and that it is my fault, not my partner's.

Set the onyx on the altar and remove the sodalite from the mixture. Hold it in your hands and say:

> *Grant me wisdom and calmness*
> *but above all, grant my partner*
> *your healing grace.*

Set the sodalite on your altar and close your circle.

Carry both stones with you when you speak with your partner, and make sure you do it as soon as possible. These things have a way of coming out, and things will go better for everyone if the news comes from you rather than from someone else.

I feel like I'm the only one doing any giving in my relationships

All relationships are give-and-take. When a relationship becomes one-sided and one person is doing all the giving and the other is doing all the taking, it can become quite stressful and overwhelming for the giver. Unless something changes, the taker ends up being seen as vampiric and eventually massive resentment will kick in.

It is entirely possible that the taker doesn't realize they aren't giving anything in the relationship. It's also possible that the giver has tried to have the conversation with the taker dozens of times saying how it feels and wanting things to change, but the taker is already perfectly aware of what is really going on and has no intentions of changing anything. How many people would really want to change a situation where they are getting everything they want? They often don't realize that if things do not change, the giver is going to stop giving and the taker is going to end up losing all their "benefits." The giver will likely move on to someone else who is capable and willing to be a giver too.

My second husband was definitely a taker and needed someone who was willing to constantly give. He needed a mother figure, which I think may have been part of the reason he was attracted to me in the first place. When he and I married, I was already raising my young twins and he seemed to want the same mothering attention on him all the time. He didn't seem to notice I already had two children to raise and one more after giving birth to our son. I needed a partner, not a fourth child! When I finally realized what was going on, I also realized our relationship was never going to change unless I changed it. He wasn't happy with any changes because he had been happy with the way things were. Unfortunately, my own happiness wasn't one of the things he wanted—he simply wanted me to be responsible for his.

Some relationships naturally involve more giving, such as a mother to a child, or if you are caring for an elderly parent. However, if you find that you are a giver in several of your relationships, such as with friends or with romantic relationships, this should be a clue that you keep attaching yourself to the same kind of selfish person, which means you may want to speak with a therapist to help figure out why.

This spell will help you figure out if the relationships you are in are one-sided, and it will help give you the strength to stand up for yourself and end these relationships if necessary. It's also possible you might realize that *you* are the one making these relationships the way they are.

For this spell you will need:

- several sheets of brown paper (for stability, balance, decision making, grounding, strength, and grace) and a writing utensil
- chamomile tea to help you with your meditation
- a fireproof container and lighter
- a silver candle for balance
- coffee grounds (for the conscious mind; used, wet grounds are fine)

Place the coffee grounds in the bottom of the fireproof container. Place the container, silver candle, and tea on your altar. Open your circle.

Light the silver candle and say:

> *Goddess, help me to find the balance needed in my life.*

Take a seat and get comfortable. Say:

> *Goddess, help me to meditate on this problem before me.*

Sip your chamomile tea. As you do, allow yourself to relax and slip into a semi-meditative state.

Once you are comfortable and relaxed, take your paper and prepare to write. At the top of the page write the name of a person with whom you are in a relationship you feel does not do any giving, only taking. Below the name, write the type of a relationship: friendship, family, romantic, etc.

Below that, write examples of times when you have needed something but the person wasn't willing to give it to you, wasn't willing to give you what you needed. How did the person act when you made your request? How did you act when you were refused? Use as much paper as you need. When you are done with examples, write next about what it is you do for that other person. Do they ask you to do these things? Do you do them without being asked? How does the other person act when you do these things for him/her? Do they thank you? Tell you not to do them?

Continue writing down everything that comes to mind. Watch for patterns such as you doing things for people without them asking, or people saying you don't need to do something. Are you doing things for people after they tell you not to?

You are going to consciously put these behaviors in the past.

Tear your sheets of paper into strips and place them on top of the coffee grounds in your fireproof container. As you do so, say:

> *The path I have followed ends here.*
> *I control my future.*

Repeat the above three times. Light the paper on fire and say the following as it burns:

> *I will no longer allow myself to be taken advantage of.*
> *It is my decision to leave the past behind*
> *and move forward into the future.*
> *I will now stand up for myself*
> *and no longer be tread upon.*
> *When I give, it will be because I want to,*
> *not because I feel I have to.*
> *I will associate with those who are*
> *willing to give back,*
> *and avoid those who spend their lives taking.*

After the paper has burned up, bury the ashes along with the coffee grounds.

My family keeps bugging me to get married, but I really don't want to yet

Though it seems these types of people are becoming fewer and further between, there are still those parents who want nothing more than for their children to marry and have children of their own—and in that order.

More and more frequently, people are putting off marriage until later in life and some have children without getting married at all. This is a personal choice that parents or other family members might not be happy with, but in order to save your own sanity, they will need to accept your decision for what it is—*your* decision.

This spell is designed to give you peace and strength when dealing with your family. Though you can't force them to understand (oh, if only it were so easy!), you can make yourself feel better about your decision and not be as affected by your family's behavior.

For this spell you will need:
- coltsfoot for peace and tranquility
- mugwort for strength
- a brown floating candle for dealing with family issues
- a black bowl filled with water

Cast your circle and place the bowl of water on your altar. Sit in front of it. Light the brown candle and say:

> *I call out to the universe*
> *to help me cope with the pressures from my family.*
> *To affirm that my choices are my choices,*
> *and not for my family to make.*

Set the floating candle in the bowl of water. Take a pinch of mugwort, sprinkle it over the water, and say:

I call out to the universe
to give me strength in dealing
with the pressures from my family.
To give me the strength to make choices
that are mine to make,
and not for my family to make for me.

Take a pinch of coltsfoot, sprinkle it over the water, and say:

I call out to the universe
to give me peace in dealing
with the pressures from my family.
To give me peace when making choices that are mine to
make, and not for my family to make for me.

Take some time to meditate. Visualize yourself making the decisions to put off marriage and feeling good about it. See yourself telling your family and being strong and firm in your decision. See yourself telling your family that you are comfortable with your life choices and that since you are the one they affect the most, *you* are the one who needs to be the most comfortable with those decisions. When you are done meditating, extinguish the candle and pour the water and herbs outside.

The next time your family approaches you with the subject, take a deep breath and relax a moment before you answer. When you do answer, think back to your meditation and how you responded to them then. Use what you learned in your meditation to help you out when you speak to your family in the future.

I was physically abused by my significant other

Domestic battery is an extremely serious and dangerous matter. If you are in an abusive relationship, you need to do whatever is necessary to get yourself out and to a safe place. This may mean involving the police or moving into a protective shelter for a while. Though it probably won't be the best experience of your life, it may very well be a life saving experience. Unfortunately, often in abuse cases, the victim doesn't leave and the abuser continues to abuse.

My second husband had quite a long arrest record. I admit I was scared to leave for a while. He made threats starting just after we had a baby. I couldn't leave him because I didn't know how I was going to take care of three kids on my own. I was in college trying to get ahead. But when things come to a crisis, we all do what we have to do. I soon learned that having him out of my life made it far easier. I had stuck around because I was under the false impression that life without him would be more difficult, not easier. Sure, money was tighter without him, but my family and friends were more than willing to help out as long as I was safe.

Several friends of mine have gone through the same or similar problems; one unfortunately let the abuser come back over and over again. At some point he stopped abusing her and moved on to the kids instead. It took a long time to get her and her family help, but they are all safe and far away from him now.

Do not leave your fate up to this spell alone! If you don't do something about your situation in the mundane world, you will be working against your spell work.

Due to the nature of this spell, I feel it is okay to perform it for others without their knowledge. Keep in mind that you will have to rework the wording a bit. If you have a family member or friend in an abusive situation—I say go ahead and work the spell for them. Some people won't agree with this, so ultimately it's entirely up to you. Do what you feel is right.

This spell is designed to help keep the abused safe, binding the abuser, preventing abuse, and banishing the negativity the abuse has built up. This spell is best done under a new moon, but by all means do not wait if you need to do the spell sooner!

For this spell you will need:
- nettle for protection, healing, and banishing negative energy
- dried ivy for binding
- frankincense for protection and banishing negative energy

- a silver candle for truth, intuition, receptivity, stability, balance, inner self, moon power, and the Goddess
- a piece of white paper and a writing utensil
- a length of black cord (18 inches should be enough)
- a fireproof container, charcoal tablet and lighter

Set up the items on your altar and cast your circle. Light the charcoal in the fireproof container. Light the silver candle and say the following:

> *Mother Goddess, I come to you for your protection.*
> *I need your strength, to help me through,*
> *to help me face my fears,*
> *and do what must be done to protect myself.*
> *Help me to use my intuition*
> *and be receptive to the choices I know I must make.*
> *Give my inner self the voice to guide me in finding truth,*
> *stability, and balance in my life.*

Sprinkle some nettle and frankincense onto the lit tablet. Take the piece of paper and at the top of the page write the name of the person who has been harming you. Write down some of the forms of abuse this person has taken against you. When you are finished, sprinkle some dried ivy leaves onto the paper and roll it up like a scroll.

Take the black cord and begin wrapping it around the scroll saying:

> *I bind you once.*
> *I bind you twice.*
> *I bind you thrice.*
> *You can do me no harm.*

Continue this chant until you have used all of the cord, then tie it off. Again sprinkle some more nettle and frankincense on the tablet. Waft the scroll through the smoke and say:

> *Banish the negative from my life,*
> *send it away and keep it away.*
> *Let me have the chance to be happy.*

> *Heal me from the damage that has already been done*
> *and keep me safe and protected.*

Set the scroll on top of the lit charcoal. If it doesn't light, go ahead and use the lighter to set it on fire. When the paper has burned, either wash the ashes down a drain or bury them in your yard.

My significant other is jealous and controlling

A significant other who is jealous and controlling is about as dangerous as being with someone who is abusive physically. Though the abuse takes shape in either mental or emotional forms (or both), it is very likely to develop into physical abuse given time. As you might guess, this kind of abuse often precedes physical abuse.

If your significant other is jealous and controlling, in a way you're lucky: this kind of behavior gives you the chance to get out before things escalate to a level of physical danger.

This spell is similar to the previous spell. It will bind the abusive actions of your partner and help give you the strength to leave—or kick that person out as the case may be. As with the previous spell, I feel it is okay to do the spell for others to protect them. Sometimes people who are in the most need don't see it and need even more help. Again, what you do is entirely up to you and your own code of ethics.

For this spell you will need:

- a purple candle for growth, self-esteem, insight,
  and inner strength
- a black candle to absorb negative energy, for protection,
  defining boundaries, and binding
- a hunk of green wax to represents jealousy (to banish it)
- dried ivy for binding
- costmary to still emotions
- dragon's blood oil for power, protection, banishing, and to
  amplify the spell
- a fireproof container, charcoal tablet, and lighter
- tongs

Place the items on your altar. Light the charcoal tablet and cast your circle. Light the purple candle and say:

Looking inside myself, I will find
the strength to move on,
to grow, and thrive,
without negativity in my life.

Light the black candle and say:

Protect me from harm,
as I set about my plans,
to begin my life anew.
Banish and bind the actions
that hurt me
both heart and soul.
Protect me from harm.

Use the tongs to hold the chunk of green wax above the flame of the black candle—do not hold it close enough to melt the wax, just close enough to soften the outsides a bit. When it is soft, roll the wax in dried, crushed ivy and costmary leaves. Squeeze the wax tightly to help the leaves stick and get embedded into the wax. As you do so, say the following three time:

I bind you, (name),
and your emotions from harming me.

Drip some dragon's blood oil onto the charcoal tablet. As it steams and smokes up, pass the wax through the smoke. Close your circle and bury the wax outside.

As with others, this spell must also be backed up with work in the mundane world. You cannot expect this spell to work if you continue to stay in the abusive relationship. Get out as soon as you possibly can. This spell helps buy you time so you can make arrangements to leave, but it won't hold off someone else's behaviors forever.

I feel like I'm growing, but my friends aren't growing with me—we just don't have that much in common anymore

If you are hanging out with friends one night and you bring up some recent news story, political event, religious topic, or other item of interest to you, and they stare at you like you've just sprouted a second head, chances are you've probably outgrown your friends.

If their only idea of a good time is to see how many shots they can down without passing out, you've probably outgrown your friends. If they sit around and do nothing but man/woman bash, you've probably outgrown your friends. Maybe they spend all their time playing video games and have no clue what is going on in the real world (yes, this kind of thing can happen at any age). If anything of substance (other than substance use) seems too deep for them, you have most definitely outgrown your friends. If they constantly talk about the things they claim they are going to do someday, and the changes they claim they are going to make but never really change or do anything, that's all there is to it—you have outgrown your friends.

This isn't necessarily a bad thing. Some people never want to mature or grow up. It's easier to sit around and blame everyone else for one's circumstances than it is to own up and face facts. Some people will use the excuse, "Oh, but we're just having fun," yet there never seems to be a time when they aren't "just having fun." They take nothing seriously.

You, however, have outgrown that. It happens sooner for some than others, and that's okay too. The important thing is that you have grown and you believe your relationships are no longer good at stimulating you in a positive manner. You may feel lonely for a while, as it may take some time to find new friends who are on the same intellectual level as you.

This spell is designed to help attract new, more mature friends into your circle. It will help you see yourself for who you really are—a growing, ever learning person willing to expand your mind.

The difference in maturity levels was a real problem in the Grove I run. Some of our members were more interested in drinking and partying it up after ritual, yet at the same time we learned they were telling others we weren't "serious enough" for them! The rest of us had wanted to start spending time after ritual and feasting working on new things—whether it was watching a spiritual sort of movie, having a discussion about different spiritual topics, mini-lessons, crafts, whatever—we were looking to add more to our spiritual experience. We had found doing so difficult due to the party atmosphere these others insisted on bringing with them.

This spell helped bring about many changes for my group and for my personal life as well. For me personally, it was truly a dawning of a new age. The old "party people" left and formed their own group and suddenly a whole new world of spiritual people opened to me. The new people who came into my life have become my spiritual partners and my closest, dearest friends.

For this spell you will be doing a candle scrying/meditation using a purple candle. Purple represents growth, self-esteem, insight, inspiration, power, ambition, and inner strength.

Set up your altar, cast your circle, and light your candle. Get in a comfortable position where you will be able to stare into the candle flame.

During this meditation you will keep your eyes open, staring continuously into the flame. Don't get too relaxed or comfortable. You don't want to fall asleep by a lit candle. Begin by saying the following:

My life has changed
and so have I.
I no longer feel connections
I once did.
Ending these relationships
is a positive step.
I will not be brought down
by those around me and
I know I must find and make
new connections in order
to continue to grow.
I will reach inside myself
to see what my future holds.
I will always continue growing
and learning, and will
find those who are capable of
growing and learning too.

As you stare into the flame, feel yourself becoming lighter, unburdened. That which has been weighing you down and holding you back has been lifted. The burden has been removed. You are free to grow in exciting new directions. You are free to try new things, to express yourself freely and confidently. Feel yourself projecting this newfound freedom and maturity into the flame. Say out loud:

I am ready to move on.
Bring those close to me
who are on the same path
to enlightenment
and knowledge.

Continue your visualization by imagining yourself saying goodbye to your old friends (you may have actually done this in real life, but do so now in your meditation as well). Say goodbye to your old life. Look into the future, into the flame. There are new people waiting there for you. You might not be able to make out their faces just yet, but they are there.

When you feel you have completed your meditation, slowly blow the flame out, sending your message out into the universe to bring these new people into your life.

My friends are too critical of me

If you feel your friends are being too critical of you, this is indeed a warning sign that you need to sit up and take notice. It's possible your friends might be critical of you because you deserve it. Are you sitting there eating your third helping of cake and ice cream ten minutes after complaining that your new pants don't fit anymore? Are you a chain smoker complaining that you can't stop coughing? Are you complaining once again what a pain your boyfriend is—the one you've been with for five years now and haven't said a nice word about in four years? If one of these or a similar situation applies to you, you need to wake up and change your life if you want it to be different or improve. No one else will do it for you.

However, your friends might be critical about other things you just don't understand. For example, they don't like your new haircut, color, or length. You lost five pounds and they complain you look too thin (though medically you may even be overweight). Your new boyfriend brings you flowers once a week, so they think he must be up to something. Maybe you have a friend or two going through a difficult time and instead of focusing on constructive ways to work matters out, they are doing everything they can to bring others down with them. Misery loves company. Are you starting to get the gist here? Friends who are critical about the good things in your life aren't really your friends. They are insecure, jealous people who are trying to put you down and minimize your good fortune in order to feel better about themselves.

These very well could be people who do care about you very much, but either (as in the first scenario) they aren't getting through to you, or (as in the second scenario) their feelings are what are the most important at this point in their lives. So what do you do about it?

For starters, you need to sit down and figure out what is really going on. Maybe even ask if you truly can't figure it out on your own. However, chances are if you can't figure it out on your own, your friends are being critical because you seriously need to wake up. Ask yourself this simple question. Are your friends trying to help you, or hurt you? If they are trying to help you, you need to listen up.

That being said, if these people are trying to hurt you, sit down and talk to them about what is going on in their lives to make them feel the way they do. This spell will help you with the latter. Either way, this situation requires some excellent listening skills, the ability to communicate effectively, and willpower to go through with the conversation. The conversation may be confrontational whether the problem is you or your friends; the goal is to set confrontation aside—don't go on either the offense or defense. Figure out how to work with your friend for the betterment of everyone. This is also going to take some adaptability on your part. If you are sabotaging yourself, you need to learn how to stop. If your friend is upset because of her failure and your success, you will need to learn how to adapt to that situation too.

Again, this spell will help you work things out for the best in whatever way that may be, depending on your situation. Plan to do your spell on a Friday, the day related to friendships.

For this spell you will need:

- an orange candle for courage, friendship, communication, success, willpower, adaptability, zest for life, and imagination
- a purple candle for growth, self-esteem, insight, and inner strength
- an obsidian stone for protection and to prevent negativity
- lemon oil for mental clarity

Cast your circle. Dress each candle with a drop of lemon oil and light them. Place the obsidian on your altar in between the two candles. Say the following:

> *Though there has been pain, hurt, and confusion,*
> *I want to set this right.*
> *Grant me the courage*
> *to be strong, find my inner strength,*
> *and deal with this as I must.*
> *Grant me the willpower to see this through*
> *though I may be in pain, or may cause pain to others.*
> *I do not do this out of hate, but out of love.*
> *Love for myself, love for my friends.*
> *I will use my own insight to*
> *help me grow while speaking with my friends.*
> *I will listen and be open to changes*
> *I may need to make to help myself,*
> *or to help my friend.*

Pick up the stone and hold it tightly in your hands. Imagine energy transferring from you and your working to the stone as you say the following:

I infuse this stone with the power of protection.
I infuse this stone with the power to prevent negativity.
This stone will stay with me
as I deal with matters ahead of me.

Extinguish your candles and close your circle.

Set up a time to talk with your friends about what has been going on and how you feel. Remember to carry your stone with you, or perhaps place it on a table or somewhere in the room while you have your talk.

This may end up being quite an emotional time for you and/or your friends. Keep your wits about you and remember, if these friendships were meant to be, they will be salvageable and things will work out.

I let my friend move in because she needed someplace to stay—now I'm wishing I hadn't and it's ruined our friendship

Several years ago, I let someone who was supposed to be my best friend move in with my family. My husband and I spent our anniversary doing the actual moving. The idea was to give her six months to get back on her feet. She would get her bills paid off and get some money saved so she could get a place of her own. She paid $200 a month to help cover her share of utilities. Unfortunately, her six-month stay turned into two and a half years. Her bills didn't get paid and she didn't save any money. She stayed up most of the night, TV blaring, and then complained about my young son making noise during the day while she tried to sleep. The $200 a month only barely covered the utilities, as once she moved in the electric bill jumped $150 a month. Money wasn't the main concern, though. Her lack of ambition to help herself and the utter disregard for everyone else in the house, however—well, that was a different story altogether. In those two-and-a-half years, which also included countless other favors such as mechanical work on her car, there were very few times when any appreciation was ever shown. We seldom received even a thank you. The relationship didn't end well, and soon after she moved out we ceased speaking to each other. We had been friends for many, many years, but our relationship as we knew it simply could not continue.

Would the friendship have ended similarly if she hadn't moved in with my family? I honestly do not know. I imagine someday I would have discovered her ungrateful, selfish nature, but it may have taken several more years. So in a way, I'm grateful it ended when it did.

Sometimes people move in together and their personalities clash. Not all cases are extreme as mine, and some of these friendships may be salvageable—if both parties want that. In my case, I didn't want or need the friend in my life; I had made a decision to surround myself with positivity, not negativity, which meant saying goodbye to her.

You will need to decide whether or not you want to try to save this relationship. Either way, this spell will help you get over the pain and loss—a necessary step before either reconciling with your friend, or moving on without your friend in your life. No matter what you choose, you must forgive and start over anew. You will feel pain from this too; no relationship ends without sadness.

If you want to reconcile, perform this spell on a Friday, the day best suited for friendships and reconciliations.

If you do not want to reconcile and instead want to put this relationship behind you, perform the spell on a Saturday, for endings.

For this spell you will need:
- a green candle to neutralize this difficult situation
- witch hazel to mend a broken heart
- cypress to ease feelings of loss, and bring solace and comfort
- a small cloth drawstring bag

Lay the items out on your altar and cast your circle.

As you light the green candle, say:

> *Feelings and emotions*
> *are running high right now.*
> *Help to bring these feelings*
> *to normal, controllable levels.*
> *To set the anger and hurt aside,*
> *and put the past behind.*

Take the cypress and crumble it as you add it to the drawstring bag. Say:

> *Comfort me in this time,*
> *this time of loss.*
> *This friendship*
> *has left me with heartache.*
> *I must forgive, forget, and move on;*
> *help to heal me so that I may.*

Pour out a drop of witch hazel on the cypress in the bag. Say:

> *Mend my broken heart.*
> *Help me put the pieces back together again.*
> *This ordeal has left me saddened and overwhelmed.*
> *I must forgive, forget, and move on;*
> *help me to heal so that I may.*

Carry the pouch with you and hold it in your hands if you feel you need an extra boost of healing energy.

If you plan to try to work things out with your friend, give yourself a couple of days to meditate on the situation before trying to speak with him/her. If you believe this relationship is beyond salvaging, pack up any physical remnants you have of the relationship, do with them what you need to. Move on with your life, putting the unfortunate incident behind you.

My best friend had an affair with my significant other

When your significant other cheats on you, whether it be your spouse, boyfriend, or girlfriend, the devastation can be astronomical. When the cheating takes place with another person who is also supposed to care about you, your frustration, pain, and anger are all doubled. Had you only been cheated on, you most likely would have turned to your best friend for support. Now that support has been completed annihilated.

Some people may be capable of forgiving one person or the other, or possibly even both in this situation. Personally, I don't believe I ever could. The betrayal would be too much, so I feel lucky I haven't had this experience. Unfortunately, I can't say that for all of my friends.

Kirsten had this very thing happen to her: a close, mutual friend of ours had an affair with her husband. This situation changed all our lives, but it was truly devastating for Kirsten. She lost her husband, whom she thought was her dearest friend, and then her home besides. This spell was written for her to help her move on. Recovering from something like this could take quite a long time, and you may want to seek professional help in dealing with the pain you are going through.

This spell is designed to help you pick up the pieces and move on with your life. It is a spell you will want to repeat, particularly when you are feeling down. This spell is also best done in the bath, since the warmth and relaxation can often help us sort through our feelings. It will be important during this time of recovery to try to eliminate as much stress from your life as you can—or at the very least, try not to add any more.

For this spell you will need:
- a gold candle (for helping you take necessary actions, and for boosting courage, strength, and self-confidence)
- your bathtub

A few drops of the following essential oils:
- witch hazel
- cypress
- lavender

This type of affair can be quite detrimental to a person's self-esteem and confidence. It's important to remember you were not the cause of these actions and you are not to blame.

Light your candle, turn out the lights, and situate yourself in the tub.

Close your eyes and do some deep breathing exercises. Inhale the lavender and cypress scents. Breathe out the bad, and inhale the good. Relax. Understand that you are hurting and allow yourself the time and chance to get that pain out. If you feel like crying, go ahead and do it. Crying often helps relieve stress. Let the pent-up emotions out. You are in a safe place with no one to judge you. Let the pain all out.

After you have had some time to relax and get yourself into a better state of mind, say the following:

The betrayal I have felt
has weighed down my heart
and shattered it into pieces.
I will be my own glue,
I will pick up the pieces,
and put my heart back together once again.
I have lost love and friendship,
but I will go on.
I will be bold and strong.
I will be courageous and
will never stop fighting for myself.
For my peace,
and my sanity.
I will build myself up again,
and not allow this pain to ruin me.
I start my life over,
and begin anew.

You may repeat this as many times as you feel necessary. When you feel a bit better, go ahead and pull the plug, and drain away all the pain. When you imagine yourself being happy and strong, you make it much easier for you to actually *be* those things once again.

I really like my best friend, but sometimes she is downright embarrassing

We love our friends, but sometimes we have to wonder just what on earth is going through their heads. Do you have one of those friends who is always making a scene? Overly loud? Drinks far too much? Yells loudly at his/her children in public? Is the friend one of those people who make customer service reps cringe in agony?

Have you ever talked to the friend about it? Have you been told there is nothing to worry about? Do you enjoy this person's company but often find him or her to be so embarrassing you just don't want to be seen together in public?

I think we all probably encounter someone like this at some point in our lives, though they may not be a close friend. It's embarrassing enough as it is, but when it is your closest friend—the one person you spend all kinds of time with, it becomes worse.

Though your friend behaves embarrassingly, what she's doing isn't life threatening, not to mention that we don't want to interfere with someone's free will. For that reason, we don't really want to do a binding…not a full-blown one, anyway. Instead, this spell is a small binding on the friend's actions—it dictates discipline and self-control, at least when you are together!

For this spell you will need:
- a yellow candle for persuasion, open communication, and to help give your friend a little "charm"
- several turquoise stones (or if you own any turquoise jewelry you can use that) for discipline and self-control

You can't force this friend into charm school, obviously, but you can hope some of your own good sense will rub off! Place the candle and stones/jewelry on your altar and cast your circle.

Begin by saying:

I light this candle to save a friendship.
I love (friend's name) dearly,
yet his/her behavior can sometime be unsavory.
I light this candle to be heard clearly
when I ask him/her to tone it down,
so s/he will understand how his/her behavior
looks to others.

Concentrating, picture your friend in your mind as you light the candle. Feel the flame reaching out.

Pick up the stone and/or jewelry and hold them in your hands, with your hands cupped together out in front of you. Say:

When (friend's name) is with me,
I ask that s/he control his/her behaviors,
that s/he be disciplined
and be conscious
of his/her actions.
I ask that s/he understand
his/her behaviors,
and how they affect others.
This is my will, so mote it be.

When you are out with your friend, wear the turquoise jewelry or carry the stones with you in several different places. You may carry some in pockets, in your purse, anywhere you can.

Remember to recharge the stones frequently. To keep up the work in the mundane world, remember to occasionally ask your friend to tone it down a bit. Don't harp or criticize, but don't let it slide either.

My friend always wants my help with her problems, but she's never around to help me with mine

Unfortunately, I've been in this position far too many times. As someone who has always been willing to go out of her way to help out a friend in need, I have often found it nearly impossible to get anything close to a favor in return.

Someone actually told me once that with the way I help everyone else out, they never once thought I would need help in return. How does this make sense? When I asked for help, what was I doing, trying to make someone else feel needed? Well, this person figured I could handle other people's problems so well, why couldn't I handle my own? Seriously? When I was helping other people with their problems, it meant I was…helping other people, period.

Unfortunately the next time I asked for help, it still wasn't forthcoming; my little explanation didn't do any good after all. I eventually realized that people who were too selfish to help a friend in need were not the kind of people I wanted as friends. After all, what's a friend if it isn't someone you can count on?

It's up to you if you want to keep someone in your life who is never there for you. If you decide to keep this friend in your life, you need to accept that you cannot change this person into who you want him or her to be. You can, however, choose your own actions and your own path. You can create equality by giving the relationship the same priority and attention the other person does. This means you may have to pull back some, which is easier said than done. But who knows, maybe if you pull back the person will be more willing to help out when you aren't always around for him or her when needed.

This spell will help you create that balance.

For this spell you will need:
• a silver candle for intuition, receptivity, stability, and balance

Cast your circle and light your candle. Begin by saying:

I will look deep inside me
to find the balance I need
in this relationship.

I can no longer give,
when nothing is given in return.
I cherish my friendship,
but feel I am more involved
than what is healthy for me.
I long for the stability and balance
that will make me whole.

Stare into the flame of the candle. This relationship has obviously left you with some hurt and possibly some anger. Let the pain and anger burn up in the flame. Project any other negative feelings you have about this relationship into the flame as well. Disappointment and maybe even jealousy may have taken up residency in your heart. Let these feelings out. Rid yourself of them, projecting them into the flame and watching them burn away.

Know that in the future, you will better delineate between what you will and will not do for others. This does not mean you are hardening your heart, just deciding when and where your energies are best used and served. Perhaps your friend has not had the opportunity to grow because she always asks others for help. Perhaps she needs to be told, "I'm sorry, I can't help out," in order to help her grow more as an individual.

In the future you will use your intuition to decide when to lend a hand and when not to. You will think about requests and ponder on them before automatically saying "yes."

Say the following to end your spell:

This is how I change myself,
this is how my interests are best served.
I will grow by learning it is okay for me to say no
and when to do so.

Close your circle.

I just learned that my friends have been doing a lot of negative talking behind my back and YES, these people are adults

You probably have more than one group of friends, and chances are your friends do as well. You may even have several friends who hang out with several other people with whom you don't associate. What happens when you find out that when your friends are with other people they talk about you behind your back? Sound confusing? Well, it is, though I know it's happened to many of you out there! We thought this kind of behavior ends after high school, but I've often said that women are their own worst enemies, and this is why! When friend A and friend B are with you, everything seems just fine and dandy, but when A and B go off and meet M for lunch, it's a whole other ball game. M might not particularly like you, so A and B do what they can to either distance themselves from you or act like you guys aren't all that close anyway.

Of course, if M had a brain in her head, wouldn't she just ask, "Why associate with her at all?" but M doesn't ask, and A and B don't offer anything positive, only negativity M feeds off.

Yes, it's immature. Yes, it's childish. Yes, it's absolutely ridiculous that anyone over the age of ten partakes in this kind of behavior, but it happens. And it happens a lot.

Maybe you don't have a problem with the backstabbing itself and only want the talk to stop so you can comfortably continue your relationship with A and B. This spell won't affect that. What this spell will do is to remove you as a conversation topic when A, B, and M get together. What you do after that is up to you.

For this spell you will need:

- slippery elm (lots of it if using a bonfire) to stop gossip
- a bonfire (if possible)
- fireproof container, charcoal tablet, and lighter (if a bonfire is not a possibility)
- a length of black cord
- a piece of paper and writing instrument

This spell is written for a bonfire. If you are using a fireproof container, make adjustments as needed.

On the piece of paper, write down the names of the people who have been talking about you behind your back. Roll the paper up like a scroll and wrap the black cord around it, saying:

> *I bind thee once.*
> *I bind thee twice.*
> *I bind thee thrice.*
> *No longer shall I be a topic of your conversation.*

After you say this, tie a knot in the cording. Wrap again while repeating the above and finish with a knot two more times for a total of three times.

Take a handful of slippery elm and say:

> *Slippery tongues shall not speak of me.*

Toss the slippery elm into the fire.
Hold the bound scroll in your hand and say:

> *The names found here*
> *are forbidden to speak ill of me.*

Toss the scroll into the fire followed by another handful of slippery elm. Again say:

> *Slippery tongues shall not speak of me.*
> *This I send to the universe.*
> *My will, my command be done.*

After the paper and slippery elm have burned up completely, go ahead and close your circle. Bury the ashes.

Someone keeps flirting with me—I've let the person know I am not interested, but he/she doesn't seem to get it…it's starting to creep me out

If a person's advances are starting to creep you out, chances are the situation is taking a turn for the unsafe. You've already told this person you aren't interested, yet they either aren't taking the hint or they are purposely choosing to ignore your wishes, which shows how little they really care for you and are only concerned with their own desires. This could escalate into a stalker situation, something very serious.

What this means magically is you need a strong spell that will not only protect you, but will set boundaries and banish your would-be stalker. You are also going to need to have negative energies absorbed because, believe it or not, they are all around you at this point. The constant flirting isn't about love or romance. It's about control and making you feel vulnerable. We aren't going to let that happen.

This spell is going to take a bit of prep work, so let's get started.

If you can, perform this spell on either a new moon (for banishing) or on a Tuesday (for its protective aspect). If the space is available to you, you should prepare a small bonfire with pine, oak, cedar, and aspen wood; all woods are for protection. The aspen also invokes a magical shield around you. If you do not have a place for a bonfire, use a fireproof container (such as a cauldron) and add small pieces of the above named woods. If you can't find all of the wood types that is fine, just try to find as many of them as you can. The aspen is the most important wood in this spell. No matter how you prepare to do this spell, it would be best to do it outside. The smoke may become overwhelming, among other safety reasons.

You will also need to prepare incense ahead of time. Use equal amounts of dried angelica, anise, burdock, clove, cumin, elder berries, frankincense, horehound, ivy leaves, juniper berries, nettle, and peppercorns. I suggest using about a tablespoon of each. You do not need to grind this incense if you don't want to but make sure it's mixed very well. Sprinkle a tablespoon of dragon's blood oil over the top and mix some more. Allow the dragon's blood to absorb into the dried ingredients.

The last item you will need to prepare before the spell is softened black wax. You can melt some black wax and allow it to start hardening again. The wax should be malleable because you are going to shape it.

You will also need:

- a large bowl of water (moon water is preferable,
  see page 4 for an explanation)
- a bowl for the incense
- either a picture of the person or his/her name
  written on a piece of paper
- a toothpick
- black cord, yarn, or string, 9 feet in length

If you have anything that once belonged to the person, this would also be very help-ful, especially if you have access to something such as hair, or something that was kept close to the person's body, like a shirt. Note that you will *not* be keeping the item you use.

Set your altar up near your fire pit or put a fireproof container on your altar. Cast your circle.

You will light the fire first. As you light it and it begins burning, say:

Through this fire, I am cleansed.
Sacred woods burn.
The fire does alight.
Work your magic around me,
protect me in my fight.

If you are able to include aspen wood in your fire, also say:

Through the smoke of the aspen a shield is formed.
It surrounds and follows me
wherever I go, whatever I do.
It protects me from harm, seen and unseen.

Take the softened black wax and mold it into a shape that represents the person you want to banish. It may be the shape of a face, a human form, or some other symbol. Just be sure to make it into a symbol that truly represents this individual. If you have an item (such as hair) from the individual, incorporate this into your wax mold.

As you make your representation, focus on the person it symbolizes and chant:

I work this wax into your form,
so at your hands I'll suffer no harm.

Continue the chant until you are finished molding the wax.

If you have a picture, use a toothpick to attach it to your form. If you only have the name on a piece of paper, tear it off and use a toothpick to attach it.

Take the black cord and begin wrapping it around the form saying:

I bind you once.
I bind you twice.
I bind you thrice.
You can do me no harm.

Continue this chant until you have used all of the cord and tie it off. Set the form on your altar and pick up your bowl of incense. Hold the bowl out in front of you and say:

These herbs are instilled with the power of protection.
I take their essences in and they become a part of me.

Lift the bowl to your face and deeply inhale the herbs. Say:

May they keep me safe and protect me.
May they keep (name) at a safe distance.

Take a small handful of the herbs and throw it into the fire. Take another deeply inhaled sniff of the burning herbs, being careful not to actually inhale the smoke—only the scent.

Set the bowl down on your altar and pick up your wax form. Say:

(Name), I have bound you from harming me.
You will no longer contact me.
To you—I no longer exist.
I cleanse you from my life.

Place the wax form into the bowl of water and hold it down (the wax will most likely float so hold it down). Swish it back and forth in the water. Say:

> *I cleanse you from my life.*
> *Take your thoughts with you.*

While holding the wax under the water, imagine your life without this person in it. Feel the calmness and serenity as you no longer have to deal with unwelcome advances.

When you are satisfied with your meditation, remove the form from the water and immediately throw it into the fire. Say:

> *By the flame that burneth bright,*
> *I cleanse you from my life.*

Continue this chant until all of the wax has melted and the form is no longer visible. Close your circle as you normally would.

You may want to do this spell for a full month—new moon to new moon and on each Tuesday in between.

Follow this working up in the mundane world by keeping a log of any contact this person still has with you. If the unwanted contact continues, go to your local county courthouse and apply for an order of protection. Hopefully it won't come to that, but I firmly believe it is better to be safe than sorry.

For those who are worried that this spell interferes with the free will of the person who has been doing the harassing, that is your prerogative. However, stalking cases have shown us just how dangerous and deadly these types of obsessive people can be. Again, better safe than sorry!

I've caught my friend lying to me several times and don't know why it continues

I hate lying with a passion. It's almost understandable when little kids do it, though how they learn, I'll never quite figure out. When it's done by adults who know better, however, I will truly never figure out why.

To tell a lie often implies knowledge of wrongdoing. It's easy to see why a child does it, but as adults we should face up to our misdeeds. Liars usually get caught in their lies anyway, and it's nearly impossible to trust someone after they've been caught on more than one occasion.

When someone lies to you, you figure if that person really cared and liked you, he or she wouldn't have lied in the first place. The liar usually doesn't see it that way and may even claim he or she was trying to protect you, when in fact they were most likely protecting themselves.

So what do you do when you catch someone lying to you, especially if it is not the first time? What if this is someone who for all intents and purposes is someone you really like and enjoy spending time with? Their only fault is, well, the lying! I admit I remained friends with someone who lied to me repeatedly for many years. It finally got to the point where I couldn't take it anymore and ended the friendship.

What you do in this matter is entirely up to you, but deciding what to do can be difficult as well as painful. This spell is going to help you decide what to do about your situation and help you stick with your decision.

For this spell you will need:
- a blue candle for truth
- a fireproof container, charcoal tablet, and lighter
- coltsfoot for visions

Set up your altar and cast your circle. Sprinkle some coltsfoot onto the lit charcoal tablet and light the blue candle. Get yourself into a comfortable position and say:

> *I have been lied to,*
> *time and time again.*
> *It is time now for me to look around*
> *and see the truth in front of me.*

Though I cannot change the actions of others,
I can decide if I will allow these actions to affect me or not.

I can decide if I continue to
keep this person in my life or not.
Great Goddess,
send me the visions I need to see,
allow me to see what I must,
so I may decide what is right for me.

Open your mind to see the possibilities in this relationship. Can you try to talk to this person about the lying? Have you before? What was the outcome? What would the outcome be if you tried now? Do you see this person in your future? What is your relationship with this person like in the future if he or she is still there? Try not to force your thoughts in any one direction, simply empty your mind and see what comes to you.

If you don't get anything after ten or fifteen minutes you might not be ready yet to see what is in front of you. This is okay—you just need some more time to deal with the situation. End the spell and try again later. Consciously set aside time to think about the questions listed above and perform the spell again in a day or two to see if you have any new answers.

Sometimes you can save a relationship like this; sometimes the person will want to change and was just waiting to be called out on his or her actions. Other times, the person has no desire to change and doesn't see anything wrong with what he or she is doing. If the latter is the case, it's really up to you to decide if the good about this person outweighs the bad or not, though it might be quite difficult.

The important thing to remember is that when someone lies to you, it is not your fault—even if they tell you it is! You didn't ask to be lied to, but you can make the decision as to whether you want to continue putting up with it or not.

Part Four

★ ★ ★ ★

PETS

My new puppy pees in the house and I can't stand it

Puppies and baby animals of any kind really are great. They are cute, cuddly, and soft. They are playful and want to give all kinds of love and are overjoyed when they get some in return. However, they need to be housebroken and that usually isn't fun for anyone.

Having a puppy pee all over your house is not the puppy's fault, not really. He or she can't help it. After all, a puppy is a baby who needs to be taught. If you are having problems with housebreaking your puppy, try reading up on different techniques or speak with an animal trainer.

If you are getting upset and anxious about housebreaking the puppy, the puppy will become upset and anxious too, which will most likely lead to even more peeing where you don't want it!

This spell is for both of you—yes, you and your puppy. It will help you both relax and remain calm so that potty training can continue in a positive and supportive environment.

Most often it is puppies who need housebreaking, but sometimes you will come across an older dog that was never trained. This spell is for them too. I myself took in a seven-year-old malamute who apparently was never housebroken. It took this older dog a while to get the hang of letting me know when she needed to go outside, but by building trust and being consistent, she was able to be trained too.

When you do this spell, you will need the dog with you. If he or she isn't very good at sitting still (most puppies aren't!) you will need to place the dog in a carrier crate or playpen to keep it in the circle with you. Make sure it can't jump up on to your altar.

For this spell you will need:

- an amethyst stone (for peace, love, and happiness)
- your puppy's collar
- a small amount of light blue material (for calmness, tranquility, and patience)
- a thread and needle
- lavender incense

Set up your altar and cast your circle with your dog inside of it with you.
Light the lavender incense and say:

This spell I cast
to help my puppy (name) and I
work together to housebreak him/her.
I come to bring closeness between the two of us—
so that my puppy will come to trust me,
and understand me,
the way I want to trust and understand him/her.

Take the amethyst stone and lay it on the blue material. Using the needle and thread,
sew the material closed tightly around the stone. As you sew, chant:

We two connect,
join together,
happiness and peace,
love one another.

When you are done sewing, attach the stone packet to your puppy's collar and then
put it back on your puppy.
If possible, pick up your puppy and hold him or her close while continuing the spell.
While holding your animal close to you, say the following:

I love my puppy (name),
and want him/her to understand that.
Even when he/she does have an accident in the house,
my love is unfailing.
I ask for guidance and patience
while training my puppy.
With peace, love, and understanding
we will both get through housebreaking,
and we will both be happier because of it.

Your puppy will probably be wiggly and not want to be held for too long, so go through the spell as quickly as you can. When you are done, close your circle and take the puppy for a walk. Remember: your puppy doesn't *want* to make a mess in the house, it just hasn't learned yet where to go to do its business.

Your puppy needs some time, patience, and understanding to get the hang of it. When you remain calm, your puppy will remain calm too.

My pets fight with each other all the time

As someone who often takes in stray cats, I know what it's like to have animals who don't necessarily get along with one another. Introducing a new animal to the mix always brings on the same pattern. The new animal is excited to be in a home—a place where it is warm, food is readily available, toys abound, and love surrounds them at all times. However, the animals already living there aren't always excited to welcome someone new to the flock. They don't want to share their food, water, toys, or their spot at the foot of the bed.

Those first few days are a little scary and time consuming; you have to make sure the animals are able to get close enough to one another to start accepting each other, yet far enough apart to keep them safe. Once they do start accepting one another they will become closer.

The last kitten we took in, Furrina, was trying very hard to fit in with my other cats, Lancelot, Quantico, and Morgaine, but Morgaine was not happy at all that she was here. Every time Furrina went anywhere near Morgaine, she would get hissed at and Morgaine would reach out and smack her with her paw. Furrina was much smaller than Morgaine so of course it was a concern. After using this spell, I went to go to bed and discovered Morgaine had not only allowed Furrina up on the bed with her, she was giving her a tongue-bath as well. If Morgaine—who is quite a drama queen—can become loving toward her "younger sister," this spell can work for your pets too.

For this spell you will need:
- a sky blue candle for calmness, tranquility, patience, and understanding
- catnip (even if the animals involved are dogs) to bring out good spirits, love, and peace
- coltsfoot for peace, tranquility, and because this is a spell relating to animals
- frankincense for banishing negative entities
- freesia for love and peace
- mortar and pestle
- fireproof container, charcoal tablet, and lighter

Set up your altar and cast your circle.

Prepare the incense. Later, you'll add it to the lit charcoal tablet in your fireproof container and walk it around your house so that the smoke penetrates every room of your house, every place that your pets will be.

Begin the spell by lighting the blue candle and say:

> *May this mixture I make,*
> *this spell I conjure,*
> *bring peace and tranquility*
> *to my pets and our home.*
> *May they find calmness, love,*
> *and comfort in one another*
> *the way I do in them.*

Add some catnip, coltsfoot, frankincense, and freesia to the mortar and grind together with the pestle. As you grind, say:

> *May this mixture I make,*
> *this spell I conjure*
> *bring peace to my pets.*
> *May they learn to live*
> *with one another in peace.*
> *May they learn to play with each other,*
> *comfort each other,*
> *depend on each other.*
> *May they love one another*
> *as I love them.*

Sprinkle the incense on the lit charcoal tablet and extinguish your candle. Close your circle. Take your container and walk all throughout your house—dispersing the smoke throughout. Be careful not to get the rooms too smoky or to set off smoke detectors! As you walk, chant:

> *This spell I do*
> *for peace for you.*

Repeat this spell weekly and also seek out advice from your veterinarian or an animal trainer.

My cat has stopped using the litter box and has ruined furniture and carpeting

When a cat who previously used his/her litter box without a problem suddenly stops using it and starts going other places in the house, this is most often a sign that the cat is having some kind of a problem—either the cat is most likely ill or is experiencing stress for some reason.

Have there been any kind of changes in the home recently? Has a new animal come into the home—or a new person? Has an animal or person left? Does your cat show any other signs of illness? Trouble walking? Maybe he or she doesn't want to be picked up? Or suddenly does want to be picked up? The first thing you need to do is get the cat to a vet to find out if there is a medical reason for the lack of litter box use. Once you have a better idea of how to work on this problem in the mundane world, whether that be through medication or just reassuring your cat of your love and helping your cat to relax, you can start performing this spell to help heal (physically or emotionally) and relax your cat. Cats know where they are supposed to use the bathroom, and when they can't do it properly they feel bad, guilty even. Just look at a cat that has been caught messing in the wrong place. They can feel downright ashamed. This spell will help take away the shame and let your animal know how much he/she is loved.

For this spell you will need:
- catnip to improve your psychic bond with your cat, to attract good spirits to watch over him/her, and love and peace
- coltsfoot for peace, tranquility, visions, and animal spells
- dried lemon peel for healing, purification, and physical energy
- mortar and pestle
- a fireproof container, charcoal tablet, and lighter

If possible, do this spell with your cat in the circle with you, or at least in the room with you—just be careful he/she doesn't get too close to the lit charcoal tablet or the smoke.

Set up your altar and cast your circle. Say:

> *My friend, (cat's name),*
> *has been having problems,*
> *and needs to be healed,*
> *physically (and/or) emotionally.*
> *(Cat's name) needs strength,*
> *and assistance in regaining*
> *his/her dignity,*
> *and knowing that he/she is loved.*

Light the charcoal tablet and while it is getting an even burn to it, prepare to grind the ingredients together with the mortar and pestle, creating an incense blend.

Begin with the dried lemon peel. Pour some into the mortar and as you grind it, say (speaking to your pet):

> *This lemon is to heal you,*
> *to give you the energy needed to recover and relearn.*
> *To help purify you body and soul.*

Next add the coltsfoot to the mortar and grind. Say (speaking to your pet):

> *This coltsfoot is to heal you,*
> *to bring you peace and comfort,*
> *to give you tranquility*
> *and to help you see what you must work on.*

Finally, add the catnip and say to you pet:

> *This catnip is to bring us closer together,*
> *to help us know what each other is thinking,*
> *so I will know when you need my help,*
> *and you will know when I need yours.*
> *It will bring us love and peace,*
> *and attract good spirits*
> *to watch over you and keep you safe—*
> *and to help heal you with love.*

Sprinkle some of the incense onto the lit charcoal tablet. Either hold your cat in your arms, or carry the incense around the room so you can gently waft some of the smoke around your cat.

As you do this, say:

> *My strength and power*
> *I share with you,*
> *to help you heal.*
> *I ask the God and Goddess*
> *to bless you,*
> *to help you heal.*
> *To bring peace back into our lives,*
> *filled with love.*
> *So mote it be.*

Give your cat a big hug and some extra love and treats. Spend extra time with your cat petting him/her so he/she will know that no matter what, he/she is loved.

When I began writing this book, I already had this chapter in my table of contents, but still ended up surprised when my ten-year-old Quantico began urinating just about everywhere but his litter box. We got him to the vet right away and found out he had a bladder infection. We had recently brought the new kitty Furrina in—who turned out to be pregnant and had two kittens of her own—so we thought it could have been a jealousy issue. The vet was able to get a urine sample and told us the results in minutes. A prescription of antibiotics, this spell, and a whole lot of extra loving later, Quantico is good as new.

I want a new pet, but I'm not sure what to choose

Getting a new pet can be quite exciting, but it can also be confusing—there are many options. Not only do you have to pick the type of animal, you will also have to pick a breed and an individual animal. Perhaps the problem with trying to choose a new pet is the fact that we often make it more difficult than it needs to be. When it comes right down to it, do we really choose the pet ourselves, or do we end up going with the pet that has chosen us instead? If you are looking at dogs, do you choose the dog that growls at you? No. But since he growled, hasn't he already told you no, you aren't the one for him? Do you go for the animal that ignores you, or the one that walks over to check you out? We only *think* we are the one doing the choosing; the animals themselves have as least as much say in the matter as we do, if not more.

This spell is going to open you up and help you to find the perfect pet. If you aren't sure if you want a cat, or dog, or even a rabbit, bird, ferret, or whatever—don't worry about that. You are going to cast this spell and then go spend time at a pet store or animal shelter (preferably the animal shelter!) walking around and waiting to see if any of the animals seem drawn to you.

There are a couple of things you need to keep in mind. For starters, animals get nervous and excited. Many of the animals you encounter are going to be very happy to see you. They want to play, they want to be loved, but you have to see through to see who is looking for a playmate and who is looking for a loyal friend. The animals will be doing the same thing!

Also remember, the animal that is right for you may not be at the first shelter or store you visit. He or she might not be at the second or third either. You might find the right animal the first day, you might have to look for a month. You will *know* though when you do find the right one. There won't be any questions or doubts whatsoever. You will just know this is the one you are meant to share your life with—it's often easier with pets than with other people. Animals tend to have a very honest nature and are very bad liars!

Perform this spell each and every time before going on your search for a new pet.

This spell is a simple chant—we don't want to use any kind of herbs or candles that could leave a scent that masks your own. Animals are very sensitive to smell—and they have different preferences too. One of my cats loves the smell of lavender. If I spray it into the air she literally stops to sniff it, her nose in the air. Another cat, however, cannot stand the smell. If I even use lavender-scented hand or body cream, he won't come near me. So because animals do have a strong sense of smell, you need to smell as much like "you" as possible. You probably shouldn't pile on a ton of perfume or cologne either UNLESS of course, you do every day anyway. Let the animals smell you as you usually smell.

Chant the following over and over, building the power. When you hit the peak, you will know when the energy is ready to be released into the universe around you.

Oh great Goddess, send to me
the animal companion right for me—
the perfect one to be with me,
to complete our lives,
so mote it be.

Don't rush the process. Spend time performing the chant. Spend time looking at different animals. As mentioned before, when you come across the right animal, both of you will know.

My pet is a special needs animal

First of all, whether you have taken in a special needs animal on purpose, or the pet you already have has become a special needs pet and you are doing what you can to take care of him/her—congratulations on stepping up to the plate! Special needs animals generally need more love and care than "normal" pets do. They need dedication—someone who will always be there for them when needed. They are often abandoned at shelters or worse. These animals aren't any less worthy of love and companionship. The fact that you are willing to give this animal the love and attention says a lot about you as a person.

Special needs animals require more care than most pets; extra care could include daily medication, special equipment to help them walk, numerous surgeries, or making adjustments for their comfort due to missing a limb or blindness.

This is difficult for the animal, but can also be difficult for you to deal with too. It may mean you can't leave the house for too long at a time, it may be a financial burden. It may also be stressful not always knowing if you are doing the right thing—if you are giving the best care you can, and sometimes it may just be the stress of having to have to do it at all. Sure, you love your pet but sometimes the stress of having to take care of a special needs animal is burdensome too. It's not that you don't love your pet, you just really, really wish, he/she was "normal."

Some special needs animals can be cured, or at least can become more self sufficient. This spell is therefore designed to promote healing for your animal along with some healing and respite for yourself. It will also help protect your pet from harm and help relax the both of you when having to deal with the stresses of the animal's special needs.

For this spell you will need:
• a sage smudge stick to purify
• crushed, dried eucalyptus for healing
• crushed, dried lavender buds for peace and love
• fireproof container/cauldron, charcoal tablet, and lighter

You need not cast a circle in this spell, as you are going to walk around your home so that every place your animal visits, s/he will be surrounded by healing and positive energies.

Begin at your front door. Light the sage smudge and begin walking around your home by turning left whenever you can. As you walk with the smudge focus your energy on cleansing and purifying your home. Say:

Cleanse, and purify, and protect
Make our home safe for my pet.

Continue to chant this throughout your entire home until you make it back to your front door.

Extinguish the sage, and light the charcoal tablet in your fireproof container/cauldron. Sprinkle some crushed eucalyptus on the lit tablet and again walk throughout your home, always turning to the left whenever you can. (Carry the eucalyptus with you so you can add to the charcoal as needed.) Project healing energies and thoughts as you go.

As you walk and waft the smoke from the smoldering eucalyptus in the air, say:

Heal us both heart and soul
keeping us healthy is my goal.

Keep this simple chant going all through your home once again, until you make it back to your front door. At this point, add the crushed lavender (again carry some with you in case you need a "refill") to the lit charcoal tablet and make your third and final trip throughout your home. Project loving and peaceful energies as you go. This last time chant:

Love, peace, hope, and faith
surround us with these,
in this place.

When you get back to the front door, take your pet for a casual stroll throughout the house. Tell your pet how much you love and appreciate having her/him in your life with you.

Repeat this spell whenever you feel necessary or if you experience a setback.

My pet has died

The death of a pet can be as traumatic as the death of any other loved one. When we send any of our loved ones on to the next world, we often feel like we are sending a part of us with them. As with any death, you will need time to grieve and you may want to hold a funeral rite for your pet. This "spell" then, is actually a combination of an emotionally healing spell for you and a funeral ritual for your pet.

If you are able to bury your pet, perform this ritual at the grave site. If you have had you pet cremated and have the ashes, place them on your altar. If you are not able to do either, place a picture of your pet on your altar.

For this spell/ritual you will need:
- a gold candle to represent the God
- a silver candle to represent the Goddess
- a candle of your choice to represent your pet
- frankincense for purification and protection
- a lighter

Begin by lighting the candle that represents your pet and say:

> (Pet's name) *has left us,*
> *and gone ahead to a new world,*
> *a new life, a new incarnation.*
> *This candle represents* (pet's name),
> *along his/her travels.*

Light the incense and waft it in the air all around you and the grave, ashes, or candle representation. As you do so, say:

> *May this frankincense help to*
> *protect you on your journey and*
> *purify you for the next world.*

Place the incense back on your altar. Say:

Lord of the wild,
Lady of the moon,
I come tonight to honor (pet's name),
and to wish him/her well,
as he/she sets off on a
new journey into the Otherworld.
While here, (name) brought great joy into my life,
and though I will miss him/her greatly,
I know he/she must travel on now without me.
Though I will mourn my loss,
I also celebrate the life of (name)
and the love we shared.
I ask that the Lord and Lady,
take both of us under their wings.
Heal my heart please,
and guide (name) safely to the Otherworld.

Use the candle representing your pet to light the silver Goddess candle. Say:

(Pet's name) becomes one with the Goddess.

Use the candle representing your pet to light the gold God candle. Say:

(Pet's name) becomes one with the God.

Say:

(Pet's name)'s life on this plane has been extinguished,
and so this candle must be too.

Extinguish the pet's candle. Say:

May (name)'s journey to the Otherworld
be safe and blessed.
So mote it be.

Take as much time as you need to say your goodbyes. When you are finished, if you do not have ashes or a grave site, you may bury the candle that represented your pet.

I raise chickens, so we often have pets that have to be buried. It is always a time of great sadness, and we do have our own "chicken graveyard"—their own special area of the yard, right by our ritual site, where all of them are buried, unless they were chicks that didn't survive. The chicks have their own special place in our fairy garden. We have had several friends who have come to help us bury them as they had never attended a chicken funeral before. They end up actually realizing what a touching and somber moment it is as we perform the above spell for our departed feathered friends.

My vet recommended I put my pet down

About a decade ago, my husband and I woke up on Thanksgiving morning and went out to the deck to have a cup of coffee and admire the light snowfall we'd had overnight. Our dog, Nakita—an Alaskan Malamute—should have been excited as possible to see the snow; she didn't like anything better. That morning, however, she lay there watching us. I looked at her closely and as she rocked a little I noticed she was on grass, not snow—she had stayed in the same position for quite a while.

I said to my husband, "I have a bad feeling. Something's wrong." We went over to Nakita who rolled over onto her back and showed us her tummy. She looked normal, except for way down between her hind legs we saw what could have been dried blood, though we couldn't tell for sure. We didn't see any wounds either, as we couldn't even find her skin through her extremely thick winter coat. She didn't want to get up, and so while I stuck the turkey in the oven and put our oldest son in charge my husband carried Nakita out to the car. We drove her to the emergency vet and waited, and waited, and waited.

Finally, we were told she was going to be sent home. They had shaved her belly completely so they could find what was wrong and discovered that a tumor in a mammary gland had exploded. We had never known she had any kind of tumor at all. They let us know that because of its location it would have been impossible to find without shaving her first. They then told us there wasn't anything they could do for her. She was going to die soon and it would be painful. They would not put her down there, but recommended we see our regular vet as soon as possible.

What a blow—and on Thanksgiving! We brought her home and she had the best dinner—for Thanksgiving or any other day for that matter. We had to explain to our children that the kindest decision in our minds was to put her out of her misery.

I realize there are some people reading this book who do not agree with the option of euthanizing a pet, and that is your prerogative. That being said, I believe it is the kindest and most humane course of action for an animal that only has a painful demise in its near future. I won't try to change your position if you won't try to change mine.

At the time of Nakita's passing, I didn't have any kind of spell or ritual to help us through it; I hadn't expected anything like this to happen.

This scenario is different than an actual funeral rite mainly because you know ahead of time what is going to happen, and of course your pet is still alive. This gives you more time to prepare your animal for their journey to the Otherworld, and prepare yourself and your family for the loss you are about to experience.

When exactly you go about this spell/ritual is entirely up to you. You may have a vet who will allow you to perform it at the office, or you may want to perform it at home in familiar surroundings. If you do perform this spell at the vet's office, you can quite literally help send your pet's soul to the Otherworld. Depending on your preferences and beliefs, this can be quite comforting to your pet, your family, and yourself. No matter when or where exactly you perform this spell, the most important factor is to have your pet right there with you while it is conducted. The whole family can read the spell together or one person can lead with others present.

For this spell you will need:
- a blue candle for tranquility, truth, honor, peace, healing, and wisdom
- frankincense for spirituality, consecration, meditation, and protection
- myrrh for spirituality, consecration, meditation, and protection
- sandalwood for spirituality, protection, and meditation
- fireproof container, charcoal tablet, and lighter

Set up your altar, bring your pet in, and cast your circle.
Begin by lighting the blue candle. Say:

> *Great Goddess,*
> *the time to say goodbye to* (pet's name)
> *is coming upon us.*
> *We ask that while you grant* (pet's name)
> *tranquility and peace,*
> *you grant the rest of us the wisdom*
> *to accept the truth of the matter at hand—*
> *that* (pet's name) *must leave us and go on ahead.*
> *Help us to heal as we have to say goodbye.*

Sprinkle some frankincense onto the lit charcoal tablet. Walk the container around the circle, wafting the smoke into the air. Say:

> *Great Goddess,*
> *We ask for you to come and accompany (pet's name)*
> *on his/her journey to the Otherworld.*
> *We ask for you to consecrate and protect*
> *his/her soul and to deliver him/her*
> *safely into the Summerland.*

Sprinkle some myrrh onto the lit charcoal tablet. Walk the container around the circle, wafting the smoke into the air. Say:

> *Great Goddess,*
> *As we say goodbye to (pet's name),*
> *and turn his/her life over to you,*
> *we ask for blessings of your protection,*
> *for us, and for our beloved pet.*
> *Help us to heal and mend.*
> *Help us to be content with the knowledge*
> *(pet's name) is going on to a better existence.*
> *An existence free from pain and suffering.*

Sprinkle some sandalwood onto the lit charcoal tablet. Walk the container around the circle, wafting the smoke into the air. Say:

> *Great Goddess,*
> *be with (pet's name) throughout his/her journey,*
> *but be with us in spirit also.*
> *As we meditate on the life of our beloved pet,*
> *help us to remember the good times,*
> *and to celebrate (pet's name)'s life with honor and joy.*

At this point, allow everyone a few moments to meditate on the life of your pet. Afterwards, each person is free to say something about the life of your pet, or to even take a moment to just talk with the pet. Let everyone have as much time as they need to say what they want. When everyone is finished, say:

Thank you, Great Goddess, for your presence,
and for escorting (pet's name) on to the
next phase of his/her journey.

Go ahead and close your circle.

My dog bit someone

One of the hardest parts about writing this book is that spells had to have come from somewhere. Some situations came from close friends I helped by writing spells for, and many of these situations have happened to me personally; this being one of them.

My dog, Foxy, was a mixed breed who often lived up to her name. She was quite foxy in a very sneaky sense. Sometimes even I felt uncomfortable around her. One day, my elderly father was at my house while I did an errand. My father had been told several times to leave Foxy outside—I would take care of her when I got home. He didn't listen. He managed to get her in the house, but when he went to take her leash off, she attacked his hand—badly. My dad didn't even realize how severe it was; when I returned home he was still bleeding. It was awful. He was on blood thinners and got so upset we had to physically restrain him when he tried to walk away from the house after we called for an ambulance. He suffers from dementia and thought we were making too big a deal. We weren't.

Animal bites often aren't stitched up because of the risk of infection, but this was bad enough that he had to have several stitches in several fingers. When the deputy sheriffs arrived at the emergency room to fill out the report, they took one look at him and the damage done and told us we had to put Foxy down. We knew we had to, but it didn't make things easier.

Was it really her fault? It was hard to say. She didn't bite him when he walked out to get her from her run. She waited until they were back inside and he was trying to remove her leash. If we had to make the decision ourselves it would have been tough to do, but as it turned out we had no choice in the matter. The police gave us twenty-four hours to take care of the matter ourselves (to take her into the vet, that is). If we didn't, they would send animal control to get her.

We didn't want to make things any more difficult than they already were, so we took her in. Our vet is a wonderful man who takes care of all of our animals, even our chickens. He knew how upsetting this was for us, and so instead of taking her into the office and putting her on a cold steel table, he came outside and met us on the grass underneath a tree. When Foxy took her last breath, her head was in my arms.

Not all animal bite stories end this way, granted, but they should end with a report to the police at the very least. If an animal bites too many times, or severely enough, your local ordinance may require the animal be put down. If you do have to put a dog down, you may want to do the preceding spell/ritual instead ("My vet recommended I put my pet down"). The situation is a bit different but could be easily adapted for your purposes.

This spell is for the *first* biting, not a serious attack that results in euthanization. How can a bite not be serious? Well, they don't always break the skin, and believe it or not, that is a good thing. It's a warning for you to get your dog some help, whether through a vet, obedience training, or other means. It is a chance to find out why the animal bites and an opportunity to take the necessary steps to prevent repeat occurrences. The same can also be said for excessive barking, growling, or other aggressive behaviors.

If a bite breaks the skin, someone is going to be in pain and there will be medical bills and possible legal matters to deal with, but again you are given a warning to try to get the animal help so that a second or more serious bite does not occur.

This spell will help you find out what the problem is and why the dog bit in the first place. It will help your dog be more receptive to training to prevent a second occurrence. It will also send healing energy to the victim, and to everyone involved to help deal with the trauma, including the dog. Remember that animals don't bite without reason—they usually do so because they are scared or feel threatened. If your dog has bitten someone, chances are it was going through a traumatic moment. It may have wrongly perceived a threat that wasn't there, it saw a threat and reacted.

Lastly, this spell is going to help prevent further problems, by setting boundaries and binding this type of behavior.

For this spell you will need:
- a black candle for defining boundaries and binding
- a green candle for healing and neutralizing difficult situations
- green ribbon
- a black collar for your dog
- lemon oil for healing and clarity
- fireproof container, charcoal tablet, and lighter

Set up your altar and have your pet with you. Cast your circle. Light the charcoal tablet.

Light the green candle and say:

Great pain has come to many
and this we need to mend.
Healing, peace, and strength for all
I ask the Goddess to send.
Calm (pet's name) *and soothe his/her soul,*
while we set things right
protect us all with your power
and your love and light.

Light the black candle and say:

Set the boundaries for (pet's name)
so that they are very clear.
Bind the bad behavior
and protect him/her from fear.

Add a few drops of lemon oil to the charcoal tablet. Swirl the fireproof container in the air to help disperse the smoke throughout the area. Say:

Clear our minds,
purge the negativity.
Give us all a fresh start.
Heal the bodies, minds, hearts, and souls,
of everyone involved.

Hold the black collar close to the black candle (but not too close!) and say:

As (pet's name) *wears this collar,*
let it bind his/her negative actions,
while he/she works on learning the difference
between right and wrong.

Take the green ribbon and tie it to the black collar. Say:

As (pet's name) *wears this,*
let it help to heal him/her,
and to keep him/her calm.

Put the collar on your pet. Finish with:

Dear Goddess, help us all
in this time of need.
Send your healing
and loving strength to us,
and into the universe,
for everyone who has been affected
by (pet's name) *actions.*
Help us all to learn from this
and go on with our lives.
So mote it be.

Close your circle. Make sure you follow up with a visit to vet as soon as possible.

My child wants a pet, but I don't know if he/she is ready for the responsibility

It seems that as soon as kids can start talking and making sentences, they start asking for their own pet, whether it be a cat, dog, rabbit, hamster, fish, bird, or ferret—they always seem to be wanting something or other. How do you know if your child is ready for the responsibility of pet ownership? This meditative spell will help tell you.

For this spell you will need:
· an indigo candle for insight, vision, and psychic abilities
· coltsfoot for peace, tranquility, visions, and animal spells
· a fireproof container, charcoal tablet, and lighter

Set up your altar and cast your circle in a comfortable location. Light the charcoal tablet. Sprinkle some coltsfoot onto the tablet and say:

> *Bring me peace*
> *and tranquility*
> *so my visions and insights*
> *will be clear and precise.*

Light the indigo candle and say:

> *I am looking for answers.*
> *My child wants a pet*
> *and yet I am unsure.*
> *Show me what the future may hold.*
> *Show me what my child is ready for.*
> *Show me how life will be for the animal,*
> *as well for my child*
> *and the rest of the family.*

Get into a comfortable position and stare deeply into the candle's flame. Shut everything else out. Look only at the flame. Do not see anything around it or behind it. This may take a little practice but eventually it will work. Continue staring into the flame until you feel it is necessary to close your eyes. When you close your eyes, your visions should appear. If they don't appear, don't worry, you just need some more practice. End the spell and try again the next day.

If days go by and you still haven't been able to get an answer through your visions, take a short break. If you try to push too hard, you won't see anything anyway. After a few days go ahead and try again. Vision spells can be very difficult, but they are also very important for when we want to see how certain actions will play out in the future if we choose to take them.

If your visions show clearly, you can gain much information without even realizing it. As soon as the vision fades, close your circle and write down everything you remember or record it on a digital player. You may see a certain type of animal. You may see your child at a different age; if your child appears much older with a young animal, it isn't time to get one yet, for example. If your child appears older with an older animal, this may very well be showing you the animal and your child have grown up together. You may see the type of animal and even the breed and coloring. Record as many details as possible, as it will help you narrow down your search—keep in mind that animal spirit you saw has a connection to your child and is on a search of its own.

We have to give our pet away

The past few years have been extremely difficult for home owners with pets. With high foreclosure rates, many families who lose their home also have to consider giving up their pet or pets when they are unable to find a place to rent allowing them to keep these family members. Sometimes people are lucky but the extra security deposit is too steep to handle, making the possible impossible once again.

Animal shelters have been overflowing with pets who have lost their homes. Sometimes pets end up being abandoned because their owners can't find a place to live with them and shelters are too full to take them. Abandonment is of course *not* something I recommend at all.

Check with friends and family first—if they can't take your pet perhaps they know someone who will be able. Also many freecycle sites that formerly banned posting animals now do so because of the sudden spike in the homeless animal population. No matter what you do, make sure your animal has been spayed or neutered—there are already too many homeless animals in the world; we don't need more being brought into it.

There may be other reasons your family has to give a pet away such as allergies or it not getting along with other pets (or even certain people) in the home. Whatever the reason, this spell will help your family deal with the pain and heartache of having to give the pet away and also help you find it a suitable home. It also eases the pet's transition into a new home—a place your pet will be taken care of and well loved. Your pet is going to miss you too!

For this spell you will need:
- an indigo candle to help you deal with change
- a brown candle to deal with issues relating to pets, animals, and decision making
- coltsfoot for peace, animal spells, and visions
- witch hazel for healing a broken heart
- cypress for comfort and easing feelings of loss
- a fireproof container, charcoal tablet, and lighter

Set up your altar and cast your circle. Light the charcoal tab. It's up to you if you want to have your pet with you while you perform this spell. It won't hurt, but it isn't necessary either.

Begin by lighting the brown candle and say:

I light this candle for (pet's name).
I work this spell in the best interest of (pet's name),
as I look for a new home for him/her.
I know this is a difficult decision,
and one I may not even have the choice of making.
It is a situation I cannot control.
I hope to find the best home possible for (pet's name).

Light the indigo candle and say:

During this time of change,
help us all adjust—
my family and my pet too.
As we search for a new home for (pet's name)
allow us to be able to see the situation clearly,
in order to find the best placement possible.

Add some coltsfoot to the charcoal tablet. Say:

I ask for assistance from the Lord and Lady,
to bring peace to my family and pet
as we go through this difficult time.
I ask for the visions to help me find the solution
best for all involved.
Send me visions that will lead me on the right path,
the path to find a good loving home for (pet's name).

Add some witch hazel to the lit charcoal tablet and say:

> *I offer this witch hazel,*
> *to help our hearts mend.*
> *As we have loved (pet's name),*
> *so has he/she loved us.*
> *The pain and loss we will all feel will be great indeed.*
> *Please help to ease these feelings.*

Add some cypress to the lit charcoal tablet and say:

> *Let this cypress help comfort us.*
> *Let it console us with the knowledge*
> *that (pet's name) will find a kind and loving home.*

You may take some time to meditate now, to see if any visions are sent to you about where you should look for a new home for your pet. When you are done, close your circle.

It is better to begin a search for a new home as soon as you can. Once you know your situation and that you won't be able to keep your pet, you need to get moving on finding a new home immediately. Time is truly of the essence. Because it can take so long to find a home for a pet these days, you need to get started on it right away.

Someone I know is abusing their pet

This can be a very touchy situation, especially depending on what your relationship is with the person. If you are close friends of yours and the person is abusing a pet, you may very well lose this friendship because the very first thing you need to do—before working any spell at all—is call the authorities. Animal abuse is illegal. If an animal is in harm's way, the first thing you must do is get that animal to safety.

Whether the person doing the abusing is a close friend, casual acquaintance, or neighbor, it is imperative that you call the police and get them involved. Only then may you do this spell that will help both the animal overcome its injuries (mental or physical) and will also stop the abuser from abusing in the future.

For this spell you will need:
- a green candle for healing
- a black candle for banishing and binding
- coltsfoot for peace, visions, and animal spells
- a fireproof container
- charcoal tablet
- lighter

Set up your altar and cast your circle. Ignite the tablet.
Light the black candle and say:

> *I use my power and energy*
> *to banish the hurt and pain this animal has suffered.*
> *I bind the abuser from harming again.*

Repeat this three times.
Light the green candle and say:

> *I use my power and energy*
> *to heal the hurt and pain this animal suffered.*
> *Bring peace to this animal and*
> *let it never suffer again.*

Repeat this three times also.

Add some coltsfoot to the charcoal tablet and say:

> *Allow this coltsfoot to bring peace to this animal.*
> *Allow this coltsfoot to bring visions to me.*
> *Visions to help me see how*
> *else I can best help this animal.*

Again, repeat this three times also.

Take some time to meditate. Visualize energy, peace, and healing being sent to the animal wherever it is at this point. Your energy and love finds the animal and surrounds it, puts it at ease. Makes it feel safe. After you feel the animal has received your energy, again send out binding energy toward the abuser. Surround the person with peace and calmness, tell him or her to banish their desire to harm. When you are finished, close your circle.

Part Five

★★★★

HEALTH

I feel like I don't have the energy
to get out of bed and face the day

While we all probably feel this way on certain days, some people end up where this becomes constant, not just a once-in-a-while funk. If you have this feeling frequently, chances are you may be suffering a form of depression, or it could be a physical problem as well.

You definitely should see a doctor, and there are other things you can be doing at home to help boost your energy level. Along with vitamins, exercise, making sure you eat right, and maybe even adding different herbal supplements, this spell can help get you back on track.

For this spell you will need:
- an orange candle for ambition, enthusiasm, energy, willpower, and zest for life
- balm of Gilead for emotional healing
- bayberry for harmony and well-being
- neroli oil for joy
- a fireproof container, charcoal tablet, and lighter
- mortar and pestle

This spell should be completed at dawn to aid in the removal of stagnation and for new beginnings. If possible, you should do this spell outside so you can be one with the sunrise. Making the rising of the sun a part of your daily life is sure to help you get back on your feet and help you give each day a fresh new start as the sun itself does each morning.

Set up your altar and cast your circle.

Light the orange candle and say:

Sun so bright,
I ask for a blessing
from your guiding light.

> *Bring to me ambition*
> *and enthusiasm.*
> *Restore to me my energy*
> *and willpower*
> *and grant me zest for life.*

Add the balm of Gilead and bayberry to the mortar and crush with the pestle. As you crush them together, chant:

> *Bring me harmony*
> *and well-being*
> *as I mend with emotional healing.*

Once the mixture is ground thoroughly, add in a few drops of neroli oil and mix some more. This time say:

> *Bring joy to my life,*
> *this I ask,*
> *please accept this as your task.*

Once everything is combined, place some on the lit charcoal tablet and end as you began, saying:

> *Sun so bright,*
> *I ask for a blessing*
> *from your guiding light.*
> *Bring to me ambition,*
> *and enthusiasm.*
> *Restore to me my energy*
> *and willpower*
> *and grant me zest for life.*

You may take some time now to do morning meditation or affirmations. Remember this spell absolutely needs to be backed up with work in the mundane world—make sure you see a doctor to ensure there is no medical cause for your lack of energy.

I know I should exercise, but I just don't feel like it

I'm sure I am not the only one out there who's had this problem! I admit that my motivation to exercise comes and goes (mainly goes!) in spurts. The key is to not sit around waiting for those spurts to show up; we can help create them with a simple spell.

When most people get into the habit of exercising, it often becomes a part of life; they really don't want to do without. The key is to do it long enough to start reaping the benefits so that the habit sticks.

This spell is best performed on the day of a full moon—a time for workings on positives and physical energy—though you can do this spell any time. If the timing is close to a full moon, all the better.

This spell should also be performed at dawn if at all possible. I know, terrible, aren't I? I want you up at dawn for all kinds of things! However, there is more than one reason for this. For starters, dawn is the optimum time for working on positives—and of course starting a new exercise regimen is a positive. It is also the optimum time for workings that have to do with physical energy. Finally, many people use lack of time to *not* exercise, so now that you are up at dawn, you should be able to squeeze in at least a fifteen-minute workout.

This spell is quite brief, simply so you will have time for that workout!

Mix up the incense, and set up your altar ahead of time so when you wake up in the morning, you are all ready to go. The herbs here all help with physical energy.

For this spell you will need:
The following dried herbs/essential oils:

- bergamot
- camphor
- cinnamon
- lemon
- lime
- nutmeg
- columbine (for willpower)
- peppermint (for energy and stimulation)

You will also need:

- a fireproof container, charcoal tablet, and lighter

Cast your circle and light the charcoal tablet.

Place a pinch of the incense on the tablet and say:

> *Help me to do*
> *what I know is right,*
> *give me energy*
> *to win this fight.*
> *Restore my energy*
> *and my might*
> *with the dawning*
> *of the sun's light.*

Close your circle.

If you can, put the incense in the room you work out in. If you take a walk or jog, add a small amount of the incense to a small drawstring bag and carry it with you.

When you exercise, try some uplifting, spiritual music—it will help motivate you and make your workout seem to go quicker.

I need help controlling my appetite

We live in a society that one minute is telling us to eat, eat, eat, and then the next minute is telling us to diet, diet, diet.

Though it seems to continually get lost on people, we should all know by now that "a diet" is not the answer. Changing *your* diet (that is, the sum of all the foods you consume) to be healthy and keeping it that way is. Of course fad diet manufacturers don't want us to know or believe that and so they keep bombarding us with their advertisements, plans, and "miracle cures."

We don't need boxed or frozen meals delivered to us a month at a time. We don't need to pop three pills in the morning, two at lunch, and another six before dinner. We don't have to have cereal twice a day for two weeks. We simply need to start being more responsible for what and how much we put into our mouths! It's hard to break old habits, however. Maybe we could use a little help in this department.

This spell is going to help you control your appetite so you aren't overeating things that aren't good for you. It isn't going to starve you. It isn't going to make you lose forty pounds in a week. It's going to help you fight cravings and not give in to them. It's going to help you stop at two servings of mashed potatoes and not go for a third—if you let it!

For this spell you will need:

- a carrier oil such as almond or grapeseed oil
- grapefruit oil
- sweet fennel oil
- an atomizer or vial for storing mixed oil

Set up your altar and cast your circle. Begin by pouring some carrier oil into your atomizer or vial.

Add in three drops of grapefruit oil and say:

> *Great Goddess*
> *I come to you for help,*
> *I ask you to bless this oil*
> *with your powers and infuse*
> *it with your strength.*

> *Known to kill*
> *cravings for sweets,*
> *I add this grapefruit oil*
> *to help keep me on track.*

Add in three drops of the fennel oil and say:

> *I ask you to bless this oil*
> *with your power and infuse*
> *it with your strength.*
> *Known to stave off hunger,*
> *I add this fennel oil*
> *to help keep me on track*
> *and distinguish between emotional*
> *and physical hunger.*

Cap the vial and shake vigorously.

Close your circle.

Rub or spray the oil mixture on the pulse points of your wrists and neck at least three times a day, and whenever you feel the strong desire to overeat!

I need help losing weight

The only true way to lose weight is to burn more calories than you consume. You do this through diet and exercise. Can you have that piece of cake? Sure you can—in moderation. You have to remember the weight loss process is twofold. Output must be greater than input. Increase your output, decrease your input, and you'll lose weight faster.

Stress plays a part in weight gain—it affects the way we metabolize food and makes exercise even more important. To lose weight the most effective way possible, we need to remember a simple equation and more importantly *follow through with it*. Output needs to be greater than input and stress needs to be minimized. When it comes down to it, the process sounds really easy, but we all know how real life can complicate things.

We need to keep our motivation up, and there is a particular oil that helps do this especially when it comes to the weight loss battle.

For this spell you will need:
• a carrier oil such as grapeseed or almond oil
• honeysuckle oil
• an atomizer or capped vial

Set up your altar and cast your circle. Add the carrier oil to the vial followed by three to five drops of honeysuckle oil.

As you add the honeysuckle say:

Great Goddess
I come to you for help,
I ask you to bless this oil
with your powers and infuse
it with your strength.
My goal is to lose weight
and I ask for you
to assist me in this task.

*I walk with the Goddess
in everything I do,
and pray for your
assistance in losing
this weight too.*

Close your circle.

Rub or spray the oil on the pulse points of your wrists and neck at least three times a day.

Your weight loss will generally go even more smoothly if you can find a friend to be your weight loss buddy. Encourage one another. If your friend is willing, perform the spell together.

I need help to quit smoking

It's easy to quit smoking—I've done it thousands of times!

Actually I have done it twice. The first time was for over two years, and as I'm writing this now, I am over a year and a half smoke-free. I have absolutely no intention or desire to ever start again.

Why would I start again after quitting for two years? When it comes right down to it I was weak. I started hanging around the wrong people—people who didn't just smoke, but people who it turned out didn't really care about me or themselves for that matter. Those people are no longer a part of my life, and that made it easier to quit.

I also felt I needed some good motivation. My husband's van was on its last legs and he really needed a new vehicle to drive to work. The cash-for-clunkers program was going on and after doing a bit of math, I discovered we could make payments on a new car for *less* than what I spent each month on cigarettes. How could I *not* quit smoking?

Saying you are going to quit and actually doing it are two different things. I am one of those people who literally tried everything—patches, pills, gum, lozenges, injections, hypnotherapy—you name, it I tried it. Nothing worked. The only way I have been able to quit smoking both times was to simply quit buying cigarettes. Yes, I still had to deal with cravings (not a whole lot of fun), but once I accepted the fact that I would just have to deal with them possibly for the rest of my life, it made it easier. And yes, from what I have heard from other former smokers—some who haven't had a cigarette in more than twenty years—the cravings simply never go away. They become less frequent and might not be as strong, but someday you will be doing something and suddenly think to yourself, "I want a smoke."

I truly believe the only way to control smoking is not to give in to the cravings. It takes willpower, which can be boosted with a spell. This spell can help kill those cravings. When a craving hits, you need to redirect your mind elsewhere and give the craving time to pass. Most cravings generally last less than fifteen minutes—not really that long to just wait out.

This spell is going to help you relax and mellow while waiting for the craving to pass. Plan to quit on the night of a new moon. If possible, perform this spell outside.

For this spell you will need:
- a black candle (for banishing)
- peppermint oil (for mental stimulation and purification)
- a carrier oil such as almond or grapeseed oil
- cinnamon red hot candies in a sealed container
  (cinnamon for success)

Set up your altar and cast your circle.

Begin by lighting the candle and say:

I come here tonight
under the darkness of the moon
to take a new step in my life.
I have come to banish
the use of cigarettes
and any form of nicotine
from my life.
I come to ask the
Lord and Lady
to stand by my side
and help see me through.

Add the carrier oil to the atomizer or vial. Add in four drops of peppermint oil. Say:

Bless this peppermint oil,
infuse it with strength and power.
Allow it to purify me and stave
off any cravings I encounter.
As I inhale its scent,
I will feel my lungs being
cleansed and purged
of the toxins that have
contaminated them for so long.

Cap off the vial and shake vigorously. Place the peppermint atomizer back on the altar and pick up the container of cinnamon candies. Hold them out in front of you and say:

> *Bless this cinnamon,*
> *infuse it with strength and power.*
> *Allow it to help me*
> *successfully stave off*
> *cravings I encounter.*
> *As I taste the cinnamon*
> *I will feel my lungs being*
> *cleansed and purged*
> *of the toxins that have*
> *contaminated them for so long.*

Go ahead and close your circle.

When you have your next craving, take a seat and breathe deeply. Rub or spray some of the peppermint mixture on the pulse points of your wrists and inhale the scent. Feel the peppermint cleansing your lungs. Pop a cinnamon candy or two in your mouth and suck on them. Don't keep watch of the time, but know that the craving will soon pass. Walk yourself through each craving, and you'll soon find yourself making it day after day without having a cigarette.

I'm a recovering alcoholic/addict

The keyword in this title is *recovering*. If you are recovering, you are not currently using. If you are currently using, this spell will not help you. If you are using, you will need to get yourself into some type of rehab for help.

This spell is for those who are in recovery. It is to help you mend and heal. The type of rehab you undergo is completely up to you. This spell helps your body, mind, and soul heal from the damage that has been done to it.

For this spell you will need:
- a piece of amber for stability, self confidence, and peace
- cedar oil for healing, courage, purification, spirituality, and self-control
- tangerine oil for strength, power, and vitality
- a fireproof container, charcoal tablet, and lighter

This spell should be done at least once a week. If you are feeling low on strength, perform it every morning with the sunrise.

Set up your altar and cast a circle.

Light the charcoal tablet and add a couple of drops of cedar oil. Say:

> *As I start off my day (week),*
> *I look to the Lord and Lady*
> *for healing energies and courage.*
> *I look to my God and Goddess*
> *to purify my body, soul, and mind.*
> *I look to regain my connection with my deities.*
> *I look to keep my self control.*

Pass the piece of amber through the smoke.

Add a couple of drops of tangerine oil to the charcoal tablet and say:

> *As I start off my day (week),*
> *I look to the Lord and Lady*
> *for vitality, power, and strength—*
> *strength in fighting my disease.*

Pass the piece of amber through the smoke again. Close the circle.

Carry your amber with you and grasp it whenever you need a boost of strength.

I've been diagnosed with a serious medical condition

If you've been diagnosed, the good news is that you are already under a doctor's care and treatment can begin. While your doctor works on treating your medical condition, you need to work on treating the rest of yourself.

There are other types of treatments you can look into—alternative, holistic, and spiritual just to name a few. If you undergo any forms of treatment other than what your doctor prescribes make sure to keep all your practitioners up to date on what is being done. Different components of different types of treatments may interact with each other in negative ways that could make you worse instead of better. We don't want that happening, so it's best to keep everyone informed. Use a notebook to keep track of your different treatments as this will make the information easy to share with each practitioner.

The spell we are going to do here is to help treat yourself with positive and healing energies.

We are going to make up a mojo bag of goodness to keep with you at all times. This bag will contain healing energies for your body, mind, and soul. If you don't have all these ingredients, don't worry—just use as many as you can.

For this spell you will need:
- A green drawstring bag

Any/All of the following herbs:
- allspice, angelica, balm of Gilead, buckthorn, bramble, burdock, calendula, carnation, cedar, clove, coriander, cowslip, dragon's blood, eucalyptus, gardenia, garlic, geranium, ginseng, honeysuckle, horehound, juniper, lavender, lemon, melon, mistletoe, myrrh, nettle, palmarosa, pine, rue, sage, sandalwood, sassafras, spearmint, spikenard, sunflower, sweet pea, tea tree, violet, willow, and yerba santa

Place all the ingredients up on your altar along with the bag.

Cast your circle and say:

I have learned a sad truth,
an obstacle I must face
and overcome.

> *I ask the Lord and Lady*
> *to take me under their wing,*
> *into their care,*
> *I ask for their protection*
> *and for the strength*
> *to fight the battle I have ahead of me.*
> *Protect me on my journey.*
> *So mote it be.*

As you add each ingredient to the bag, remain silent. Focus on being strong and healing yourself. Focus on the inflicted or affected areas of your body. Visualize those areas becoming clean and pure.

When you are finished, close your circle.

I've broken a bone

Depending on your age and your overall health, breaking a bone may be considered a routine medical problem, or it can be something extremely serious. People who already have certain problems with their bones can suffer tremendously when a bone breaks. Healing times can vary from a few weeks up to several months. Then there is the inconvenience caused by things like casts, slings, crutches, or special shoes.

If you haven't broken a bone, chances are you at least know someone who has. It is quite common, and if you haven't broken one yet unfortunately you still might someday.

This spell will help your healing move along while giving you the patience to put up with the inconveniences you will have to deal with along the way.

You will need:
- a hematite stone
- an amethyst stone
- light blue cloth
- needle
- thread

Set up your altar and cast a circle.

Depending on which bone is broken, you will need to figure out what you are going to attach the cloth to (this will also determine how much cloth you need). For example, if you have a casted arm and a sling, you can sew a small amount of the cloth on to the inside of the sling. If you have to wear a specially fitted boot, you can attach it to the boot somehow. For other casts you may have to use a larger amount of cloth and wrap it around the cast itself. You want to be able to keep the cloth as close to your body as possible.

Before you attach the cloth, you must first sew the stones into it.

Lay the cloth out on your altar and say:

Though my bone is broken
my spirit is not.
I know I must take it easy and relax
in order to aid my healing.
I should not push ahead
of my recovery rate
and need to remain at peace
in order to heal completely.

Place the amethyst and hematite on the cloth and fold it up however you need to in order to sew the stones inside. As you stitch, chant:

Each stitch I take
seals the fate
of mending my bones again

Once it is completely sewn, attach it where you need it and close your circle.

I've had a heart attack

You've had a heart attack, and luckily you have recovered. Having a heart attack can and should have a very profound effect on a person. When you have a heart attack and survive, it is often a warning—a warning that you need to immediately change something (or several things!) in your lifestyle. Your doctor is going to be able to give you a good idea on what changes you must make.

Making those changes is often the hardest part. You have to keep in mind what these changes ultimately mean. If you want to give yourself the best chance at surviving for as long as you can, you need to follow your doctor's orders, no matter how different and inconvenient they may seem.

Heart disease runs in my step-mother's family so I have seen many of my relatives on that side suffer from heart attacks and other heart conditions. The attacks are scary, but if mild, can actually be quite the life-saver, acting as huge warning signs flashing "Change your life now or next time it won't be as easy!" Ultimately, it's up to you to decide what to do with the information the universe hands you.

This spell is designed to help you heal body, mind, and soul. It's also going to help you accept changes you have to make and keep you at peace while doing so.

For this spell you will need:

- an indigo candle
- apple blossom for peace and celebrating life
- balm of Gilead for emotional healing
- bergamot for peace, happiness, restful sleep, and for breaking hexes (just to make sure)
- cedar for healing, courage, purification, protection, spirituality, and self-control
- bay berry for peace, harmony, and well-being
- a small green drawstring bag

Set up your altar and cast your circle. For this spell you are going to make a small gris-gris bag to carry around with you. Lay all the ingredients on your altar. Begin by saying:

My heart has been broken
and needs to be repaired.
It needs healing energies
to mend the damage done.
I come today to ask for strength
and the assistance of the
Lord and Lady
in putting my heart right.
I ask for your blessings.

Silently and with focused intent, add a pinch of each ingredient to the bag. As you add them, visualize your heart getting stronger, working more efficiently. It has more power than it did before. Visualize your heart becoming more robust with each beat. You can feel yourself and your heart becoming healthier.

After you add all of the ingredients to the bag, close it and tie it tight.

Hold the bag close to your heart and say:

I may not always have taken
care of my heart as well as I should have.
I pledge to take better care and
to love myself
as I always should have.
To remember my body is a temple unto
the God and Goddess
and revere it
and worship it
while caring for it
the best I can.
As my heart heals and mends,
I will not forget
the damage it has seen,
the pain it has survived.

Bless my heart,
Lord and Lady.
Keep me safe
in your loving embrace.

Carry this gris-gris bag with you. You already know how important it is to back up your working in the mundane world by taking care of yourself and following your doctor's recommendations.

I've been diagnosed with cancer

As the saying goes, "Cancer sucks!" but luckily it isn't always the death sentence it was a couple of decades ago. Though there are still some forms that simply can't be defeated, many forms can be these days. It is extremely important to *not* give up the fight. You have to fight in order to win. If you give up, the cancer will beat you, and no one wants that.

Most of my family has had cancer. Seriously. While some died of it a long time ago, others have battled it with great success. The odds for survival get better all the time. I won't be surprised if I end up with some form of cancer at some point in my life with so much of it on both sides of my family. I see it as another "wonderful" trial I will just have to deal with when it happens. The most important aspect of fighting cancer is to simply keep up the fight. Some days are easier than others, but every day you do have to fight.

A friend of mine has a son who had a rare form of cancer she was told he would not survive. His chances were given as less than 5 percent. But he fought it and he fought hard—a 5 percent chance was all he needed. He has been cancer-free for several years now.

This spell was written for him. It will help you keep that willpower up, to keep the fight inside you alive. As long as you still have that inside of you, you have a good chance of winning your battle.

In this spell we will make a mojo bag you will be able to carry with you at all times. Make sure you use small pieces, for starters you want them to all fit in the bag and you don't want it to be too heavy.

For this spell you will need:

- a small green drawstring bag
- dragon's blood oil

Small pieces of different stones (if you don't have access to every stone listed, use as many as you can for added power)
- agate for courage and strength
- amethyst for courage and healing
- aquamarine for courage and peace
- aventurine for peace and healing
- beryl for energy and healing
- bloodstone for courage, strength, and victory
- calcite for peace and calming fears

- carnelian for courage
- hematite for healing, strength, and calmness
- jade for healing and courage
- rose quartz for healing and peace
- tiger's eye for courage and to ease depression
- tourmaline for courage, energy, and peace
- turquoise for courage

Set up your altar and cast your circle. Say the following to begin:

*I have just learned
my body is being ravaged
by a terrible disease.
But I have no intentions
of letting it win.
I will fight against this
in every way I can,
and I ask
the Lord and Lady
to fight with me,
to protect me on my path and
to guide me in my battle ahead.*

Take each stone and place it in the bag. As you do so, say what each is for (as printed here).

After placing each stone in the bag, take the dragon's blood oil and sprinkle it on the stones inside the bag. Say:

> *This dragon's blood I add*
> *to intensify*
> *and boost*
> *the work I do.*
> *Give it the power*
> *to aid me in my journey*
> *and fulfill my quest*
> *to make myself*
> *whole and complete*
> *once again.*

Keep the bag with you whenever possible and recharge under the full moon. Good luck in your fight!

I'm sure my spouse is suffering from depression but he/she won't talk to anyone

Having a spouse with emotional and/or mental issues can destroy your relationship if treatment is never sought. You've heard the saying, "You can lead a horse to water, but you can't make it drink." Not that your spouse is a horse, but I think you understand my meaning! You can hope, plead, beg, or threaten someone to get help but even if they do go to therapy, it won't do much good if they aren't ready to accept they need help.

Even if you do manage to cajole someone into getting help, he or she may resent you at first. As much as you may want your spouse to get help, it isn't something you can control. You can only decide what you are going to do *yourself* about this situation—and make no mistake, this does involve you too. One option is to see a therapist yourself to learn how to better deal with your situation.

Depending on how bad things are, you may need to make the decision about whether or not to even stay in the relationship. While some people may think it's a terrible thing to leave a person with mental issues, I honestly don't believe it is—especially if kids are involved! Children need a stable environment and if they aren't getting one in their current situation, something *needs* to change to give them a chance at a good life. Mental illness is a terrible thing and it can create awful situations, but if the person who is suffering refuses to get help, that doesn't mean everyone else around him or her should have to suffer too. We all have our own lives to live and if you are a parent, you are also responsible for your children's. They are already suffering from having one parent who can't possibly give them the proper care they need; your job is to make sure their other parent—you—can.

You need time and space to make decisions for yourself. You need to figure out what you are going to do for you and your children, if you have any. What decisions do you need to make to handle living with this situation?

This spell is going to give you the peace of mind in a meditative state to work on those decisions.

For this spell you will need:
- a sky blue candle for calmness, tranquility, patience, and understanding
- an indigo candle for insight, vision, change, and flexibility
- fireproof container, charcoal tablet, and lighter

The following herbs:
- costmary for stilling emotions
- gota kola for meditation
- magnolia for meditation
- myrrh for meditation
- sandalwood for meditation

Set your altar up in a comfortable location—someplace you will be able to sit quietly and meditate for a while, where it will also be safe for the candles to burn while you do.

Begin this spell by saying:

I have found myself in a problematic situation.
The one I love needs help,
and I am unable to help him/her.
I know the only person
I can force into action is myself,
but I do not know what actions to take.
I do not know what step to take next,
and so I come tonight to meditate on this situation.

Light the sky blue candle and say:

I come tonight to meditate,
to find calmness, tranquility, patience, and understanding.

Light the indigo candle and say:

I come tonight to meditate
for insight, vision, and flexibility,
and the strength to make changes
that may need to be made.

Place a large pinch of the incense on the lit charcoal tablet. Get comfortable and let all thoughts go from your mind. Say:

I come tonight to meditate
on my problem at hand.
I'm not looking for all the answers,
just help and guidance for the next step I must take.
I know my spouse is suffering,
and I know I cannot stop it—
I can only control my own actions,
and must let (spouse) make his/her own choices.
I come tonight to find the right answer for me.

Allow yourself plenty of time to drift into a place of clear mind. Visualize possible steps you could take and follow through the visualization to possible outcomes of those steps. How does each step and outcome make you feel? Don't only pay attention to ones that make you feel happy—those may only be wishful thinking. Pay attention to the small details in your meditation: what other signals do you receive on which course of action you should take? Don't look for too many answers at one time; you can repeat this spell and meditation as often as needed, so look for short-term steps to take now to help you with long-term goals. Remember, you cannot change someone who is not willing to change. You cannot help someone who does not want your help.

When you feel you have an answer for what to do next, go ahead and close your circle. If you have spent a lot of time in meditation and nothing has come to you yet, it may mean inaction is your best strategy at this point. Don't make any choices yet; continue meditating and doing what you can until future options present themselves.

I'm going through perimenopause

…and is it ever a joyous event! Yes, that was sarcasm. I myself have been experiencing symptoms for almost two years now, and I must say the hot flashes and night sweats are my all-time favorites. There's just something about waking up in the middle of the night doused in sweat that makes you want to rip your own hair out! I know some people like to call hot flashes "power surges." Honestly, I think those people must be nuts. Hot flashes complete wipe me out when I stand in the kitchen with my head stuck in the freezer. Luckily, it's currently winter so I can roll around and melt all the snow in my driveway—don't even have to shovel. I also *love* how my metabolism apparently got completely burnt up in those hot flashes too, all the additional weight I've put on over the past two years has just been fantastic. I'm pretty sure sarcasm is probably a symptom of menopause too. If not, it probably should be.

There are medications and herbal supplements that offer some relief, so of course talk to your doctor about any treatment options. You can also do this spell to help bring the symptoms under control and help you deal with the changes your body, mind, and quite possibly soul are going through. It's important to remember that menopause is just another step along life's journey. It comes with some negatives, but of course there are positives too. This new step in life brings you to a new level in all things. The croning period of your life is a beginning.

This spell is best performed outside under a new moon.

For this spell you will need:

- a silver candle to represent the Goddess and lunar deities
- a red candle to represent life cycles
- violet oil for healing and peace
- cinnamon for spirituality
- a fireproof container, charcoal tablet, and lighter

Set up your altar, light the charcoal, and cast your circle.

Begin by lighting the silver candle. Say:

Great Goddess of the Moon and Mother to us all,
I come tonight to celebrate
the change in my life,
the beginning of my croning.

Light the red candle and say:

Great Goddess of the Moon and Mother to us all,
I come to ask for help in dealing with
the changes surging through
my body, my mind, my soul.

Place a few drops of violet oil onto the lit charcoal and say:

Great Goddess of the Moon and Mother to us all,
purify and bless me in your own light.
Grant me peace,
and allow my body to heal
and adjust to its new status,
its new standing in both the physical and spiritual worlds.
Help my symptoms to subside,
to controllable levels.
Though I am ready to take my place as crone,
I ask for sympathy in my symptoms.
Allow them to diminish and be subdued.

Sprinkle some cinnamon onto the lit charcoal tablet and say:

Great Goddess of the Moon and Mother to us all,
I am ready to move on to my new role,
to live my life as a crone.
Endow me with the wisdom
to pass on my knowledge to those
who look to me for enlightenment.

Guide me on my spiritual path,
and help me to become an elder
in all respects.
Guide me now, oh Great Goddess
of the Moon and Mother to us all.

When you are done, close your circle.

Perform this spell each full moon. Remember that along with the good, we also have to accept the bad, but you can help keep those symptoms under control.

I'm pregnant—and happy about it

For starters—congratulations! If this is your first pregnancy, you probably have all kinds of concerns and questions. Your doctor or midwife will be able to help you out in those areas. You can also read books and Internet articles to help you find answers to your questions. One of your biggest concerns right now is probably about having a safe and healthy pregnancy, birth, and baby—which is where this spell comes in. I have yet to meet an expecting mother who wasn't the least bit anxious or worried about the upcoming birth.

Our intent with this spell is to make sure both baby and mom are healthy and happy. Being nervous is a part of any pregnancy, but we don't want to focus on negative emotions. This spell will help keep you calm and relaxed. It will also help to build a spiritual connection between you and your baby. We use this spell to focus on and accentuate the positive, overriding any negative feelings of anxiety or nervousness.

For this spell you will need:
- a gold candle for the God and strength
- a silver candle for the Goddess
- a green candle for growth, healing, and fertility
- a sky blue candle for calmness, tranquility, patience, and good health
- a blue candle for tranquility, protection, peace, and healing
- a white candle for peace, protection, and tranquility

You will only use candles for this spell, as you may have noticed how strongly your sense of smell increases when pregnant. Using any incense, herbs, or oils may make you feel nauseous!

Set up your altar and cast your circle. Put the gold and silver candles at the rear of the altar, and arrange the others left to right: green, sky blue ,blue, and white.

Begin by lighting the gold and silver candles. Say:

Great God and Great Goddess,
I give my thanks
for the life inside of me.

Light the green candle and say:

> *Help my baby to grow inside of me,*
> *strong and healthy.*

Light the sky blue candle and say:

> *During my pregnancy and birth,*
> *help me to remain*
> *calm, tranquil, and patient.*
> *Grant both my baby and me good health.*

Light the blue candle and say:

> *During my pregnancy and birth,*
> *protect both my baby and me from harm.*
> *Give us healing peace and tranquility.*

Light the white candle and say:

> *During my pregnancy and birth,*
> *grant my baby and me peace and tranquility,*
> *protect us both on this most important journey.*
> *Great God and Great Goddess,*
> *Every day I shall give thanks for the*
> *blessings you have bestowed upon me.*
> *Your blessings and love*
> *are happily accepted and returned.*

If you would like to, take some time to meditate on the life growing inside of you. Visualize both you and your baby surrounded by a protective white light. Do this spell any time you feel jittery or nervous—which is a normal part of pregnancy. This spell will help to soothe any fears.

I'm pregnant—and don't know what to do about it

Not every woman is going to be thrilled to find out she is pregnant, and that's okay. Whether it was an unexpected mistake, a birth control mishap—or the result of something worse—unplanned, unwanted pregnancies do happen. For some women, becoming pregnant can create a very serious health risk. Whatever the reason for your uncertainty about what to do next, this matter is very personal. What you do now is *your* choice and *your* business. It is very difficult for me to fathom that in this day and age, so many political agendas still center around this extremely delicate and most importantly *personal* situation.

If you feel confused, know that you have options. You have the option to terminate the pregnancy, to give birth to the baby and keep him or her, or you can put the baby up for adoption. These are tough choices—I had planned on putting my twins up for adoption when I found out I was pregnant with them. I was told I was sterile after a bad infection from an ectopic pregnancy—so to hear I was pregnant was a real shock! Friends and family stepped up and insisted they would help, so I decided to go ahead and raise the twins on my own. My ectopic pregnancy I had no choice but to terminate—if I hadn't, it would have killed me. I personally understand the tough decisions this situation leaves with you.

This spell is to help calm you, allow you to meditate on different options, and reach a decision.

For this spell you will need:

• a green candle to neutralize difficult situations

Set up your altar and cast your circle in a location where you will be able to sit quietly and meditate with the candle safely burning.

Light the candle and say:

> *Great Goddess,*
> *Maiden, Mother, Crone.*
> *I have found myself*
> *in a position I did not expect,*
> *or plan,*
> *or want.*

Now I must make a decision
as to what to do next.
Help me to see my future,
to plan ahead,
to see what I must do.

Get into a comfortable position and stare into the flame of the candle. Allow all other thoughts to fall away. Focus only on the flame for a few moments, draw your attention to your womb area and focus on how you feel. Do you feel pain? Sadness? Anger? Maybe even a hint of joy? Think about your different options—how does each one make you feel? Look into the flame and into your future. Where do you see yourself a year from now? Is a baby with you? Spend as much time as you need with this meditation. You may need to perform this meditation more than once. Perhaps each time you will be able to eliminate different options. If you don't feel comfortable with a choice yet, don't make one—you should have a little time yet to decide. If you can't find a decision the first time you do this spell, take a day off and try again the day after. Don't rush yourself into any decision about which you aren't completely sure.

My partner and I are unable to conceive

This can be a devastating blow for any couple. Several sets of friends of mine spent tons of money on fertility specialists only to find they just aren't going to be able to have biological children on their own.

There is always the possibility of surrogacy or adoption, but that doesn't ease the pain you are going through, and for many people, when they first learn of this problem, the alternatives aren't yet an option. You need to grieve, and grieving takes time.

This spell will help you deal with the loss—and this is indeed a loss—and to move on with your life to entertain other options.

For this spell you will need:
- balm of Gilead for emotional healing
- cypress for comfort, solace, and easing feelings of loss
- witch hazel for mending a broken heart
- a small glass bowl, light blue in color

Set up your altar and cast your circle.

Take the bowl and hold it out in front of you in both hands. Say:

This bowl represents my heart.
Right now it is empty and it needs to heal
so it will be full again someday.

Set the bowl back on the altar. Add some of balm of Gilead to the bowl and say:

Our infertility has left us childless.
I add this balm of Gilead
to bring emotional healing to my spouse and me,
to help us work through our grief.

Add some cypress to the bowl and say:

Right now in our lives
we feel at a loss.
I add this cypress
to help comfort us,

to bring us solace,
and to ease the pain of our loss.

Add some witch hazel to the bowl and say:

We will go on with our lives
and eventually put the pain behind us.
I add this witch hazel
to help mend our broken hearts.

Mix the ingredients in the bowl and say:

The God and Goddess
are always here to protect us.
They always see us through.
I ask once again,
for the God and Goddess
to take my spouse and me,
under their protective wings.
Heal our hearts,
and make us whole once again.

You may spend time meditating if you like. Close your circle when you are done.

My child has an eating disorder

Any kind of illness our children suffer is always going to be a major event—but when it's a life-threatening one, we have to take every action possible to do whatever we can to help.

While there are different types of eating disorders, all of them can have extremely devastating results. Your child needs both medical and psychiatric help, and you yourself may need to speak with a therapist to help you understand the disorder better and figure out how to deal with it.

This spell is going to help put you into the best frame of mind to give your child the support he or she needs. You need to be at ease, which isn't easy in a situation such as thi., However, you have to do everything you can to keep yourself in a state of mind that will enable you to help your child to the best of your ability. If you are extremely stressed out, your child is going to pick up on that and be more stressed too. This is a meditative bath spell in which you will work on relaxing and putting yourself at ease. If you use oils, add a few drops directly to the water. If you are using dried herbs, tie them in a piece of cheesecloth and let it float in the tub.

For this spell you will need:
· chamomile for meditation and peace
· coltsfoot for peace and tranquility
· freesia for peace
· gardenia for peace and emotional healing
· jasmine for peace
· lavender for peace and the conscious mind
· lily for peace
· magnolia for peace
· narcissus for peace

Add the ingredients to your bath and step in. Get into a comfortable position and feel the warmth around you. Inhale the peaceful, relaxing floral scents and feel them working their way through your muscles. Feel yourself unwinding. Feel yourself more at ease. Say:

Great Goddess,
loving mother,
as a parent,
I have found myself
in a terrible situation.
The very food that should
nourish my child
is instead the source of great pain.
Though I am frustrated and
extremely concerned,
I know that it is up to my child
to overcome this disorder.
Though I cannot do it for her/him,
I can be supportive.
I can keep my feelings
under control and focus
instead upon my child.
I ask for your assistance
in helping me to remain calm
and focused on my child.
Please give me a clear mind
to deal with everything
we encounter,
each step of the way.
This is my wish,
so mote it be.

Spend some time meditating, not on the eating disorder itself, but on your child conquering it, your child having a healthier attitude about food, your child happy and whole once again.

Perform this meditative bath spell when you start to feel overwhelmed. Keeping yourself at ease will help show your child you are in control of yourself and encourage him or her to have self-control too.

I've sustained a serious injury

Injuries are a pain, quite literally! I have torn my rotator cuff, and more recently I tore cartilage in my knee. These kind of injuries (along with many other kinds) are time consuming and expensive to deal with. First are all the tests to determine exactly what the injury is and to what extent the damage has been done. Then there is the treatment, whether it's surgery, medications, physical therapy—again, time consuming and expensive. On top of all of that is the actual pain you have to deal with. I can definitely think of better ways to spend my time!

This spell is designed to help you heal faster, while minimizing the other suffering (emotional, physical, and financial) you are going through. This spell is going to take place in a bathtub so you can immerse yourself in healing waters. Since Sunday is a day for healing and replenishing your strength, perform this spell each Sunday until you are fully recovered.

For this spell you will need:
- a green candle for healing, finances, neutralizing a difficult situation, and for stability—place it as close to the tub as you can
- cheesecloth
- a hematite stone for grounding, calming, healing, and physical strength
- quartz for healing and cleansing
- angelica for healing and cleansing
- carnation for healing, strength, and physical energy
- eucalyptus for healing
- lavender for healing

Take the herbs and the stones, and wrap them in the cheesecloth. Place the cheesecloth into the tub and then get in.

As you soak in the tub, feel the healing stones and herbs take effect. Concentrate on the area of your body that was injured. Visualize it healing in your mind's eye. Whatever the injury, see it getting better. See it repairing itself. Feel the pain subsiding.

As you concentrate on your injury, say the following:

Oh God and Goddess,
instill these herbs
with your healing grace,
to relieve my suffering
and replenish my strength.

Repeat this chant over and over. Stay in the water until it becomes too cold for you.

My child has been diagnosed with a serious illness

Thirty years ago, my cousin Clint was diagnosed with diabetes at the age of ten. When he was diagnosed, his mother was told by the doctors not to worry about saving money for college because he would never live long enough to go. Clint not only went to and graduated from college, he recently celebrated his forty-first birthday—and he is in excellent health. He is an only child, but his mother raised him exactly how she would have raised any child. The only difference was that he had to learn how to give himself insulin injections.

I've known other people who also had children diagnosed with a serious illness. One such person's son was diagnosed with cystic fibrosis. This woman felt that since there was a chance her son might not live to be an adult, she would basically allow him to do whatever he wanted, whenever he wanted. When his little brother was born, she ended up allowing the same for the younger brother because it wouldn't be fair to raise them differently. Her son's prognosis is still pretty good and the doctors believe at this point he could live to be in his forties. Ten years ago, they gave him about half of that. Who knows what strides could be made in the next twenty years?

The problem is that because this child has spent his whole life thus far doing whatever he wants whenever he wants, he is totally unprepared for the real world. As a young teenager, he had *the* most foul mouth I had ever heard. Behavior like this won't get him very far in life, and could make things like holding a job pretty difficult. This boy was already given a bum deal by having a disease such as cystic fibrosis to begin with, but then he was dealt another blow by having a parent who wasn't strong enough to raise him as though he would ever have any sort of a future whatsoever.

I know of another family who has a daughter with muscular dystrophy. They were told Erin would never be able to walk without assistance. While it did take her longer to learn to walk than normal and she required the assistance of braces and a walker for a couple of years, she has not only learned to walk unassisted, but is now in her teens and a cheerleader. She still has a bit of a limp, but she has worked very hard to overcome her handicap. Even though there were times her parents felt like giving up, they didn't. They continued to raise her the same way they did her two older sisters, and they encouraged her to work for what she wanted. All their hard work—and Erin's—has paid off.

Yes, it's terrible to have your child diagnosed with a serious illness—one that may claim his or her life someday, but if you let that disease win and take over the child's life as soon as the diagnosis is given, you are doing your child quite a disservice. You aren't preparing him or her for any future that's still possible. There will be days when you will want to just give up, but remember—*you* are the parent. Your child needs you to be strong for them. Remember that no matter how hard it is for you to watch your child going through all of this, they are living it every day. You may see the pain in their eyes, but they are feeling it. Don't give up on your child!

This spell is to help you get through the bad days, the days when you don't know how to continue being strong. The days you want to give up. You don't get the option to give up, so this spell will help build your resolve and give you strength so you can help your child carry on.

Do this spell whenever you feel it is necessary. Don't put it off hoping things will get better, just do it so you *know* they will.

For this spell you will need:

· a red candle for courage, willpower, passion, energy,
   and strength

Set up your altar and cast your circle. Get into a comfortable position and light the red candle. Say:

> *Oh loving Goddess*
> *of strength so bold,*
> *be with me now.*
> *Grant me the strength,*
> *the courage,*
> *the passion,*
> *the energy,*
> *and the willpower*
> *to carry on through these days*
> *when everything seems so rough.*
> *Remind me of the strength I had before,*
> *and help it to build within me once again.*

Visualize yourself as being strong. What does this look like to you? See yourself as being brave and strong for your child. Be the rock your child needs you to be. Repeat the above over and over again until you feel that strength surging through your body and mind once again.

When you are done, extinguish the candle and close the circle. You can perform this spell whenever you need a boost. Again, don't wait until you are so far down it's hard to pull yourself back up. Keep yourself charged for your child so you will always be there when he or she needs you.

Part Six

★ ★ ★ ★

HOUSE
AND HOME

We had a fire in our home

Having a fire occur in your home is a tragic and devastating event. Even small house fires can really shake a person up. When the damage is more severe or amounts to utter destruction, it's truly heart wrenching.

The element of fire is powerful. It gives us life. It gives us food and heat. It gives us passion. It can also take everything away, leaving nothing but ash in its wake. Some fires we know the exact cause: faulty electrical work, intentionally set, a knocked-over candle. Some fires we have no clue how they start: "Everything seemed fine … " "No evidence was found … " These are phrases that leave us with more questions instead of answers.

While this spell isn't going to give you answers, it is going to help you in a couple of other ways. You may have a fear of fire now, which is of course completely understandable. This spell will help you with that. It will help you protect your home. It will also help you reconnect with the element of fire and bring elemental balance back to your home.

For this spell you will need:
- a red pillar candle
- a bowl of water
- a sage smudge
- a bowl of dirt, sand, or salt
- a fireproof container to catch ashes from the smudge and a lighter

Set up an altar in a central location in your home. You will be walking each element throughout your entire home, so a circle is not necessary. You will begin at your altar site, and walk to your front door. You will face away from your front door as if you had just entered your home. Then you will turn to your left and will follow along the wall as close as you can, always turning to the left.

Begin at the altar and pick up the bowl of water. As you walk through your home, dip your fingertips into the water and flick it around you.

As you disperse the water throughout your home, chant repeatedly:

Water, water, purify,
balance, and wash clean.
Purge away the fear.
Purge away the pain.
Balance and wash clean.

After completing the entire course around your home, go back to the altar and set the bowl down. Pick up the salt/sand/soil bowl and go back to the front door and begin the course again. Sprinkle a small amount of the earth element on the floor as you go. Chant repeatedly:

Earth, earth,
stabilize and ground.
Purge away the fear.
Purge away the pain.
Stabilize and ground.

Again walk the same route and return to your altar. Set down the earth element and pick up the sage smudge. Light it and carry it over the ash catcher. Begin the rounds, waving the sage all around to let it fully penetrate the area, this time chanting:

Air, air, all around,
blowing right on by.
Purge away the fear.
Purge away the pain.
Blow it right on by.

After completing the course, go back to your altar, return the smudge to the altar (extinguish it with the ash catcher). Pick up the red candle and light it. Begin the final round chanting:

Fire, fire purify
balance in control.
Purge away the fear.
Purge away the pain.
Balance in control.

Complete the course. Return to the altar and extinguish the candle. Say the following:

> *As the elements rebalance,*
> *they bring stability together*
> *forming a protective barrier.*
> *I am safe in my home.*
> *My family is safe in our home.*
> *Our home is safe from danger,*
> *from inside and outside forces.*
> *The elements combine together*
> *and make our home whole*
> *and complete*
> *once more*
> *So mote it be.*

Keep this altar set up in a central location. You don't have to continually light the sage or candle—the representations will help hold the elements in balance. Repeat the spell whenever you feel it is necessary.

Our home was severely damaged and we lost everything

Whether caused by fire, flood, hurricane, mudslide, tornado, earthquake, or some other disaster, losing your home (along with just about everything in it) has to be one of the most devastating events that could happen to anyone. These types of events happen unexpectedly and take you by surprise. While you may feel lucky and grateful to have escaped with your life, it's sometimes hard to keep that feeling of gratitude alive when you survey the devastation and take account of what was lost.

As much as you may want, you can't turn back time or wave a wand and make everything come back—magic doesn't work that way. You *do* have magic to work, but instead of miraculously bringing everything back, it is going to help you start your life over and take advantage of a new beginning. When everything else is gone, and you think there is nothing left, you always have a chance for a new beginning. Every ending brings a new beginning.

As a child, my mother always talked to me about hoping for the best and preparing for the worst—which is why my house is well-insured. I understand that not everyone has this luxury, but I must emphasize just how important insurance is—whether you are a home owner or a renter—always try to have at least some form of insurance. If you have insurance when disaster strikes, it makes starting over that much easier. If you don't, you are going to have a more difficult time, but you are still in for a new beginning—it just may be tougher to dictate how that new beginning will take shape and form.

Since this spell is about helping you take best advantage of the new beginning set in front of you, this spell is best performed during a waxing moon. If possible perform the spell outside on a Sunday for added strength and protection.

Because this spell is about new beginnings and starting from scratch, you aren't going to use any "supplies" other than your own energy, voice, and power.

Cast your circle.

Before you begin this spell, take a moment to calm and ground yourself. You may want to sit directly on the ground. Feel the good, strong, positive, energy come up through the earth and fill you. Feel the negative energy drain away from you. Feel the energy inside you become replenished with good, clean, positive energy. The negative, the hurt, the loss, the pain, washes away and is absorbed into the earth to be cleansed and renewed later on.

Stand up and stretch toward the moon. Reach your hands high above your head into the air, toward the sky, toward the moon. Feel the energy from the moon stretch out to your fingertips. Feel it cover you, wash over you, absorb into your skin, and replenish you. You are cleansed. You are pure. You are whole. You are alive.

Say:

> *My life has taken a turn for the worse,*
> *a disaster I did not expect.*
> *My life and the lives of everyone in my family*
> *have been drastically changed.*
> *We have lost our home,*
> *our material possessions,*
> *our mementos from the past.*
> *But we are not broken.*
> *I am not broken.*
> *It is time for a new beginning,*
> *It is time to start anew.*
> *The past is gone,*
> *taken away,*
> *put aside.*
> *Only the future now remains.*
> *This hidden gift*
> *can be hard to see, yet I catch a glimpse of it.*
> *I am able to start again,*
> *to start anew.*
> *My new future will be promising and bright.*
> *I will learn from past mistakes,*
> *so that I don't make the same mistakes again.*
> *I will start over in every sense I can.*
> *I will renew all aspects of my life.*

I will understand everything happens for a reason,
whether I know or understand that reason or not.
I will accept my fate and my future.
I ask for protection, strength, and guidance
as I begin my life on this new path
on the new road that is set out before me.
I ask for the Lord and Lady to protect me
and guide me in all the days of my life,
and to help me help others who
find themselves suffering a similar fate.

Take as much time as you need to meditate, and then close your circle.

While this is probably the most difficult time you will ever go through, remember you are not alone. Look to your deities for guidance and support whenever you feel a need.

We lost our home due to foreclosure
and now we have to downsize considerably

"Foreclosure" is the new dirtiest word in the English language. It's cold, evil, and just plain nasty.

Some people out there welcome a foreclosure, as it's a chance to get out from under their mortgage and lower their monthly costs. For most people, however, foreclosure is a terrible, stressful time. Their home is being ripped out from under them, in some cases after having lived there for decades. Family homes that were passed down for generations and mortgaged to pay for repairs are being lost. New homes that were built for couples just starting out are being reclaimed by the banks and at alarming rates.

As so many people are losing their homes, many have had to downsize. Garage sales and estate sales are happening all the time to pass on a lifetime of accumulated possessions for which there is simply no more room. With the economy the way it is, chances are there isn't money to pay for a storage facility either, so families are eliminating wants and focusing on needs instead.

Material possessions aren't the only thing being reduced…you may have had to eliminate sports, lessons, after-school activities, even medical care. All this is a part of downsizing living expenses, and maybe your lifestyle.

Going through this time is a real eye-opener. It forces a person to examine what is important in life and what can be done without—what is a necessity and what is not. Saying goodbye to possessions and a way of life can really be difficult. Times change, circumstances change, and we have to learn to accept those changes if we want to be able to pick ourselves back up, start over, and be successful. Chances are you may notice even your definition of "successful" changes too.

This spell is to help comfort you in your time of change. It is to help you set your priorities straight so you can better distinguish between a want and a need. It is to help relieve the stress of losing your home. Because this spell is to help you deal with loss, it should be performed during a waning moon.

Because this spell will help you distinguish between needs and wants, you won't be using any spell components. While for many people spell components help the caster focus and they can add to the spell's power, the most important component here is you. If possible, I would suggest doing this spell outside at night under a waning moon, but if that isn't possible, find a quiet location inside your home.

Begin by casting your circle.

Take a seat and spend a moment taking some deep breaths and let the stress roll away. You are probably pretty stressed and tense right now, so give yourself a few minutes to get yourself into a better, clearer state of mind.

As you exhale, feel the stress lift away and your body becoming lighter. You don't have any pressures weighing you down. Most people find this time of life to be very stressful, but what they don't realize is that their path has already been set, they no longer have to worry what they're going to do day to day. They now know what they are going to do—move to a smaller location. The stress you find yourself under now isn't so much about what you're going to do, it's about *accepting* that the choice has been made for you. The foreclosure took care of that, so now you have to accept it and move on to the next steps of your life, often the hardest part. Human nature often prevents us from looking forward to change. We often associate change with bad things, but we aren't going to do that anymore. With that in mind as you breathe in, breathe in change and embrace it. It is clean, new, and fresh. Breathe out the stress of unknowing, fear, and stagnation. Breathe in change, a new start, a "do-over." Breathe out the filth of accumulation and stress. Let all the bad go and focus on bringing only good into your lungs, into your body, into your life.

When you feel more relaxed (with everything going on right now, I certainly don't expect you to become fully relaxed—don't expect it from yourself either or you will only get stressed out about not being able to relax!), take a couple more deep breaths and then say:

> *My life has taken a major change,*
> *one I fought to keep from happening,*
> *but I was unable to succeed.*
> *Now I am losing my home,*
> *and my life starts anew.*
> *Help me to see the silver lining,*
> *the new beginning I have been given—*
> *the opportunity to redefine*
> *my priorities, my life.*
> *The chance to give my life new meaning—*
> *new meaning and new hope to myself*
> *and to my family.*

Guide us, watch over us, and protect us
as we begin this new chapter.
Assist my family and me in making decisions now
and in the future.
Bring us peace, strength, contentment, and hope.
So mote it be.

While this is a short ritual, it is a very important one. Feel the words as you say them. Put a lot of your own emotion into this spell. Be honest with yourself and with your deity/ies as you perform it. Repeat this spell as often as needed. Feel free to have the entire family participate. You are going through this as a family, you should heal as a family too. Now is the time to pull together like never before and support one another the best you can.

Our home was broken into

If your home has been broken into and if you have been robbed, you know the complete, utter feeling of helplessness. The feeling of being violated, taken advantage of, possibly even betrayal if the burglar was someone you know. Knowing that someone has come into your home, gone through your possessions, and decided to take what they wanted for themselves or to fence them for money is a terrible, terrible feeling.

I was robbed by a trusted employee—the person who took care of my children. This person not only stole and cashed checks out of my mailbox, she stole checks out of my checkbook and wiped out my checking account, overdrawing my account by thousands of dollars. I had to get a new checking account, was late in paying some bills because of my missing income, and had to deal with many other unpleasantries because of what this person had decided to do to me.

The woman was caught, but it took her over a year to pay restitution. She had committed several felonies but didn't serve any jail time whatsoever. I was left feeling less than vindicated; I did not feel justice had been done. Even though she was caught right away, the feeling of betrayal, being taken advantage of, and distrust among everyone I knew at that point was overwhelming. The police couldn't help me, and the courts let her go with a slap on the wrist.

It can take a while to feel safe in your own home. It's not like starting from scratch; starting from scratch would be easier. Instead you are starting from a place of fear—a place that once had been happy and safe.

If the robbery took place while you were at home, this fear can be even worse. You may have been held against your will. You may have been assaulted or abused.

Friends may suggest to you to just move and start all over again, but in this day and age, how realistic is that? If you own your home, you most likely would have to sell it before being able to get into another location, and that could take years. If you are renting, it might be easier if you have a landlord who is willing to let you out of your lease. And though a new location may help, it will not take away all of the pain or make you feel completely safe once again, not unless you can move into Fort Knox or some other highly secure location! So what do you do?

For starters, you do all of the mundane things you need to do to get your life back on track. You work with the police and the insurance company (if applicable). Perhaps check with a safety consultant on what you can do to make your house more physically safe. Install an alarm, flood lights, better locks on windows and doors, or even surveillance cameras. Do what you can physically to make your home safer, and then do what you can spiritually, emotionally, and magically. Realize that you may never find the justice or closure you want from the legal system. Sometimes it just doesn't work out that way unfortunately. The sooner you accept that, the sooner you will be able to move on with your life.

Do this spell as soon as possible to protect your home and as often as necessary to build and strengthen the level of protection.

For this spell you will need:
- a large black pillar candle to absorb negative energy and for protection
- a sage smudge for protection
- fireproof container and lighter
- a small black bag

The following gemstones:
- hematite stone for calming and grounding
- agate for protection
- beryl for protection
- calcite to calm fears
- jade for protection
- jasper for protection
- malachite for protection

The following herbs:
- anise for protection
- black pepper for protection
- blessed thistle for protection and to break hexes
- clove for protection
- cumin for protection
- cypress for comfort and to ease feelings of loss and promote healing
- dragon's blood for protection and to amplify power
- frankincense to banish negative entities
- myrrh for protection
- rosemary for protection

Take all the stones and herbs (everything but the black candle and the sage smudge), and place them into the black bag. Tie it shut.

Set up an altar by your front door and include the bag, the candle, and the sage smudge on the altar.

Light the black candle and begin walking clockwise around your home. Every time you can take a left turn take it. (You may also do this part of the spell widdershins if you prefer.) This way you will walk all around the outer wall of your home.

As you walk, say the following:

> *Banish the negativity from my home,*
> *take the sadness, the pain,*
> *the betrayal,*
> *the feelings of helplessness,*
> *and the feelings of being violated.*
> *Replace them with safety and security,*
> *love and hope.*

Continue this chant as you walk throughout your home. When you get back to the altar at your front door, place the candle into the holder and go outside. Walk the entire outside of your home clockwise, again repeating the chant as you go. When you get back to the beginning, to the front door, walk out to the property line and this time walk the entire property line in a clockwise direction repeating the chant a third time. You are in the process of building layers of protection from the inside to the outside of your home.

After completing this round, return to your altar. Extinguish the candle. Take and light the sage smudge and begin another walk around the inside of your home turning left every chance you get. As you walk, say the following:

> *Protect this home and the people inside.*
> *Keep us safe, day and night.*

Again, once you get to the front door, go back outside, and walk around the outside of your home the same way as before, continuing with the chant. Once you get back to the starting location, head to the property line and make the third path, the third border of protection, repeating the chant again. When you finish this walk, return to your altar. Extinguish the sage.

Pick up the bag with stones and herbs and make another clockwise trip around the inside of your home. This time chant the following:

> *Help us to move on,*
> *help us find peace,*
> *help us deal with the loss we have suffered.*
> *Above all,*
> *protect our house and home.*

Shake the bag as you walk along, dispersing the magic as you go. Visualize the boundary building up and strengthening as you go, like a force field—ill will cannot pass through it.

Once you return to your starting point, again go outside, walking the outer walls of your home and then the property line—all the while chanting and shaking your bag of stones and herbs. When finished, go back inside and place the bag in a highly visible, high-traffic area of your home. Place the candle and sage bundle next to it. Any time you feel like strengthening this spell, perform it again, using the same bag, sage, and candle. Do not use this candle for any other spell, only for this one protection spell. Even if you feel safe, continue to perform this spell once a month; at the full moon is best.

My adult child has moved back home— and brought his or her family with

I have been extremely lucky—I have not had to either move back to my parents' home with any of my children nor have any of my own adult children needed to move in bringing their families with them. Though I still haven't been able to get quite all of my own adult children out the door, the ones who have left have been able to stay independent.

A brother of mine, on the other hand, moved back home with our parents on several different occasions, and I have taken in my adult siblings along with their families.

This really isn't an easy situation for anyone, and I imagine having to swallow your pride to go back and live with mom and dad must be pretty tough. That being said, I was brought up in a home where the main rule was "As long as you live in my house…" followed by whatever happened to come out of Dad's mouth that day. He had a good point—as long as people are going to live in a home owned by someone else and the bills are being paid by someone else, the occupants need to be respectful and honor the homeowner's wishes.

When adult children move back in with mom and dad, they of course are still legally adults, but that does not give them the right to treat their parents poorly. This was a problem with my brother; I constantly argued with him when he would move back in with our folks. He wanted certain things done one way, Mom and Dad another way.

My argument was that it was Mom and Dad's house and they were the ones paying the bills. They were doing him a favor by letting him stay there. My brother couldn't see it that way, insisting he should be able to do what he wanted when he wanted. Eventually he moved out because everyone was so miserable.

There has to be some kind of a happy medium when the "kids" move home again, though it may be a very difficult and fine line to walk. The parents own the house. The parents are paying the bills. They don't want to see their kids or grandkids out on the street, but they are taking on more in expenses—even if the kids are helping to pay the bills. It's important to remember *respect*. No law says a parent has to take their forty-year-old child in along with his or her entire family. Parents do it because they want to help.

When your child brings his or her family to live with you, the first thing you need to do is sit down and discuss rules and whether there is going to be help with paying the bills and if so, the amount. Starting off with clear, established rules and guidelines should make things easier, though this will be a difficult transition for all those involved.

You may be used to a certain level of privacy; your grandchildren may have to change schools; your child and his/her spouse may be unemployed and trying to find work. You may have to crowd several people into a small area, such as making grandchildren who are used to their own rooms share with one another, or perhaps the entire family now sleeps in an open basement. There are a lot of adjustments to be made on everyone's part.

This spell is designed to help make that transition as smooth as possible, define the boundaries and set limitations, and assist your child and his or her family to get back on their feet as soon as possible.

For this spell you will need:

- a large black pillar candle for setting limitations and defining boundaries
- a large brown pillar candle for family issues
- a large green pillar candle for neutralizing difficult situations, finances, security, and career
- basil oil for harmony
- bergamot oil for peace, happiness, and money
- a fireproof candle plate you can keep the three candles on in a central area of your home
- a small bowl to mix the oils in

Cast your circle. You are going to work this spell by blessing the candles at your altar and then placing them in that central locale of your home. You are using large pillar candles because each morning when you wake up and each night before you go to bed, you will light them and do a brief affirmation.

First, however, we are going to bless each candle for the purpose we want it to serve.

Begin by taking the basil and bergamot oils and mix a small amount (just enough to dress three candles) in the bowl. As you mix them, say:

> *Blend together to bring my family*
> *peace, happiness, and harmony*
> *while we share this home.*
> *Bring to my child and his/her family*
> *the money and resources they need*
> *to be able to build their own home again.*

Take some of the oil and dress the black candle. As you do so, say:

> *Charge this candle with the power to*
> *help us all not overstep boundaries.*
> *Help us to realize*
> *limitations exist all around.*
> *In order to coexist to the best of our abilities,*
> *these limitations and boundaries must be respected.*
> *Charge this candle with the power to remind us all.*

Set this candle on the fireproof candle plate.

Take the brown candle and dress it with the oil. As you do so, say:

> *Charge this candle with the power to remind us*
> *that we are all family.*
> *We are always here for one another,*
> *and no issue that arises cannot be dealt with.*
> *Our love and ties will always hold true.*
> *Charge this candle with the power to remind us all.*

Set this candle on the fireproof plate.

Take the green candle and dress it with oil. As you do so, say:

> *Charge this candle with the power*
> *to help us all remain calm when tempers start to flare.*
> *Keep our home at peace and keep negativity at bay.*
> *Charge this candle also with the power*
> *to bring the resources*
> *to my child to support his/her family*
> *on his/her own once again.*
> *Charge this candle with the power to remind us all.*

Set this candle on the fireproof plate.

Close your circle and take the candles to that location in your home where everyone will see them every day.

Each morning, go to the candles and light them. As you do so, either say out loud or to yourself:

Remind us all we are family.
Love and family survive all.

Take a few moments to meditate on your situation. Look into the future, seeing it turn out how you want—the family at peace, your child working and successfully finding a new home. Give yourself just a few minutes and blow the candles out, releasing the good intentions into the universe.

Each night before you go to bed, come back to the candles, light them, and repeat the affirmation again. Again, briefly meditate and blow the candles out, releasing the energy into the universe.

Remember that this situation was most likely a long time in the making unless there was a sudden disaster like a fire that destroyed your child's home. His or her situation most likely didn't happen overnight. Similarly, new opportunities to regain independence are not going to arise overnight either. It may take a while for the universe to say "Okay, enough's enough. Time to move on."

Our house needs a lot of work,
but we just can't afford it right now

One of the problems that arose as a result of the housing market crash was that many people learned their houses weren't worth as much as they thought they were, partly due to repairs that needed doing in order to make the house sellable. In some cases, the repairs may be so costly that there's no way to get the house into selling condition and not list it as a "fixer upper."

Often we don't notice the things in our home that need replacing—we put up with them. Some of my carpets are more than twenty years old, having weathered seven kids, and a total of seven cats and three dogs. Would anyone else want to buy my house with the older carpets and actually keep them? Not if they had any choice in the matter.

Some repairs are more important than others; a leaky roof is not something you can blow off, but old carpets you can continue to ignore for a while. On the other hand, an ignored leaky roof doesn't remain a leaky roof. It's a problem that grows exponentially in severity and repair cost. But what do you do when you are all tapped out and have no equity even to borrow against? What if financing isn't available? You are in dire straits and need a miracle.

While you continue to pursue options to finance your repairs (don't stop looking!), use this spell to help reveal hidden opportunities. Remember, this situation is sort of like the story about the lottery ticket in the introduction. The "winning ticket"—in this case, the money to fix your home—is not going to just fall into your lap. You are going to have to do some work to find it. This spell is going to help reveal to you places you would not have thought to look for help.

For this spell you will need:
• a green candle to neutralize difficult situations,
  and for money and finances

In this spell, you are going to do a candle meditation. We want to keep the supplies needed for this spell to a minimum—you are short on the supplies you need to improve or repair your home, so let's make the spell fit the situation.

Begin by casting your circle. Get into a comfortable position.

Light your candle and say:

> *Supplies are low,*
> *but work needs to be done.*
> *My home is in disrepair.*
> *Funds are nonexistent*
> *and I don't know which way to go.*
> *I bring to the universe*
> *my request to help me find a way*
> *to fix the things I need to fix.*
> *I come to ask for help,*
> *to reveal what is hidden to me.*
> *I ask for aid in finding the money*
> *to make the necessary repairs.*

Take time and meditate on the repairs you have to do, visualize the project being completed, and the bill paid in full. See the work being done and the finished result. Feel the relief of having the repair completed.

When you have finished the visualization, close your circle. When any ideas pop into your mind, take note of them and follow through immediately.

We are being evicted from our apartment

Though most evictions are for non-payment, they can also be the result of other lease violations. When you sign a lease, make sure you read everything and know exactly what you are signing. If you don't agree with something in the rules, don't sign it. Find some other place to live. If you are going to live in property owned by someone else, it is imperative you respect the rules dictated.

If you have fallen on hard times and are unable to pay your rent or are unable to work out any kind of a deal with your landlord, you will end up getting evicted if you don't move first. Finding another place may not be easy either. You may have to move into a smaller place in order to make ends meet. While this is never fun, you have to do what is necessary to keep a roof over your family. A small roof is better than no roof at all!

This spell is designed to help you quickly find suitable living arrangements for your family and to help you get back on your feet. If you weren't evicted for non-payment, and instead it was for some other lease violation, it will also help open your eyes to the rules of a new place and to be more aware and respectful of them in the future.

For this spell you will need:
- a mirror that can stand on its own
- a green candle for abundance, security, finances, and growth

This spell requires minimal components. We want our spells to reflect our situation and if we are low on funds, spells that are extravagant in a material nature are simply counterproductive. If you can, do this spell outdoors or near a window.

To begin this spell, place the mirror on your altar with the candle about six inches in front of it in the very center. Cast your circle and get into a comfortable position where you will be able to easily gaze into the candle's flame once it is lit, and into the mirror itself.

Light the candle. Stare into the flame and through it into the mirror. Focus on seeing the image in the mirror through the flame. You will only have a small spot on which you are focusing. You won't be able to block out the rest of the image around that focal point, but remain focused on that one small area. This may take a little bit of practice before you can confidently do it.

As you focus on the image, say the following:

I must focus my attention and energies
on finding a suitable place to live
for my family and me.
I pour my focus, my strength, into this one area.
While I notice what is going on around me,
I don't let it distract me.
I ask the universe to show me what it is I need to see.

Clear your mind and continue to stare into the flame. Though you could use this to try to scry an answer to your housing situation, it's unlikely you will "see" anything that will lead you to a certain apartment complex or landlord, though it isn't completely out of the question. Instead you are simply concentrating on focusing your attention and energy into that one spot you see through the flame—almost like you are condensing your energies into that one location. As you stare into the flame, imagine what an ideal place would be like. How much room do you really need? What kind of rent are you able to pay? Do you need to find a rent-free place to stay (like staying with a friend or family) until you can get back on your feet? Do you need to find a place that won't mind, for example, if your band practices there, because it is how you make a living and you need to be able to practice? Do you need a place that will allow you to keep your pet? Whatever it is you need, focus that into the flame.

When you feel you have concentrated all your energy into the flame, take a deep breath and slowly exhale blowing out the candle as you do. Feel your energies swirl in the smoke and out into the universe. Watch the smoke swirl and disperse into the air. Your needs are being carried through the universe on the wind.

Remember to back up your work in the mundane world by actively looking for an appropriate place to live within your budget. Don't waste time looking at places that ultimately you know will not work for you right now even if they represent the type of place you would like to have someday. This spell is about necessity: needs, not wants. Work on satisfying your basic needs for now; wants can come later once you are in a better situation.

My house doesn't feel like a home

I will admit that when my husband and I got married, I didn't feel at home in our house at all. In fact, it took several years. He and his ex-wife had built the house. She had picked out things like the carpeting, paint, curtains, much of the furniture—she even had the kitchen shelves arranged to her liking, differently from how I wanted.

Unbelievably, the walk-in closet was still filled with clothes of hers that she kept saying she would clean out someday but hadn't. Though it had been two years since she lived in the house, her things were still sitting there because my husband hadn't wanted to deal with them. I had to pack them up myself in order to have room for my own clothes! It was uncomfortable to say the least.

It seemed everywhere I turned was something else that said this was *her* house, not mine. The storage room in the basement was filled with possessions she had never picked up—yearbooks, boxes of pictures, and other memorabilia. Even the bathroom contained old prescriptions. It took me a long time to rid the house of her presence and turn it into a home for my husband, myself, and our family.

Even after packing up her belongings and getting them to her—which took several weeks—the house was still full of her decorations. The next step was rearranging and adding our own touch. For example, the dining room had been painted mauve with a floral border. We tore off the border, patched and sanded, painted the walls white and removed the blinds from the sliding glass doors. We took the room from being dark and almost foreboding, to a bright room we filled with plants, a refurbished china cabinet filled with Belleek Irish pottery, and framed photos of family and friends on the walls.

Each room in the house had to be redone and redecorated in a way that showed it belonged to my husband and myself. We had to "claim" the house for ourselves. Despite our efforts, something was still off. I needed to do a cleansing on the house to remove any last traces of her energy in the home, which is where this spell comes in. This spell is designed to rid your house of any residual energies left by any previous occupants. It will also help you claim the house as your home.

To back this spell up in the mundane world, you will need to do what you can to incorporate yourself (and family if applicable) into this living space to claim it as your own. Fill it with your favorite things—pictures, flowers, scents even. The sense of smell is very powerful—filling your home with scents that put you at ease and that you associate with home will make your home feel more cozy.

I believe that part of my problem feeling at home was the fact that my husband's ex-wife's father had died in the home while they were still married. I often felt his presence, as if he was still looking for his daughter but didn't know where she had gone. If you have a situation like this one also perform the spell "I think my house is haunted" (p. 261). While our ghost wasn't invasive or disruptive really, he did bring the environment down around him as if he was heavily depressed and confused. Between these two spells, my husband and I were able to successfully claim the house as our home.

This spell is going to be a little different than usual because of the items we are going to use during it. You are going to collect items that say "home" to you, and place them on your altar. This can be anything that means "home,"—a special pillow you use on your couch, a certain family picture, perhaps an heirloom that has been passed down for generations. Gather together as many of these items as you wish to place on or around your altar.

You will also use a sage smudge, but you need to pick a scented candle or spray to use as well. Pick the scent that says "home" to you—check at different candle stores or other places that specialize in air sprays. Many people say that baking scents make them feel at home—pumpkin pie, sugar cookies, spiced cider—whichever one you feel is best. You may prefer a floral scent or even something like fresh linen. Everyone is different, so spend some time picking out what you want to use.

If you are doing this spell with a spouse, significant other, or family, allow each person to pick their own scent and items too.

Place all the items on your altar and cast your circle. You will begin by charging the items here at your altar. After closing your circle, this spell continues in a second part as you walk your home.

Cast your circle.

Pick up the sage smudge and say:

> *Bless this sage and purify it.*
> *Let it wash away the old*
> *and prepare for the new.*
> *Let it vanquish negativity.*
> *Bless it to refreshen and renew.*

Set the sage smudge down and pick up the candle/spray/or other type of scent you have chosen and say:

When I think of a peaceful and contented home,
I think of (name scent).
This scent makes me feel safe and secure
in a warm loving home.
Bless this scent,
and as it fills my home,
let it bring with it the love and security I need
to feel safe and happy at home

Place this scent back on your altar. Each person who has a scent should also take a turn and repeat the above.

After everyone takes a turn, you will bless the other items you have collected that convey "home" to you.

Select an item. Hold it close to you and say:

Bless this (describe the item—
for example "photograph")
and keep it safe.
This (item) *calls home to me.*
It helps me feel connected to the place I live.
It surrounds me with peace and love.

Do this with each item. If you are doing the spell with others, allow them to bless their own items.

Once all of the items are blessed, say:

I (we) *bring these items together*
to make my (our) *house a home.*
Though a home is not just the things in it,
it is the people and the love
these items represent to me.
These items bring me peace, happiness,
contentment, and joy.
As I place them throughout my home.
I place love throughout my home with them.
Each time I see one of these items,

> *I am reminded my house is my home.*
> *I am safe and at peace.*

Close your circle. Next, take the sage smudge and light it. Starting at your altar, go from room to room, smudging the entire house. As you walk, chant the following:

> *Wash away the old,*
> *refresh and renew.*

After you go through out the whole house, bring the smudge back to the altar and either place it in a fireproof dish to burn out or extinguish it. Next you will follow the same path you just walked, this time with the scent you have chosen—whether in candle or spray form. If you are doing this spell with others, they will go right behind you with their scent. If you are using a spray, use it sparingly, especially if there are others with you. You don't want to overwhelm anyone with fragrance. When you go through different bedrooms, have only the person who sleeps in that room spray their chosen scent. As you walk with your scent, chant the following:

> *My house becomes my home.*

When you are finished with the scent being dispersed throughout your home, once again return to the altar. At this point you will pick up all of the items you had blessed and place them in their proper place throughout your home. As you do so, again chant:

> *My house becomes my home.*

Once you have everything in its place, take some time to just sit back and relax. Let yourself get comfortable in your "new" home.

I think my house is haunted

There are many different types of hauntings you could be dealing with, and so there are different steps you will need to take in order to deal with this rather interesting dilemma.

For starters, you may want to have an investigation done to see if you can get more information about what you are dealing with. Going this route is also going to open you to several different choices. You may want to go with a local ghost hunting society or try to contact one of the more prominent groups. If you truly believe your home is being haunted, and you don't feel you are being threatened or harmed in any way (and again this is going to have a lot to do with your own personal beliefs), I would recommend trying several different local ghost hunters. One—it's going to give you different perspectives of what is going on in your home, and two—it's going to give the ghost hunters a place to investigate and practice their craft. Look for ghost hunters who specialize in different areas. Some may be more into proving existence, some may be more skeptical and will try to come up with other possible explanations for any disturbances you have experienced. Not too far from where I live is a ghost hunter group comprised of pagans, and so they look at things a little bit differently than how a non-pagan group might look at things. Look for local mediums who may be willing to come in and give you information about who the ghost may be and/or what it might want.

You can find these type of people and groups by doing Internet searches, checking at your local metaphysical store, and asking around through local metaphysical email lists. Many of these people and groups will do the work for free or by donation. If someone wants to charge you for their work (and they are giving their time, after all), make sure they have verifiable references you can check—especially if they are asking for hefty sums of money.

The more research you can do beforehand, the better you know what you are dealing with. Contact your recorder of deeds, find out who owned the house before you. Check obituaries or death records to see if any of those people could have died in your home or at least while living there. Again, the more information you have, the better you are informed about the situation you are dealing with.

In my case, the ghost we had visiting was my husband's former father-in-law. He had been ill with a terminal disease and since my husband's ex-wife had been a nurse, they had moved him in to care for him in his last days. I was lucky as I had complete access to any information I could possibly want about who the man had been when he was alive.

My first impression about the presence in our home was that he was very tall and also depressed. I soon learned from my husband that, yes, he had been over six feet and suffered from depression. He often made his presence known by opening the garage door. I asked my husband about this and learned that when he had lived at his own house, he had turned the garage into a kind of den he spent a lot of time in. I felt like he was wandering around our home trying to find something familiar. He seemed to become far more active after we had started changing things in the house such as rearranging and buying new furniture and painting. I also often felt like he was standing over me trying to figure out who I was and where his daughter was.

I knew he needed to move on from our home because he simply wasn't finding what he needed there—if he had found what he needed I don't think he would have been so active. I want to point out that I do not believe it was up to me to decide *where* he should have moved to. It was simply becoming more and more obvious that he did not belong there with us, but didn't know how to move on or where to.

I wrote this spell not just to remove him from the premises. It also wasn't to send him to the other side. Some people out there believe their calling is to help souls over to the other side, but I do not believe it's for me. I am sure there are people far better suited for it and if you think about it, it's not something just anybody should be messing with. Sending souls to a final resting place? I don't think it's something just anyone can or should do; it's sort of like brain surgery. You may want to be able to help someone, but that doesn't mean you have the knowledge or power to help them.

This spell was designed to simply remove him from our home and send him to a place that was better suited, a place he needed to go to. Perhaps it was moving on to the Summerlands or Otherworld. Perhaps it was moving to where his daughter had moved so he could see that she was still okay. The point is, I was not the one who specified where he should go. It was up to fate, the gods, destiny, or even the man himself to decide where that should be—the only qualification was that it be a place better suited for him.

We were able to send him on his way and though I know he stops in for a visit every now and then when his grandkids are at our house for a holiday or other family event, he is only checking in on them and joining in when they are all in one place. He then goes about on his merry way again to wherever it is he needs to be.

This spell can do the same for you, just remember it is to send the spirit to a location that is better suited for the spirit. Do not try to cross this spirit over yourself if you don't have the proper experience.

For this spell you will need:

- apple wood shavings and dried dandelion leaves—
both for spirit communication

- frankincense resin for protection and to banish
any negative entities

- a fireproof container (such as a cauldron), two
charcoal tablets, and a lighter

Set everything on your altar and cast your circle. Put both charcoal tablets in your cauldron and light them. (I use two when working with wood shavings or other heavy items as it helps get them burning better.)

Sprinkle some frankincense on a tablet. As the smoke swirls in the air, say:

Great Goddess,
protect me and mine as
I perform this spell to help this spirit
move to a place better suited for him or her.
Help guide them on their way,
help them find what they are looking for.

Add the apple wood shavings and the dried dandelion leaves. Make sure you have enough on top of the charcoal tablets to get a good smoldering going. Give it a moment to get good and smoky. Pick up the cauldron and gently swing it around your circle letting the smoke disperse all around you. Once you get a good amount around you, set the cauldron back on the altar.

Call out to your spirit by name if you know it. If not, that's okay too. Say the following:

Your presence is known and felt around me.
I wish to communicate with you today to say goodbye.
It is time for you to move on from here, from this house.
There is nothing left here for you.
There is no way for us here to help you.

There is a better place out in the universe for you.
You have a place you need to be,
a place I do not know,
but it is waiting for you.
It is time for you to move on.

If you have a personal message to give to this spirit, do so now. When I performed this spell, I informed the spirit that his daughter had moved from here and even told him what her new address was. I told him it was okay to stop by and see his grandchildren from time to time when they were here, but that ultimately it was time for him to move on. If you have a connection with the spirit, you may want to give them a message or just say goodbye privately. When you are done, continue:

I have asked the Goddess
to help you on your way.
Travel now to where you need to be.
Fare thee well,
so mote it be.

Go ahead and close the circle. With some spirits you may have to perform this spell more than once. If you have a spirit that doesn't seem to be very friendly, you may have to call in someone who specializes in removing negative entities, but we'll all be hoping it doesn't go that far! In my experience anyway, most spirits aren't nasty; they are, however, often confused. Turning your spirit's journey over to a higher power, should help them move right along.

My neighbors constantly trespass

I live in a rather rural area. We have 2.5 acres of land and have let a lot of the backyard grow, letting it go wild again. We mow paths through it, along with our outdoor ritual area, some specially planted trees (along with hundreds that seeded themselves!) and a mud pit to play in. It's really like our own private park. Most of the time it is private. Our land is situated such that several houses back up to our backyard.

The last house—the one farthest away from our actual home—was for years occupied by an elderly woman. The home was owned by her son, who lives right next door. When the woman passed away the family decided to keep the home and rent it out instead. Over the past couple of years there has been one particularly problematic tenant who does not seem to understand simple things like "Private Property" or leash laws for that matter.

The problems began with his rather large dog roaming our yard. For some people that might not be much of a problem, but it bothers me for several reasons. For starters, this area of my yard is my personal sanctuary. It is designed to help reconnect myself and my family with nature whenever we need it. It is a wildlife refuge right next to a corn field, where we know animals come and feel safe. We have an area that is a natural retention pond—it's not wet year round, but it is for the majority. We have plenty of trees and tall grass to offer protection from other animals. We often see deer, raccoons, opossums, skunks, geese, hawks, ducks, many other birds, and even coyotes. Though the coyotes unsettle me a bit, they come by with their own message to give. When this neighbor's dog runs wild, it scares these animals away. I've had people recommend we fence it in, but doing so rather defeats the purpose of it being a wildlife refuge. Any fence the animals would be able to get over, the dog would too—not too mention the cost of putting up a fence that large! The dog also seems to only use the mowed paths to do his business as we often find large "surprises" waiting for us. These surprises aren't coyote scat, it's rather easy to tell the difference. Third, my son enjoys walking the path and is very afraid of large dogs, always has been. It's not right that he shouldn't be able to use his own yard to take a simple walk because the neighbor refuses to follow leash laws and his dog likes to stray from home. Fourth, I raise chickens! This dog has on several occasions come after my chickens and I have had to run it off with a broom.

I've tried to talk to my neighbor, but he has literally shut the door in my face, showing me he has no inclination whatsoever to start following leash laws or to even pay attention to where his dog is. His response was to actually start mowing down part of the overgrown grass in the back! Then, instead of roping in his dog, he decided to give his son the same free access to my backyard. I have caught the child not only in the mud pit (which honestly you think that alone would bug his dad but apparently it didn't), but he and his friend also brought their ATVs through the paths, tearing up the ground right through my produce garden.

Since "Dad" had already shown in the past that he had no intentions of doing the right thing, I decided it was time to protect my property the best way I could, with this protection spell that blocks anyone "unauthorized" from coming into my yard.

After performing the spell, I also made a nice little sign and stuck it in the ground so it is clearly visible from the neighbor's house and yard. It says "Private Property—Do not enter!"

For this spell you will need a sage smudge. If you have a large area of land, make sure you have a jumbo size smudge. You are going to walk the property line a total of three times with the sage, so this spell will take a bit of it—and a fair amount of time if you have a larger yard.

You will also need a lot of black salt. You will only walk the property line with this once and you will be scattering it as you go—don't try to pour a steady stream—you would need a ton! But depending on your yard size, you still may need quite a bit. If you cannot afford or find enough black salt, use regular table or rock salt…whatever you can find, just as long as it's salt!

Start at the very beginning of your driveway—where the driveway and road meet. Facing your home, light the sage smudge and say:

> *My home is my haven.*
> *Protect it from all unwanted visitors.*
> *Keep all trespassers away.*

Turn to your left and beginning walking your entire property line chanting these same three lines over and over again. Once you get back to the driveway, do the entire walk twice more for a total of three with the sage. If you need to light another smudge, go ahead and do so.

After returning from the third trip around, extinguish the smudge (or put it into a fireproof container so it can safely burn out), and pick up your salt. This time you will walk the property line scattering the salt about you as you go. Say:

No unwanted visitors
shall cross this line of salt.
My property, yard, and home
always remain safe.

You will have to repeat this spell occasionally since salt does eventually break down—especially out in the environment. You may still get some trespassers, but when they enter, they will get an uneasy feeling. They will know they aren't supposed to be there and soon they will not want to come back at all without being invited.

I'm happy to report that since performing this spell, I haven't seen the kids or the dog!

Part Seven

★★★★

CAREER AND
WORK LIFE

The guy who sits next to me at work does absolutely nothing all day while I work my fingers to the bone, yet he always gets away with it

A dear friend of mine, Sue, works in a call center and though she works more than three times as hard as her fellow employees (she knows this thanks to the company's rating systems and quality controls), she doesn't get the recognition she deserves. She also sits next to someone who averages about one tenth the amount of work she does, and that's if this person is having a good day!

Why does the company put up with of this? Why don't they start insisting people boost their performance or fire those who are not working anywhere near up to par? Neither she nor I can figure it out for the life of us. While Sue is hard at work doing her job and getting more work done than almost half of her department combined, the guy next to her sits and does the absolute bare minimum, if even that.

This has been a huge source of frustration for Sue, and not because she would like to be lazy. She knows what kind of work she is capable of putting out and feels she has a good grasp of what other employees should be able to produce as well. When they sit there and complain about having too much work to do, her supervisor often pulls her off of her own assignment and puts her on another one to help someone else out. Of course she still has to complete her own assignment also.

This spell was written for her and for anyone else who finds themselves in a similar situation. It's designed to help even things out, allow for some peace, and to ask karma to kick in and deal out some justice.

For this spell you will need:

- something that represents justice you can place on your altar
  and on your desk at work (a small model of a balanced scale,
  a gavel, or the Justice card from a tarot deck, for example)
- a silver candle for balance

Place your representation of justice on your altar, cast your circle, and light the candle. Say the following:

> *I send my request out to the universe.*
> *I feel things at work are out of balance,*

that I am not treated fairly.
I know I work far harder than my fellow employees,
yet it seems to go unnoticed.
I do both my work and the work of others,
often without any thanks at all.
My request to the universe is for karma
to take notice and even the score.
Those who don't pull their own weight
should feel the consequences of not doing their job.
I feel I deserve some recognition,
not the same or less,
as those who do one-tenth the amount of work I do.
I know karma moves according to its own schedule,
I ask that it take a moment to hear my case
and dole out justice as the universe deems fit.

Spend some time visualizing what justice means to you in this situation. Be wary of your thoughts though—don't get too extreme. When you are done visualizing, close your circle and take the symbol of justice to work to place on your desk.

I'm not happy with my chosen career

If you aren't happy with what you do for a living, it truly makes it difficult to be happy, as your lack of joy for work can spread into all other areas of your life.

The problem is that you can't afford to just up and quit your job to start a different career if you're like most people today—one that may very likely require schooling. So what do you do? Like most people, you have to stick it out, unfortunately. This doesn't mean that while you are working you can't start looking around for other options or start taking classes in another field. Go right ahead and do those things, but *don't* quit your job thinking something else will quickly come along. It won't. I've seen too many people in this situation lately. You may hate your job but for now, be content with the fact that you have one. Continue your search and work on making any necessary changes that will allow you to move into a new career someday, hopefully soon.

This spell is designed to give you insight into what field might suit you better and the patience and ambition needed to make changes that will allow you to find a career where you will be far happier.

For this spell you will need:

- a purple candle for self-esteem, growth, insight, ambition, and success in business
- a turquoise candle for creativity, discipline, self-knowledge, and idealism
- a gold candle for employment
- a green candle for careers
- some dried alder leaves or bark for divination and scrying
- hibiscus for scrying
- cheesecloth
- a black bowl filled with moon water (see page 4 for an explanation)

Set up your altar with the bowl of moon water and the candles—one on each side of the bowl, front and back. Wrap the hibiscus and alder in the cheesecloth and let it soak in the water for fifteen minutes. Remove the cloth from the water and then cast your circle. You are ready to begin.

Begin by lighting the purple candle. Say the following:

I feel the need to grow and
expand my horizons,
my life,
I want to be successful and happy in my chosen career,
and so I need a change.

Light the turquoise candle and say the following:

I need both my creativity and discipline
to help see me through this change.
I will look into myself to find what I am looking for.

Light the gold candle and say:

While I keep the job I am currently in,
at the same time I will begin to look for something new.
Grant me the strength and patience
to keep the employment
I have now while it is still needed.

Light the green candle and say:

Help me to uncover my perfect career.

When all the candles are lit, pick up the purple one and tilt it over the bowl of water allowing some wax to drip into the water. We're only after a couple of drops; the wax should harden as soon as it hits the water and we don't want to obscure too much of it. When you're finished, extinguish the candle. Repeat with the other three candles.

When all four candles are extinguished, scry with the bowl of water and look for answers for what career may better suit you. If you don't yet see a career, just visualize yourself happy in a new field. Imagine coming home and being happy and feeling accomplished after a day of work.

Continue performing this spell until you see a vision in the bowl that helps you make up your mind about a new career. As always with scrying, look for any other messages as well.

I don't know how to cope with losing my job

Losing your job may very well be one of the most stressful events you will ever go through in your life, next to the death of loved ones. Unfortunately it has happened to many, many people, so you aren't alone. There are plenty of people who will be able to sympathize with you, though sympathy isn't going to get you your job back. If you don't have anything in savings or don't qualify for unemployment, this only compounds the stress you are already suffering.

Last winter, my husband was laid off for almost three months; I had been out of work for a while already. We didn't have much in savings to begin with—raising seven kids makes saving a pipe dream, and we felt just lost. He had worked for the same company for almost twenty-five years at that point and had never been laid off before. Though he was able to go back to work eventually, our taste of unemployment was devastating.

The uncertainty of not knowing from one day to the next how you will pay the bills or feed your kids is downright gut wrenching. We lost a lot of sleep and didn't know what to do with ourselves.

You get to the point where you realize just about everything you do costs money in one way or another and it makes you even more nervous. You don't want to turn on the television because you know it's adding to the electric bill—the electric bill you have no idea how you are going to pay. You turn the thermostat lower (or higher—depending on the season and where you live) and throw on a sweater (or a tank top, again), and you try not to let the little things get to you.

You suddenly realize a can of cranberry sauce and a can of carrots can actually be made into dinner. Just add some spices you seldom use to the carrots one night; on the next you can add different spices and have an entirely different meal. Okay, well, maybe not *entirely* different, but you still have something to eat as you totally wipe out everything in every cupboard of your home. You quickly learn how to make soup out of just about anything!

You feel like you are becoming desperate, and in reality, it's because you are! However, desperation isn't pretty and it can often lead people to make scary or bad, life-altering mistakes. You need to keep your head on straight and keep a cool head during this time.

This spell pulls together different aspects: we are going to need to work on finances, patience, self-esteem, employment (of course), and some good old stability. This spell then will not only help you deal with losing your job, but also help you find a new one.

If you're strapped for cash, don't worry about finding all the components of this spell. Remember that the real magic is in you.

For this spell you will need:

Several candles of different colors:

- gold for employment, strength, success, action, courage and confidence
- green for employment, calming energies, finances, security, and career
- orange for courage, pride, ambition, success, opportunities and enthusiasm
- brown for stability, endurance, strength, and grace

You will also need:

- a bloodstone for courage, strength, wealth, self-confidence, and business affairs
- bayberry incense for money, good luck, harmony, and well-being
- bergamot oil for money, peace, and happiness

Find job openings you are interested in applying for, whether in your local newspaper or online through job or company websites. Cut out the job ads you want to apply for or print them out.

Dress each candle with bergamot oil and arrange them in a diamond shape on your altar, with one at each of the four directions, leaving plenty of room on the "inside" of the diamond. Place the gold to your left, green at the back of the altar, orange to your right, and the brown to the front of the altar. Place ads for the positions you plan to apply for inside of the diamond. Set the bloodstone on top of the ads. Place your incense holder in the diamond shape also.

After casting your circle, light the incense. While holding it, walk once around your altar, dispersing the bayberry smoke into the air. As you walk, say the following:

> *Grant me the harmony my heart does seek*
> *while I set myself upon this new task.*
> *Help to set me apart from the others*
> *as I search for my new place in the world.*

Set the incense in the holder on the altar. Light the gold candle and say:

> *Grant me the strength, courage, and confidence*
> *to take the actions necessary*
> *to be successful in my search.*

Light the green candle and say:

> *While I seek employment,*
> *grant me the calming energies I need*
> *to deal with my finances.*
> *Help me to focus on my career and*
> *obtain financial security for myself and my family.*

Light the orange candle and say:

> *Grant me the enthusiasm, courage, and ambition*
> *to be successful in my search for a new position.*
> *Allow me to keep my pride in check*
> *while seeking out new opportunities.*

Light the brown candle and say:

> *As I go through this difficult time,*
> *please grant me endurance, strength, and grace*
> *as I seek out stability in my life.*

Pick up the ads you have collected and pass them through the incense smoke. Say:

> *Grant me luck in finding a stable position.*

Set the ads down and pick up the bloodstone.
Hold the bloodstone in the smoke of the gold candle (be careful!) and say:

> *I charge this stone with strength, courage and confidence.*

Hold the bloodstone in the smoke of the green candle and say:

> *I charge this stone with calming energies and security.*

Hold the bloodstone in the smoke of the orange candle and say:

I charge this stone with courage, ambition,
success, and enthusiasm.

Hold the bloodstone in the smoke of the brown candle and say:

I charge this stone with endurance,
strength, grace, and stability.

Hold the bloodstone in the smoke of the bayberry incense and say:

I charge this stone with good luck and harmony.

Now, take a seat on the floor and relax for a few minutes. Hold the bloodstone in your hand and imagine yourself working in a position where you are happy and secure. Visualize the job you are doing and how you feel doing it. Meditate on this for as long as you need to, just don't forget about your lit candles.

When you are done meditating, blow the candles out to release the magic into the air—you don't want to snuff them out, as you are probably feeling a bit suffocated after losing your job in the first place. Close your circle.

Immediately go apply for those jobs! Don't waste time, apply right away.

Keep your bloodstone with you at all times—carry it in your pocket or wrap it with wire to make a pendant to wear on a necklace. The important thing is to keep it with you. You have charged the bloodstone now with different energies, so make sure you make good use of them.

If you start feeling depressed, out of control, scared, or any negative emotion associated with being unemployed, take a moment to hold on to your bloodstone. Meditate on all the good things you want coming into your life—including that new job!

I have a crush on my boss

Generally the best-case scenario you can expect out of having a crush on your boss is to get fired. Seriously. What else is going to happen? The vast majority of workplaces have rules against fraternization to protect the company in case of sexual harassment lawsuits; chances of a "fairy tale" relationship are slim to none. If you and the boss decide to bend the rules and mess around anyway, someone *will* find out, they always do. The boss then must protect his/her own behind to avoid getting the axe and will likely claim the attraction was one-sided and a violation of company policy. You'll promptly be shown the door. If it doesn't happen exactly that way, don't worry, it will still be close enough to be a very, very bad idea.

"But I can't help myself," you might say. "[My boss] is so friendly and caring and flirty and blah blah blah."

It doesn't *matter* what the boss is except for that little four-letter word—BOSS. This person is off-limits. What matters more here are your feelings and how you are capable of controlling and changing them.

Therefore, in this spell you are going to do a binding…on yourself.

For this spell you will need:
- dried ivy, clover, and costmary
- a piece of paper and writing utensil
- a black cord (about 18 inches in length)
- a fireproof container, charcoal tablet, and lighter

Cast your circle, light the charcoal tablet, and on the piece of paper write:

My feelings for (boss's name)

Roll the paper up like a scroll and wrap it with the black cording. Each time you wrap the cord, tie it off with a knot. As you do this, say:

I bind myself from having feelings where I shouldn't.
I bind myself from getting involved where
I have no right.
I bind myself from having feelings that
will only cause pain in the future.

Take a pinch of dried ivy and place it on the lit charcoal tablet. Pass the scroll through the smoke and say:

I bind myself from continuing on
a course that leads to destruction.

Place a pinch of dried costmary on the lit charcoal tablet. Pass the scroll through the smoke and say:

I bind my emotions for now, until my
mind is in control instead of my heart.

Place a pinch of dried clover on the lit charcoal tablet. Pass the scroll through the smoke and say:

I pledge my fidelity to myself.

Place the scroll in the fireproof container. If the charcoal tablet doesn't light it, use your lighter.

It is extremely important to follow up this work in the mundane world. If you notice your feelings getting out of control, get them in check immediately. Focus on life using your mind for a while; let your heart take a break so it can mend.

I keep getting passed over
for promotions I know I deserve

If you keep getting passed over for promotions, there must be a reason. Are you truly qualified for the new position? Is someone else more qualified? Does the boss not want to let you go because you are a good worker and the promotion means replacing you? Does your boss not like you? Is he or she passing you over based on personal feelings even though you are the most qualified for the job?

Clearly *something* is going on, and the only way to really find out the truth and come up with a plan to fix it is to set up an appointment and talk to your boss about it.

Before you do that, though, you want to be completely prepared—mentally, emotionally, intellectually, and of course magically.

This spell will help put you in the right frame of mind. You don't want to go in and accuse your boss of anything. You want to be able to speak in a level-headed manner. You want to present yourself at your best when you ask what is it you aren't doing correctly in order to be promoted. Your phrasing in this conversation is important; you don't want to be putting your boss on the defense and you don't want to start this conversation by making your boss feel like she/he has to defend herself/himself.

For this spell you will need:

One candle of the following colors:
- gold for success and employment
- purple for success in business
- green for career and employment

You will also need:
- hematite for grounding, calming, and intuition
- tourmaline for business

Place the items on your altar and cast your circle.

Light the three candles and place them in a triangle formation close to one another—but not so close they melt each other.

Say the following:

I call upon the universe
to assist me in my quest.

I seek knowledge
as to why I have been passed by
for a promotion at work.
I believe my work and professionalism
deserve the reward of a promotion,
however, it has not yet happened for me.
I will go before my supervisor to discuss this.
Grant me strength, sincerity, and understanding,
when I go into this meeting.

Take some time to meditate. More than likely your supervisor is going to ask you why you believe you deserve a promotion. Even if he/she doesn't, you should be ready to tell him/her why you deserve one anyway. Spend some time thinking about what your answer will be. Think of qualities you possess and specific examples of your work that speak to your character and work ethic. Remember these so you will be prepared to talk about them if needed.

Cupping the tourmaline stone in both hands, hold it over your head and say:

I call upon the universe to charge this stone
with a vibrant energy to help me succeed at work.

Cupping the hematite stone in both hands, hold it over your head and say:

I call upon the universe to charge this stone
with a vibrant energy to help me remain calm
and to use my intuition positively to
help me in my search for a promotion.

Close your circle. After you are finished, carry these stones with you to your meeting. When you speak to your boss, you should be giving information that will help you succeed in attaining a future promotion.

Obviously, there are some situations where this might not be the case. If your supervisor is unable to provide you with an explanation or suggestions on what actions you should take in the future, you may want to consider speaking to your human resources department or your supervisor's supervisor, depending on your organization's setup and policy. Good luck!

I can't stand my coworkers/supervisor

Working with people you don't like is no fun at all. It generally makes you feel more stressed out, makes the day seem longer, and it's uncomfortable. More than likely, you can't afford to quit or find a job someplace else, because if these actually were possibilities, you already would have done one or the other or both.

Unfortunately, there are people out there who like to make other people's lives miserable. You are bound to run into several of them throughout your lifetime, and some of those will be at your workplace.

I have been in this situation as have plenty of my friends. It can be miserable to go to work every day knowing you are going to have to deal with someone who makes your skin crawl.

The good news is that there are ways to make the situation a little less painful, and this spell will help. You are going to make a type of gris-gris bag (mojo bag) to either carry around with you at work or place in your desk.

This bag will help keep a shield of peace, patience, happiness, and grounding energies around you while blocking out negative energies that would only upset you. You will find when using this bag that certain things will start happening. Someone might come to your desk—most likely to say something unhelpful—but upon reaching the shield, will simply forget what it was he or she was going to say or it won't come out as planned. You will be able to make your days more enjoyable and your coworkers will have less of an effect on you.

Because we want this to be a powerful spell, we are going to use several different ingredients. You will need to fit everything into your bag, so make sure the stones you use are small; you will only need a pinch of each herb.

For this spell you will need:

- a small drawstring bag—green would be a good color as it helps to neutralize difficult situations
- a wooden spoon or scoop
- a pestle
- a small cauldron

You will also need:

- calcite for grounding and peace
- celestite for verbal skills and compassion
- hematite for grounding, calming, and intuition
- apple blossom for peace
- aspen wood to invoke a magical shield
- basil for happiness and peace
- bergamot for peace and happiness
- chamomile for peace
- coltsfoot for peace and tranquility
- costmary for conscious mind and stilling emotions
- horehound for banishing negative energies
- ivy for binding, and protection from psychic attack
- juniper for banishing negative entities
- lavender for peace and happiness

With a black permanent marker, write your name on the bag—black is for banishing so we are banishing the negativity away from you.

Lay the items along with your cauldron and your bag out on your altar. Cast your circle.

Begin by saying:

> *These elements I combine*
> *to do magic indeed*
> *are here to protect me*
> *and create a shield to surround me.*
> *The shield I invoke*
> *keeps the good in*
> *and the bad out.*
> *I will be filled with peace and happiness,*
> *and negativity will have no grasp on me.*

Slowly and deliberately add each item to the cauldron and announce what it is, and what it is for. For example as you add the calcite you will say:

Calcite for grounding and peace.

Do this for each item as you add it to the cauldron. When you are done adding everything, mix the contents together using a wooden spoon or pestle. Chant the following three times as you stir:

> *These elements I combine*
> *to do magic indeed*
> *are here to protect me*
> *and create a shield to surround me.*

Use your wooden spoon or a wooden scoop to pour the mixture into your bag and tie it shut with a tight knot.

Hold the bag above your head and say:

> *Goddess, grant me protection.*
> *Infuse your power and love*
> *into this bag,*
> *and let your power and love surround me.*

Close your circle. Keep the bag on you or your desk and recharge during each full moon.

I hate my job but can't afford to quit

With the state our economy has been in for the past few years, it's easy to find people out there in the same boat as you when it comes to how they feel about their job and the lack of financial ability to be able to leave it.

My daughter lost her job a while ago and needed to find a new one immediately, as she's paying her own way through college. She put out dozens and dozens of applications which led to one interview and luckily, she got that job. It's in the fast food industry at a burger place—she's a vegetarian. Though they had originally hired her as a cashier, they started her off assembling burgers. She's a cashier now, but she spent months putting burgers together. When she comes home, she smells like burgers; the smell of grease is imbedded in her uniform.

I performed this spell for her and she has since received another part-time job, (though it's only temporary), and it helped to get her moved off assembly and up to the registers. She now works both jobs while she waits to see if the temporary job will turn into something more permanent. Though she still dislikes the first job, it has become more bearable for her and she still keeps looking for something else all the time.

In this day and age it's a simple fact that as long as you don't have a different job to go to, you need to stick with the one you have. Sorry, but that's just the way it is.

I'm not going to just leave you hanging, however! This spell is going to help speed up your job search and make your current job more bearable while you are looking for something else. You might not be the happiest person on the planet, but you don't have to be the most miserable either.

For this spell you will need:

- a green candle for neutralizing difficult situations; also represents employment, finances, and career
- a gold candle for success, wealth, and employment
- lavender oil

Place the items on your altar and cast your circle. Dress each candle with the oil and place them on the altar. (Do not light them yet.)

Say the following:

I come today to send a request out to the universe.
I am unhappy with my job,
though my finances prevent me from leaving.
I need assistance in finding a new position,
and maintaining my sanity while staying
at my current one.

Hold the green candle in prayer hands and say the following:

Assist me in my search for a new position,
to find a place where I feel at ease.
While I search,
help eliminate the distress I feel where I am now.

Take a moment to meditate on this request. Return the candle to the altar and light it.

Hold the gold candle in prayer hands and say the following:

It is my desire to find
a position in which I can be
happy, helpful to the company,
and satisfied with my success.
I ask the universe to help guide
me to where I need to be
to find my heart's desire.

Take another moment to meditate on this request, return the candle to the altar and light it.

Say:

Help me to see
the path to take
for a future bright—
show me the way

with your guiding light.
To make my future
plans come true
grant me this blessing
I ask of you.
Water, fire, earth, and air
my desire is in your care.
Show me guidance
to find my path.
Fulfill this wish sent to thee,
work this magic sent from me.

Take some more time to meditate on your request. Think about what kind of position or place of employment would make you happier. What can you do now to make your current position more bearable? What more can you do to look for a new position? Use this meditation time to do some brainstorming. When you are done, extinguish the candles and close your circle.

I'm being harassed at work

Harassment is a serious matter, and at many workplaces, it is grounds for termination. Depending on the type of harassment, it can also end up in criminal or civil court. Unfortunately harassment is often difficult to prove—especially if the person doing the harassing is sneaky about it; it then becomes a case of your word against the other person's. Depending on who that person is could make it tricky. If your boss is harassing you, the company might not be much help, unless you're willing to go above your boss's head. If you are in a small company and your boss is *the* boss, you may feel hopelessly trapped.

You can always try different legal avenues, but more than likely it won't make your work situation any more comfortable than it currently is—though it may be a necessity. Harassers should not get away with what they are doing, but we all know that sometimes things don't work out the way they really should.

Some people may tell you to just quit. Easier said than done; you may be depending on that job, and due to our current economy, finding another one isn't always that easy.

As any magic needs to be backed up in the mundane world, you should probably be looking for another job, or if possible reporting the harassment to a supervisor or HR department while working with this spell.

While you are working through the problems at work, this gris-gris bag will help keep the harasser at a distance and give you some peace. If possible, do this spell under a full moon.

For this spell you will need:
- a small black drawstring bag for binding, setting boundaries, protection, and to absorb negative energy
- dragon's blood resin or oil for amplifying the spell's power
- a cauldron or container to mix ingredients
- a wooden spoon or scoop

The following herbs for protection:
- acacia, black pepper, angelica, blessed thistle, cedar, clove, frankincense, hyacinth, ivy, mandrake, mugwort, myrrh, and nettle

Place all the components on your altar and cast your circle.

Begin with the following:

> *Oh Great Goddess,*
> *I call to thee*
> *to use your might*
> *and accept my task*
> *to aid in my fight.*

Slowly and deliberately add each ingredient for protection to your cauldron, reserving the dragon's blood for last. As you add each ingredient, sprinkle it all around inside the cauldron. Feel the power present in the ingredient and yourself.

Visualize power and energy from inside you traveling up your arm, down into your fingers, out through the tips and into the cauldron along with the ingredient you are sprinkling at the time.

As you add each ingredient, state its name and that you are asking for it to bless you with protection. Following this example:

> *I add black pepper—bless me with protection.*

Do this for each ingredient until you get to the dragon's blood. When you are ready for the dragon's blood, sprinkle it all over the other ingredients and say:

> *I add dragon's blood, to amplify the power*
> *of all the other ingredients combined.*

Scoop the mixture from the cauldron into the bag and tie it tightly, knotting it.

Hold the bag over your head and say:

> *Great Goddess, infuse your strength into*
> *this concoction in order to keep me safe.*

Carry the bag with you at work or store it in your desk to help shield you from any unwanted contact with your harasser.

I was downsized from my previous job and have taken a position I feel is beneath me and my qualifications

This situation is an unfortunate side effect of our country's recent economic disaster. As companies now tell people things like "unemployed need not apply," things look pretty bleak.

That being said, the first thing you need to do before performing this (or any) spell is this: get over yourself! You have a job. Be happy. Millions of people don't, so stop thinking the job you have is below you. It's a job and that's what is important. For quite a while Americans have been concerned with "what can I get?" but now a whole lot of us are being faced with "what do I need?" instead. It's about time we figure out the truly important factors in life—and let me tell you, it's not whether or not you can watch TV on your cell phone.

Now, the position you are in might not be enough to cover your expenses the way your last position did, so while you are still looking for something with better pay, you also need to find a way to cut expenses. Prioritize. Figure out what you really need, and what you can do without.

Generations ago, people had to do things they probably weren't particularly happy about doing, be it work, chores, whatever. People today seem to forget how easy life is for us. If you want to eat you go to the grocery store and buy something or to a restaurant. You *don't* have to grow the food yourself or starve (though I highly suggest growing as much of your own food as you can!). We have grown up thinking we should never have to do something we don't want to. We should pay people to do the jobs we don't want—from hauling away our trash to scrubbing our own toilets. We don't know nearly as much about sacrifice as our ancestors did. While you are working this job that you feel is beneath you, remember that. This is your sacrifice. Perhaps you ended up with this position to learn a life lesson. Think about it.

This spell is going to help you speed up your search for a higher paying or more "suitable" position, but it's also going to help you understand and appreciate the position you are in and what you can learn from it.

For this spell you will need:

- green candle for finances, employment, career, and security
- indigo candle for insight, vision, change, and flexibility

· a small memo or notepad to write in (you will continue
using this to keep notes in after the spell has been completed)

Begin by placing the candles and memo book on your altar. Cast your circle.
Open with the following:

> Situations change,
> circumstances transform,
> standings distort.
> My life has changed
> and I must now change my priorities
> to survive, to cope.

Hold the green candle in prayer hands and say:

> Though I am employed,
> I am still searching for something
> I feel better suited for.
> I ask for success in finding
> a more challenging
> and fulfilling position.

Return the candle to your altar and light it.
Hold the indigo candle in prayer hands and say:

> Grant me the wisdom,
> insight, and vision
> to see the changes
> I must make,
> and the flexibility
> and adaptability
> to follow through with them.

Return the candle to your altar and light it.

In the memo book you will be making several lists, so put a heading at the top of a page and dog ear it. Leave several pages to write in at a later time. Write the next heading, dog ear it, and again leave several pages.

Your different headings will be:

1. What I like about my current position.

2. My current position allows me to: (finish the sentence with as many different phrases as you can)

3. I want a different job because:

4. I am thankful for:

5. I need:

6. I want but don't really need:

Go ahead and answer as many of these questions as you can now, being thoughtful with your answers. When you are done, extinguish the candles and close the circle.

Keep your memo book with you so you can add to it later. Take time every day to review your answers and see where your priorities are and how they change over time.

My job is very demanding, and
I don't know if I'm up to the challenge

You searched for the perfect job. You wanted something challenging and rewarding, something that would stretch you to your limits and test your abilities.

And then you got it.

Now you don't know if you can handle it.

You know the old saying: be careful what you ask for—you just may get it. What you need to do is give it everything you've got and try your best. You need to increase your courage and ambition, restoring them to the level they were at when you went looking for this job in the first place.

This situation is something people often go through when they have been out of the workforce for some time and begin working again. When you aren't used to doing something, it seems more difficult than something you have been doing for a while.

In my mundane life, I have done most of my work in two different fields—public relations (for which I received my degree) and retail. The area I live in doesn't have a whole lot of work in the public relations field so most of my work has been in retail. After not working for a couple of years, I recently started again as an assistant manager in a store. Starting all over again is nerve-wracking. As for being up for the challenge … well, it can be scary. I've been there too! Getting that confidence back makes all the difference in the world. It makes you happier and your work stronger.

Right now you might feel a bit shaken up, so you need to get yourself back on track and start proving that, yes, you are up to the challenge. You can do this job, and you can do it quite well.

This spell will help bring that zing of confidence back into your life.

For this spell you will need:

- a sky blue candle for calmness, tranquility, patience, and understanding
- a purple candle for success in business
- an orange candle for courage, pride, ambition, enthusiasm, success, opportunities, and willpower
- a calcite stone for centering, grounding, peace, and calming fears
- lavender oil for happiness, peace, your conscious mind, and serenity

- peppermint oil for mental stimulation and energy
- a carrier oil such as almond or grapeseed oil
- a container for mixing
- atomizer
- something to contain the oil mixture you will be making

Set up your altar with all the ingredients. Cast your circle.
Begin by lighting the sky blue candle and say:

> *Grant me tranquility, patience,*
> *calmness, and understanding*
> *so that I may begin again*
> *and start my job fresh;*
> *so that I may feel renewed and refreshed*
> *each day as I go into work.*

Light the purple candle and say:

> *May I be successful in my work.*

Light the orange candle and say:

> *Grant me courage, ambition, and enthusiasm*
> *so that I may retain my pride and be successful.*
> *Grant me the willpower to take advantage of*
> *the opportunities set before me.*

Pour some carrier oil into the bottle you are going to use.
Add three drops of lavender oil and say:

> *To bring happiness and peace back into my life,*
> *to calm me, and to open my mind to*
> *face the challenges in front of me*

Add three drops of peppermint oil and say:

> *To stimulate my mind and*
> *provide me with energy throughout the day*

Replace the cap on the bottle and shake well. Pick up the calcite and spray or pour a very small amount of the oil onto the stone. Rub the oil all over the stone and say:

This stone is for centering and grounding me when
times become difficult or tough.
When I hold this stone, it will bring me peace
and calm my fears.

Carry the stone with you at work. Hold on to it when you need a moment to relax. Rub or spray some oil on the pulse points of your wrists when you need a quick pick-me-up.

Remember to support this magical working in the mundane world—make sure you are getting plenty of rest at night, and take advantage of opportunities for help from your coworkers. You can succeed at this job, you just need to keep yourself in a positive frame of mind.

I like my job, but the pay is ridiculously low

I think we all have one of these types of jobs at some point in life. It pays minimum wage, but we love it. Unfortunately, we can't live off of the wages we end up getting from it.

Is it possible you can find a similar job with better pay? Is a raise possible? Are there other benefits you can take advantage of that would make the job more attractive?

These questions require a little research on your part. If you can't seem to find anything beneficial to make the job more worthwhile, maybe once you find something else, you can still keep it but reduce your hours.

To help you come up with a reasonable solution, use this spell.

For this spell you will need:
- a green candle for finances, security, abundance, and career
- honeysuckle oil for money and prosperity
- almond oil or another carrier oil
- a small bottle, vial, or atomizer for storing mixed oil

Set up your altar and cast your circle.

Light the candle and say:

> *Money doesn't buy happiness, I know,*
> *and while I love my job,*
> *I'm finding it difficult to make ends meet.*
> *Money may not buy happiness,*
> *but it pays the bills I need to pay,*
> *and right now I need to find a way*
> *to increase my income.*

Pour some carrier oil into the container you will be using to hold the mixture. Add three drops of honeysuckle oil, replace the cap, and shake it vigorously.

Hold the container in your hand and say:

Bless this oil with prosperity,
so that I draw enough abundance toward me
to keep me comfortable.
I am not asking for a lot,
just what I need to get by
without having to struggle all the time.
I ask for strength, courage, and wisdom
to help me in my search for
a reasonable solution.

Extinguish your candle and close your circle.

Each morning before you go to work or search for a job, rub a little of the oil on the pulse points near your heart.

We are extremely understaffed at work so I'm doing my job in addition to the jobs of X other people

While this probably sounds like a terrible curse at first glance, working this hard isn't necessarily the worst thing in the world—at least you won't be bored. Depending on your job, there can be other benefits besides. At one retail job, I lost fifty pounds in six months from running around the store so much when we were short-staffed. Needless to say, that was a nice bonus!

Being in this situation can be quite stressful and exhausting, but it also gives you the opportunity to prove to yourself and your employer just what you are capable of. As for me, all that hard work got me a promotion.

The worst part about this kind of situation is knowing that while you are doing the work of three people, you are still only getting paid for being one person while the company is saving a whole lot of money. However, it's important to remember there's a silver lining to these rain clouds if you look for them. Talk to your boss, maybe you can get a raise, even if only temporary until the other positions get filled. Don't ask for it immediately though; you need to show and prove that you actually are doing the job of several people. Once your boss sees what you are capable of and what you are doing for the business, he or she will be more likely to want to help you out for helping the company out. In my situation, my promotion also came with a hefty raise for proving myself an asset to the company.

This spell is going to help you adjust to the stress and pressure of working short-staffed as well as opening up new opportunities for you.

For this spell you will need:

- an orange candle for energy, success, opportunities, and enthusiasm
- a green candle for finances, calming, neutralize difficult situations, security, and career
- peppermint oil for mental stimulation and energy
- lemon oil for physical energy
- rosemary oil for mental powers and to stimulate the conscious mind
- lavender oil for calmness and peace
- a carrier oil such as almond or grapeseed oil

· two atomizers or vials to keep prepared oils in (you are going to be making two different oils to use)

Set all the items out on your altar and cast your circle.
Begin by lighting the orange candle and say:

> *During this difficult stress-filled time,*
> *bless me with energy and enthusiasm*
> *to take advantage of the opportunities before me*
> *and be successful in my work.*

Light the green candle and say:

> *During this stress-filled time,*
> *help me to neutralize the difficulties*
> *I have to deal with and*
> *bless me with financial security in my career.*

Add carrier oil to each atomizer.
To the first atomizer add three drops of peppermint oil and say:

> *Bless this oil with energy*
> *and the ability to stimulate my mind.*

Add three drops of lemon oil and say:

> *Bless this oil with the power*
> *to increase my energy.*

Add three drops of rosemary oil and say:

> *Bless this oil with the power*
> *to stimulate my conscious mind*
> *and to increase my mental powers*
> *to get me through each day successfully.*

Cap the atomizer and shake it vigorously.
Add three drops of the lavender oil to the second atomizer and say:

Bless this oil
with calmness and peace
to help me unwind at the end of a long day.

Cap this atomizer also and shake to mix.
Hold both atomizers and say:

Great Goddess,
infuse these oils with your
magic and love to help me reach
my goals throughout the day.

Extinguish the candles and close your circle.

Carry the peppermint oil mixture with you at work. Spray on pulse points whenever you need a boost of energy at work.

Use the lavender spray when you get home from work to help you relax, unwind, and put the day behind you.

I work in customer service—
I spend all day listening to people complain
and it's really starting to bring me down

I have worked this job and know firsthand how depressing it can be. Sometimes you spend all day long being yelled at by people who want your help and don't realize that screaming at you is not the best way to get it. Occasionally you will get some great customers who understand it's really not your fault their Internet connection went out or their refrigerator broke down, and they don't actually take it out on you. Unfortunately it seems that these type of customers are becoming fewer and farther between. Customer service very seldom deals with happy customers. They deal with people who are upset, angry, and often downright miserable. It is often a thankless job that can leave the representative feeling under-appreciated and as if he or she is indeed the one to blame for all the customers' problems.

This isn't a job you want to bring home with you. You want to be able to leave the workplace and leave the foulness there. Oftentimes it follows you home anyway. This spell will help you relax at the end of the day and put the headache and heartache of your day behind you.

For this spell you will need:
- a sky blue candle for calmness, tranquility, patience, and understanding
- lemon oil for positive thoughts
- jasmine oil for peace
- a fireproof container, charcoal tablet, and lighter

Set up your altar and cast your circle.

Light the sky blue candle and say:

My day has been hard,
difficult, burdensome,
challenging, irritating,
and problematic.
I come now to refresh and restore
my body and soul.

Light the charcoal tablet and pour a few drops of lemon oil on it. Allow the smoke to scent the air all around you. Say:

> *Cleanse the negativity from me;*
> *purge the anger, resentment, and depression from my soul;*
> *leave me refreshed and renewed.*

Sit in a relaxing position and meditate to wash away the negative and recharge with positive energy instead. Imagine the lemon scent is cleansing you, your aura, your mind, your body, and your soul.

Feel it washing away the bad and bringing in new, positive thoughts and feelings. Let the negativity of the day be rinsed away. Let it flow out of you, and into the ground where it can be cleansed and recharged. Take some time to complete this part of the spell work. Make sure you feel renewed and all the negativity is gone before moving on.

When you are ready, drop a few drops of the jasmine oil onto the charcoal tablet (light a new one if needed).

Again allow the smoke to scent the air all around you. Say:

> *Bring peace to me,*
> *let it surround me*
> *and comfort me.*
> *Let it make me*
> *whole and strong again.*

Return to your relaxed position. This time meditate on being peaceful and at ease. With the negative energy gone, this should be quite easy to do now. Let the jasmine scent flow around and through you. Feel any remnants of tension slide away. Feel yourself completely at peace.

When you are done, extinguish the candle and close your circle.

Any time you have a particularly difficult day at work, use this spell to wind down, purify, and recharge.

I've been out of the workforce for a long time because I was raising my children, and now I'm finding it impossible to find a job

Many mothers end up facing this dilemma. It's a shame that some people don't see motherhood as a full-time job, but consider this: do you really want to work for someone who doesn't understand the work and sacrifice that goes into raising children? That person is not someone I would want to work for.

You are entitled to weed through employers the same way they weed through applicants. People who aren't willing to consider the work you did as a mother as "real work" don't deserve you as an employee. This might not be very comforting while you are still out of work, but don't give up—your perseverance will eventually pay off and you will find the right place.

When I married my current husband, I moved away from a great job in public relations. We had a sitter for a while, but could not find anyone who was reliable enough and didn't want more money than what I was making. The kids were ages five through thirteen at the time, and because there were seven of them, sitters wanted large sums per hour. With me commuting two hours a day, it ended up making more sense for me to leave my position and take care of the kids instead.

A few years later when I began looking for work again, I was turned down left and right for not having a steady work history. As if during those few years all of my brain cells had shriveled up and died. How could I possibly work? It was truly frustrating trying to find someone who was willing to take a chance on a mother reentering the workforce. My chance finally came in the form of a retail position with a manager who had several brothers and sisters of his own. He knew what it was like to raise a large family.

There are understanding people out there, but they might not be the easiest to find. This spell is designed to help find opportunities that are just right for you.

For this spell you will need:
- a bag or can of candied/crystallized ginger for courage,
  money and prosperity

Three ribbons, one of each of the following colors:
- orange for opportunities
- gold for employment
- green for employment and career

Cast a circle and get into a position that will be comfortable for you to braid the ribbons.

Hold the package of ginger in your hand and say:

> *Bless this ginger,*
> *and help it bring me the courage and perseverance*
> *needed to find me a position*
> *to bring prosperity and money to my family.*

Place a piece of the ginger in your mouth and suck on it while you braid the ribbons together.

As you braid, say the following:

> *Grant me the opportunity*
> *to find employment*
> *and a successful career.*

Continuing braiding the ribbon to the desired length. You will be wearing this, so decide if you want to wear it as a bracelet, anklet, or maybe even around your waist. You could also pin it to your shirt.

Continue the chant throughout the entire braiding process.

When you are done, tie it off and put it where you want to wear it. Eat another piece of the ginger and close your circle.

Continue to wear the braid until you get hired for the position you want. Before walking into an interview, eat a piece of the ginger to boost your courage and draw prosperity toward you.

I'm working two (or more) jobs and starting to feel the burnout big time

Working more than one job is exhausting, but sometimes that is what it takes to be able to take care of our families. Needless to say, you probably can't just up and quit one of your jobs. Instead, you need to find a better way to balance work, relax at the end of the day, and reenergize in the morning.

I've had to do this often myself, especially while attending school full time. My daughter, a full-time student, is currently in the same situation as well. In the mornings she does stock replenishment at a retail store. At night she works at her fast food job, and one night a week she teaches belly dancing, her "fun" job that helps her unwind in a physical way while also rejuvenating her mind.

This spell has two parts. The first part will help get you going at the beginning of the day, while the second part helps you wind down at the end of the day.

For this spell you will need:
- peppermint oil for mental stimulation
- lemon oil for energy and mental clarity
- patchouli oil for mental energy
- rosemary oil for energy and healing
- a carrier oil such as grapeseed or almond oil
- an atomizer or vial
- jasmine oil for peace and restful sleep
- lavender oil for peace and restful sleep
- a vial to store mixed oils
- fireproof container, charcoal tablet, and lighter
- chamomile tea bags

This spell is used to bless the items you will be using on a daily basis, so you will need to repeat this spell whenever you need to replenish your supplies.

Cast your circle.

Add carrier oil to the atomizer or vial, add three drops of each oil to the atomizer, and recap it. Shake it vigorously to mix it well.

In the other vial, mix equal parts jasmine oil and lavender oil (but no carrier oil) and cap the vial. Shake this well also to mix it together.

Set the atomizer, vial, and tea bags on your altar.

Hold the atomizer with the peppermint mixture in prayer hands and say:

> *Each day I wake*
> *and prepare myself*
> *for the long day ahead.*
> *I ask for blessings upon this oil*
> *that it may help to recharge me*
> *throughout the day.*
> *That it may help to*
> *keep my energy*
> *and spirit soaring.*
> *I am blessed to be able to*
> *work (number of) jobs,*
> *now I ask to be blessed*
> *by being able to perform them all*
> *to the best of my abilities.*

Place this atomizer on your altar, pick up the other one and say:

> *Each day I come home*
> *and need to take the time*
> *to refreshen and renew,*
> *to relax and put the day behind me.*
> *I need to be able to sleep in peace*
> *so my body and mind can*
> *heal, repair,*
> *and prepare for the next day ahead.*
> *Infuse this oil with the power*
> *to help me restore myself at the end of the day.*

Replace this atomizer on the alter. Now hold the tea bags in your hands and say:

Bless this chamomile tea
with the power to relax
and unwind me at the end of the day.
Before bed each night,
I will drink a cup,
and as the warmth penetrates within,
let it cleanse away the
stress and negativity of the day.
Let it replenish as it hydrates.

Close your circle and store your tea bags in a special basket separate from any other tea bags you have.

At the beginning of your day, use the peppermint spray to get you going and any time you need a boost throughout the day. At the end of the day, wind down and relax with the lavender spray and a cup of tea before bed.

Remember throughout your ordeal that even though it is stressful having two jobs, you are also extremely lucky to have even one—so be grateful for your positions, and always be thankful for what you have; the universe doesn't appreciate ungratefulness!

I try not to be too sensitive, but when my friends complain about their jobs— when I haven't been able to find one—it burns me up

I admit I have been in this situation: unemployed, trying to find work, filling out application after application and waiting day after day. Occasionally I would get an interview only to be told I was either under-qualified—or my all-time "favorite"—over-qualified.

I knew it was only a matter of time before the right job came along, but that doesn't mean I wasn't going nuts all along anyway! When my friends and I would get together, conversations often turned toward work and as people often do, they would complain about their work lives: coworkers, bosses, customers, whatever happened to be driving them crazy at the time, they let it all out. I admit that if I had been employed at the time, it probably wouldn't have bothered me as much, though I still believe we should be grateful for what we have!

To be going through a time of unemployment and hear others complain almost appears like they are complaining about their own good fortune. They don't seem to be very grateful for what they have and in fact, seem to be looking the proverbial gift horse in the mouth. This situation can get you down for more than one reason; not only does it feel like your unemployment is being rubbed in your face, it can also shake your faith in humanity when you see people being ungracious for their own good fortune.

People may tell you that you are being overly sensitive, but when it comes right down to it, perhaps the complainers aren't being sensitive *enough*.

This spell won't change the fact that you are unemployed any more than it will change the fact that your friends are employed, but it will make it easier for you to understand the frustrations your friends are feeling so perhaps you can offer words of support instead of feeling distressed when work-related conversations occur. Due to the intellectual and emotional aspects of this problem, we are going to work with aspects of air for this spell.

Set your altar up facing the east and perform this spell at sunrise. It's the dawning of a brand new day after all—what better way to start it than with a fresh step toward a more positive future?

For this spell you will need:

- a white candle and a yellow candle, each to represent and invoke the element air
- frankincense oil to banish negative energy
- lavender oil for happiness
- lemon oil for healing your faith in humanity
- a fireproof container, charcoal tablet, and lighter

Cast your circle.

Light the white candle and say:

> *Air around me*
> *swirl and swell,*
> *raise my spirits*
> *from where they fell.*

Light the yellow candle and say:

> *Bring me guidance*
> *on the air*
> *restore my faith*
> *so I will care.*

Light the charcoal tablet and add a drop of frankincense oil. Say:

> *Take the negative*
> *far away,*
> *with the dawn*
> *a brand-new day.*

Add a few drops of lavender oil to the charcoal tablet and say:

> *Happiness and peace*
> *I see,*
> *to be reconciled*
> *within me.*

Add a few drops of lemon oil to the charcoal tablet and say:

> *Heal the view*
> *of those I see,*
> *restore my faith*
> *in humanity.*

Take a moment to watch the sun rise, and remind yourself that miracles happen every day. Once you remember to appreciate the things you do have, it will make it easier for you to be sympathetic toward your friends' problems. Perhaps once they realize you are being sympathetic of their situation, they will be more understanding (and considerate) of your situation too.

I was forced into early retirement

Being forced into early retirement brings with it a lot of emotional turmoil. Someone is basically telling you that you are either too old to work, or you are simply not needed anymore. There is the fact that you may have committed years of your life to a particular company and then have them thank you with a kick in the pants. My brother is looking at this possibility very soon, and unfortunately the retirement package is not good. The company he works for does retirement through stock. He has worked for this company for thirty-four years, and in the last few years the stock has plummeted. It's worth one-tenth of what it was just a few years ago. He is now faced with a layoff. Indeed, we are quite famous as a society for not giving respect where it is due.

Early retirement can be a mixed blessing—as long as there is still a decent retirement package in place! On the upside, you get a fresh start on life. You can try something new, find a different job, or move to a new city, state, or country. You get to reinvent yourself, embark on a new life. You are given a new beginning.

This spell is going to help you see the positive side of having no choice but to retire early. It will help new plans come to mind so you can set out on your new journey.

For this spell you will need:

- a rhodochrosite stone for energy, peace, calmness, mental activity, and emotional balance
- yarrow for courage and to banish negative energy
- vetiver for money and prosperity
- tangerine oil for strength, power, and vitality
- a fireproof container, charcoal tablet, and lighter

Place the items on your altar and cast your circle.

Using a mortar and pestle, grind the yarrow and vetiver together, and add in a couple drops of tangerine oil. As you grind and mix these together, chant:

Today life begins again for me.

When the mixture is well ground, light the charcoal tablet and sprinkle some of the mixture onto it. Say:

Today I begin again,
I will search and find a new path,
a path that will bring me
happiness and joy,
as I find a new way
to express myself
in life.
I will seek out
that which I will
find the most fulfilling.
I will turn my life
in a new direction,
and find a new me.
I will forgive those who have
let me go,
and not let them
make me feel worthless
or shamed.
I will find my own worth
and shine once again.

Spend some time meditating on your future. What would you like to do? Do you have any ideas yet? Let the ideas and good energy flow and you will soon find yourself on the way to your new life.

I was unjustly fired

Living in an at-will employer state can be nerve-wracking sometimes. You can be fired at any time and really for any reason. Not too long ago, my daughter who worked as a waitress served a "secret shopper." On her previous "secret shop" she scored 100 percent. On this one, she was told she scored 30 percent but was denied access to the report, which graded her, the food the person ordered and ate, the amount of time it took the cook to fix the meal, and the cleanliness of the restaurant both inside and out. In other words, it was entirely possible that her part of the report was just fine; we don't know.

In fact, the first my daughter heard about the 30 percent report was when the assistant manager told her he was ordered by the manager to fire her due to her score—the report she wasn't allowed to see. Not really fair, is it? My daughter was at that job for almost two years. Never once was she late, and in that amount of time, she had a single customer complaint—not too shabby considering she had dealt with literally thousands of customers during her time there.

We don't know if she was justly fired or not since she was not allowed to even see the report—but if the firing had been "just," wouldn't they have shown it to her? What were they trying to hide? Earlier in the month, the manager hired six new people and was reprimanded for it. A week before my daughter was fired, another girl about her age was also fired. Again, no real reason given. It sounded to me like these firings were more about getting the manager out of trouble than they were about anyone's performance.

So what happens when you get fired for a reason unrelated to your performance? Or for no discernable reason? For starters, it affects your ability to get a new job—a double dose of unfairness. It can make you feel as though something is wrong with you, only you have no idea what! Being fired can mess with your chances of receiving unemployment—or if you aren't eligible, it can leave you with no income whatsoever. It can throw your entire life out of balance. The balance in your life needs to be restored and this spell will help you do that.

Perform this spell on a Saturday—the day for endings. We want to put this ending in the right light and also end the imbalance of justice.

For this spell you will need:
• a black candle to absorb loss, confusion, and negative energy
• a green candle to neutralize the situation and restore order
• a mirror
• dragon's blood incense

Set up your altar and cast your circle.

Begin by lighting the black candle. Walk your circle three times with the candle and chant:

> *Loss and confusion surround me,*
> *I will it to go away.*
> *Negative energy around me,*
> *keep it held at bay.*

Light the green candle. Walk your circle three times with the candle and chant:

> *The imbalanced shall be balanced,*
> *order shall be returned,*
> *karma shall be rendered,*
> *justice shall be served.*

Light the dragon's blood incense. Walk your circle three times with the incense and chant:

> *The power that resides within me,*
> *and throughout the world,*
> *shall set right this offense.*

Take the mirror and hold it facing away from you. Walk the circle three times and chant:

> *This mirror reflects the injustice done to me*
> *back to those who committed it—*
> *order shall be returned.*

Take a few moments to meditate on the working. It is important to remember you are returning the injustice done to you and nothing more. You are not sending out punishment, only the negative energy back to where it came from so you do not continue to suffer from it.

When you are done with your meditation, close your circle and begin your search for a new job.

I've been laid off with no return date

Over the past several years, there have been literally millions of layoffs in the United States, most of them without a return date. While you may be able to collect unemployment for a while, it won't last either and you still have to figure out what you're going to do. Obviously you may need to find a new job. The problem of course is not knowing how long you will be laid off.

My husband was in this position last winter. His company laid everyone off, then asked everyone back to work but only for a couple of days, and then off again for almost a month. After that it was a day here and a day there. It was quite frustrating to say the least!

Dealing with this type of layoff requires a great deal of patience and most importantly, a stash of funds to help see you through it. It doesn't hurt to have some other kind of work to do—even if it's unpaid work—to help keep you busy and feeling useful. I now have a list of projects for my husband to do if he ends up getting laid off again this winter, such as repainting the bathroom, sanding our wood floors, and other home maintenance projects he is too busy to get done during the rest of the year. Supplies were all purchased while the money was still coming in, so all he needs is the time off and he can begin working on projects that need to be done.

If you don't have other work to do, look into volunteering, especially if you get laid off in the winter because of the weather. Plenty of people need your help. Elderly people need sidewalks and driveways shoveled and possibly plastic sealant on their windows to keep out drafts. Maybe people in your neighborhood need firewood brought and stacked near a doorway. Check with your neighbors or a local United Way office.

Keep yourself busy while looking for work or waiting for your call back and things won't seem quite as bad.

This spell will help give you that patience and keep your spirits up while you wait things out, and if necessary, while you look for a new job.

For this spell you will need:
- a sky blue candle for patience
- some bayberry incense for drawing money, good luck, peace, harmony, and well-being

This will be a quick spell you can perform whenever you feel yourself getting a bit fed up or down and out.

Set up your altar and cast your circle.

Light the blue candle and say:

> *Without my work*
> *I am at a loss.*
> *I am not at peace*
> *and need to be.*
> *My days are empty*
> *and I need them to be filled.*
> *My heart must be content.*

Light the bayberry incense. Take a relaxed, meditative seat and say:

> *Grant me the patience,*
> *peace, harmony, and well-being*
> *to get me through this ordeal.*
> *Help me find the funds to keep*
> *my family fed, warm, and safe.*
> *Grant me the good fortune*
> *to find a new position,*
> *or be able to return to my old one swiftly.*
> *Let the work return*
> *to fill my days.*

Let the incense burn out while you meditate on what your future may hold.

Use the time while you are laid off wisely. Finish those neglected chores. Better yourself through reading or classes. Use this time to expand your knowledge and wisdom.

The small company I work for was bought out by a large company, and now everything is changing

Small or family businesses sometimes get bought by larger companies, which is great news for the owners, who stand to profit from the sale, but not necessarily for the employees who stay. Many may lose their jobs, while those who are still able to stick around may find everything from the company name to rules and regulations being changed. Titles and job descriptions may not even be the same and people may have to reapply for positions they've already held for years.

Many changes happen in our lives, sometimes out of our control. What we can control, however, is how we react to those changes. While we often fight against change, we often also forget that change may end up being for the better; it doesn't necessarily have to be for the worse.

This spell is for helping us deal with those changes. After all, sometimes we need to be reminded how lucky we are to have any job at all; having to make some changes in our jobs shouldn't be our most important concern.

For this spell you will need:
- a sky blue candle for patience and understanding
- an indigo candle for flexibility and dealing with change

Set up your altar and cast your circle.
Light the sky blue candle first and chant three times:

Changes come and changes go.
Give me patience to go with the flow.

Light the indigo candle and chant three times:

Changes come and changes go.
Give me the flexibility to go with the flow.

Take a seat in a comfortable position and visualize yourself being patient, understanding, and dealing well with change. Continue repeating the chant, the first verse then the second over and over. Feel the energy build, feel the chant becoming true. Build the energy, release it out into the universe, and close your circle.

I lost my job due to an injury

In some places, it is illegal to be fired for a medical reason/leave, but not all. There is also the possibility that your injury will leave you unable to perform the functions of your job to the best of your ability.

When I injured my knee, I was immediately out of work for a week. Then I had to make the decision as to whether or not I was going to return to my job. The damage to my knee was moderate, but not severe enough for surgery. Since I was on my feet all day and doing a lot of bending and lifting, working only aggravated my knee. Though the doc said it wouldn't necessarily do a whole lot more damage to my knee, it would sure make it hurt. What's a person to do? Many people can't afford to simply quit. I was lucky to have a choice, but many people who go back with injuries are then let go because they aren't capable of performing their jobs. Usually injury lets a person qualify for unemployment, but this isn't always the case.

When an injury results in you having to change your job or possibly even your entire career choice, life can get pretty stressful. You may have to go back to school to learn a completely different set of skills.

The good news is that you get the chance to reinvent yourself. When I injured my knee, I decided it was time to stop working retail jobs—I can't be on my feet all day. Currently, I am reevaluating my life and looking into new alternatives. You can do this too. Take a little time to figure out what it is you want to do that you can. Life is too short to be miserable. Don't sit around and wait too long. Put the past behind you and look toward the future.

This spell will help you deal with what has happened and help you move on with your life. It will help open your imagination and possible doors to a new life. It is best to perform this spell on a Thursday, the day related to business matters.

For this spell you will need:
- an orange piece of paper and a writing utensil
- coltsfoot for visions
- a fireproof container, charcoal tablet, and a lighter

Set up your altar and cast your circle.

Light the charcoal tablet and place some coltsfoot on it. Say:

The path before me has taken a turn,
and a new life awaits for me.
I don't know yet what lies before me,
but I come now to see what may be ahead.
May this coltsfoot bring me visions of my future to come.

Get comfortable and close your eyes. Spend some time meditating. Open your mind's eye. Imagine what your future may be. See yourself in different roles. Brainstorm in your mind different ideas of what you could do, what you can be. Spend at least half an hour visualizing plans for your future. What would it take to get you to each of these different futures? What were the outcomes? Go through each possibility following it as far as you can.

When you are done, take the orange paper and write down everything you can remember from your visualization that seems like a real possibility. If something did not turn out well in your visualization, don't write it down. Perhaps later this will become a more viable option, but it looks as though it isn't for now.

When you are done writing everything down, take the piece of paper. Hold it in both hands and say:

These are options for my future.
In the days ahead I will explore each one more fully.
I will research and find which one suits me best—
which one will bring me the most fulfilling future.

Take the piece of paper and keep it in a location where you will see it frequently. Begin your research as soon as you can. Repeat this spell every Thursday until you have decided what to do.

My coworker stole my ideas and then took credit for them

This is something that really gets my goat. In the past, coworkers of mine took credit for my ideas and hard work, and it is nothing less than infuriating behavior. Your boss might not even believe you if you try to tell him/her. Even if you are believed, there's a chance you will be labeled as "petty" because it's not necessarily about who thought up the idea, just what it will do for the company.

Bosses of mine have taken credit themselves for my work and ideas, so this kind of sneakiness isn't necessarily reserved for coworkers. It's unfortunate when those above us in the chain of command are below us in terms of decency.

While you may not be able to get credit for the work you've done, you can still cast this justice spell. Remember: what you send out into the universe comes back to you. This spell is going to ask for the universe to speed up that return to the one (or ones) who wronged you in the first place.

For this spell you will need:

- a brown candle for justice
- a brown piece of paper and a writing utensil
- a fireproof container and a lighter

Set up your altar and cast your circle.

Begin by lighting the candle. Say:

Someone (you may use a name if you know it)
has taken it upon himself/herself
to claim my work as his/her own.
The ideas I shared
were stolen and used
without my knowledge,
without my consent,
without my credit.
I have been wronged
in this intellectual theft.

Take the paper and writing utensil and write down what exactly happened to the best of your ability. Keep the account as fact-based as possible and don't add in any embellishments such as name calling. Though the person may be a real snake in the grass for stealing your work, we don't want that put down on the paper.

When you are finished writing, say:

I send my account into the universe,
so that the universe may judge,
and deal out justice as it sees fit.

Place the piece of paper into the fireproof container and use the brown candle to light it.

Allow the paper to burn up completely, relighting if you need to. Say:

I ask the Gods
and Goddesses
to hear my case,
to make judgment,
and sentence
concisely and quickly.
So mote it be.

Take the container outside and allow the ashes to blow away in the wind. Because this spell is turning this matter over to the universe and the Gods and Goddesses to deal with, you probably won't ever know what the actual result was unless you hear the person involved talking about some twist of fate or strange happening. Be satisfied with knowing that you put your request out to the universe and leave it at that, don't go digging around for answers. The universe will take care of this matter as it sees fit.

My coworker has been lying about me to my boss

I know this sounds like something you would hear about with high school kids, so believe me when I say I was completely shocked when it happened to me very recently. I knew immediately after starting my last job in retail that one of my coworkers, a fellow assistant manager, did not like me. I still have no clue why, and thinking about it now, I don't really care what her reasons were. From my first day of work she was foul and nasty. She flat-out lied to our manager that she would show me how to do certain things required of my job, but she never would actually show me. Instead she made up excuses every time I would ask, or she would go ahead and do things while I wasn't there even though she had been directly told by the manager to wait until I got there so she could show me too. Not only was it frustrating because I wasn't learning everything I needed to do my job properly, the manager never seemed to care that this was happening. When my manager went on vacation, the situation became even worse because no one listened to me when I tried explaining that I still hadn't been taught several things I needed to know to be able to run the store. She made her excuses and for some unknown reason, her attitude and actions were again overlooked.

Needless to say, working in an environment such as this is complete and utter hell. I like to work in environments where employees form a team, on the same side trying to help each other out. This woman was not only competitive, she was vindictive as well. I couldn't continue to work at a place like that.

I was lucky to be able to leave, however. Many people have to continue working in a toxic environment and have to justify and prove themselves over and over again simply because someone wants to tell lies and slander others.

This spell is for those who don't have the option to quit. You may need to stick with a job for as long as possible, or until you can find another to take its place, no matter how much it feels like you're being picked on.

This spell is going to help get you some justice because, quite frankly, it hurts when people tell lies about you—not to mention it's extremely ugly behavior. This spell is also going to help control the gossip being spread about you.

For this spell you will need:
- a brown candle for justice
- slippery elm to stop gossip
- a fireproof container, charcoal tablet, and lighter
- a brown piece of paper and a writing utensil

Set up your altar and cast your circle.

Light the candle and say:

> *I have been wronged by someone I work with—*
> *someone who should be working with me,*
> *not against me.*
> *(Name) has made my job more difficult*
> *by telling lies about me.*
> *I come today seeking justice, not revenge.*
> *May the universe see this situation*
> *and judge accordingly.*

Take the brown piece of paper and write on it any details you know about the situation. You might not know exactly what was said, but write down as much as you know. Keep this account as factual as you can, and refrain from putting any emotion or judgment into it. The universe will do the judging—you don't need to. When you are finished, say:

> *This is my account of the situation,*
> *I send it to the heavens,*
> *to the very Gods,*
> *a testament to my side.*

Set the paper in the fireproof container on top of the lit charcoal. Sprinkle slippery elm on and around the paper and say:

> *I bring to the universe*
> *this request,*
> *and ask that along with justice being served,*
> *the flapping tongues are ceased.*
> *I ask that the mouths which have lied*
> *and spread rumors against me be silenced,*
> *and speak unwell of me no more.*

The paper will burn along with the slippery elm. After it has burned completely, say:

I ask the Gods and the Goddesses
to hear my case
and to make judgment
and sentence
concise and quick.
So mote it be.

Take the container outside and allow the ashes to blow away in the wind. Because this spell is turning this matter over to the universe and the Gods and the Goddesses to deal with, you probably won't ever know the actual result. Be satisfied with knowing that you put your request out to the universe and leave it at that, don't go digging around for answers. The universe will take care of this matter the way it sees fit.

Part Eight

***

FINANCES

I have buyer's remorse and the store won't take back my purchase

Many stores are changing their return policies. While some stores are becoming more and more lenient, others are tightening up on returns because of the shape of the economy. These stores want to keep the money you already spent with them. Others want to ensure you will continue coming back again and again and as a result are broadening their customer service.

I once knew a person who was a shopaholic who suffered from buyer's remorse about 90 percent of the time. Lynn would spend a ton of money every week, often money she didn't have to spend, and then would try to take back most of what she bought. After a while, the stores she shopped at finally caught on to her ways and began limiting how many returns she could make in a month, telling her she had exceeded her "return privileges." Of course she thought it was just crazy that they wouldn't give her money back (she didn't fully realize that once she handed the money over to a store, it actually ceased to be hers). Soon she ended up with maxed-out credit cards and an overdrawn bank account. Instead of seeing it as a shopping problem, she saw it as the stores' problem—they refused to process her returns.

While this may be an extreme case, I have seen similar ones—especially when I worked in retail. The words "I want my money back" are frequently used by people who have over-spent and want it to be someone else's problem.

To follow up this spell in the mundane world, there are a few key factors you must address in the future. First of all, before you buy anything, check with the store to see what their return policy is.

Second, before you buy anything, ask yourself if it is a need (food, shampoo, toilet paper, laundry soap) or a want (purse, cute shoes, perfume, new shade of eye shadow). If it is truly a need, go ahead and get it. If it's a want, wait a few days and give yourself time to think about it. Be honest with yourself too. "I can't live without that makeup" is not being honest with yourself.

Finally, if need be, get yourself some professional help. Compulsive shopping is a symptom of something else. Perhaps you may be trying to boost your self-esteem. Maybe you feel like your life is spiraling out of control. There are many psychological reasons a person turns to shopping therapy. If you find you can't stop shopping, get some help immediately.

In this spell, you have already gone and spent your money. The store won't take the item back, nor will they return your money. You may feel angry. You may feel guilty. You may be in a tight spot because you ended up spending money you didn't have. This spell will help you overcome those feelings, learn from this experience, and think before you buy the next time you go out shopping.

For this spell you will need:
- a green candle for calming, finances, and neutralizing difficult situations
- a gray candle for anger and absorbing negative energy

This is going to be a meditation-type spell. Set up your altar and cast your circle.

Light the gray candle and carefully hold it in your hands making sure not to drip any wax.

Stare into the flame, and pour your negative feelings into it. Visualize the feelings leaving you and going into the flame where they are burned away. Burn away any anger you have toward the store for not refunding your purchase, burn away any anger you have with yourself for making the purchase in the first place. Realize as the anger leaves you where the blame actually lies. Feel yourself accepting responsibility for your own actions. When the anger is gone and you feel you have accepted the choices you've made, set the gray candle down on the altar. Extinguish the flame.

Take the green candle, light it, and hold it in your hands as you did the gray one. As you hold the candle, stare into the flame. Visualize a calming energy coming from it. It surrounds you and comforts you. You feel yourself becoming more at ease.

Continue staring into the flame and say the following:

In the future,
I will take the time to think before I buy.
I will control my impulses.
I will remember that I am responsible for my actions
and not expect others to change or bend
the rules to fit my needs.

Feel free to say this several times, really feel it sink in. When you feel ready, place the candle back on your altar and extinguish the flame. Close your circle. Save these candles for this same purpose in case you need to perform this spell again. Chances are if you have a shopping addiction, you will need to perform this spell repeatedly. Make sure you seek professional help if you ever suspect or are told your shopping has gotten out of control.

I have champagne tastes and a beer budget

Whether it's a case of wanting the best and not being able to afford it or Keeping Up With the Joneses syndrome, we often want what we can't have. You may want a luxury car but are stuck with a ten-year-old economy car. You may want a fur coat but can only afford a $10 coat from the local resale shop. Perhaps you love shrimp and steak for dinner but can only afford macaroni and cheese.

The phenomenon is becoming more and more common—we want more than we can afford. We want "better" than we can afford. The key to successfully handling this situation is to allow yourself a couple of treats to help even out the "wants." Have a fancy meal, but not every night. Maybe you'll be able to only once a month, or maybe even every other month. Try shopping at thrift stores and consignment shops—you can often find brand names at far lower than retail prices. Work small indulgences into your budget to figure out what you can afford. Figure out in what other areas of your life you can cut back to even things out.

There are lots of tips on how to spend less, but the most important factors to re-member are these:

1. Life is not about material possessions.
2. You will never be truly happy until you learn to be happy with what you have.

These two statements are what is truly going to get you through life and ensure your happiness. Once you realize that stuff is just stuff and that the saying "the one with the most toys wins" really isn't true, you will start to feel better about yourself and see those tastes change right before your eyes.

For this spell you will need:

- a gray candle for dealing with greed and envy
- a brown candle for stability, integrity, grounding, strength, grace, and decision making
- a gray piece of paper and a writing utensil
- a brown piece of ribbon or yarn
- fireproof container and lighter

Set up your altar and cast your circle.

Begin by lighting the gray candle and say:

> *I often see something I believe I want.*
> *Something better or bigger than what I have now.*
> *Help me to get over the greed and to be happy*
> *with what I already have.*
> *When I see something someone else has,*
> *I do not have to be envious.*
> *I do not have to want it for myself.*
> *I can and will be happy with what I have.*

Take a minute to meditate on what you have just said. Think about it deeply.

On the piece of paper, write out some of the things you have wanted that you couldn't afford. Include everything you can think of and be as specific as you can. Take your time. Make this list as complete as you can. When you are done, roll the paper into a scroll and tie it up with the brown ribbon or yarn.

Place it on your altar for now. Take the brown candle and light it. Stare into the flame. Feel the energy leave the candle and come into you. As you do, say:

> *Give me the strength to rise above.*
> *Give me the strength to make the right decisions.*
> *Give me the integrity to know there*
> *are people worse off than me,*
> *and instead of wanting everything for myself,*
> *I should do what I can to help others instead.*
> *Give me the grace to ground my wants*
> *and to be strong and*
> *stable in my decisions.*
> *I can learn to tone down my tastes and desires.*
> *I can learn to do without the things I don't need.*

Take some more time to meditate on what you have just said. Think about what it would be like to eliminate things from your life—things you thought you needed and had to have but probably don't even use any more.

Place the candle back on the altar. Pick up the scroll and, using the brown candle, carefully set it on fire and place it in the fireproof container. You are burning all the things you have wanted in life that you don't need. Watch as those unnecessary wants go up in smoke. Release them from your mind and your life. When you are finished, close the circle.

To really boost this spell, it would help to show the universe just how serious your intentions are. Go clean out a room in your house, maybe your closet, a bedroom, even go through a storage area. Figure out which of the items you have are needs and which are wants. Pack up some of the "wants" and either donate them to charity or sell them and donate the money to charity.

Any time you feel your desires for "wants" are getting overwhelming, perform this spell. Remind yourself there are others who don't have everyday "needs." If you help someone out instead you will truly feel better, as will the person you have helped.

I totaled my car

The very first car I purchased was a 1981 Plymouth Reliant. I bought it in 1987 at seventeen with money I had saved from working in a restaurant. The car wasn't stylish and it wasn't pretty—it was a tan box on wheels. The day before my eighteenth birthday, it was totaled in a ten-car accident while I drove home from school in a blizzard. The car was fully insured, but we all know insurance only really pays what the car is worth to someone else—not what the car is worth to you.

My stepson had a rather old car that, while not in the greatest shape, ran well. When a guy in an SUV pulled out in front of him one day, my stepson T-boned the SUV, knocking the SUV over on its side. My stepson's car was a small economy type, so needless to say it was toast. What the insurance company paid for it wouldn't even had filled its gas tank.

When you total your car, you are out not only a car, but the financial (and sometimes emotional) investments as well. If your insurance company only pays you a small amount of money for a totaled car, how on earth do you get another car to replace it?

In my and my stepson's cases, it took months to save up the money to get another car again. Our cars had run fine. They got us from point A to point B, with no problem. For us that alone was priceless. To the insurance company, however, the cars weren't worth $100. There is no way in today's world anyone is buying (or selling) a reliable car for a hundred bucks! If you don't have much money saved or can't get a loan, you are stuck with starting over again.

This spell is designed to help you deal with starting over and to give you a financial boost to help your new car come to you with less of a wait.

It's important to remember when backing up this spell in the mundane world to not only look for hidden opportunities for money, but also to look for hidden opportunities of where to find another car. Dealers are by far not the only place to look—check with family and friends; they may know of someone who is selling something reliable.

For this spell you will need:
- a candle in the color of your totaled car
- a green candle
- an orange candle
- an orange piece of paper and a writing utensil
- an orange piece of yarn or ribbon

· someplace to plant the paper in the ground or in a deep
planter (when you are done with the spell)

Set up your altar and cast your circle.
Light the candle that represents your old car. Say:

> *This candle represents the car*
> *that was taken away from me,*
> *the car that I no longer have and now have to replace.*

Light the green candle and say:

> *This candle represent the funds I need*
> *to replace the car I once had.*

Light the orange candle and say:

> *This candle represents the opportunities*
> *I wish to present themselves to me.*

Take the orange paper and write on it what you are looking for in a car. For example, you might write:

> *I am looking for a car that is no more than eight years old.*
> *It needs to be an automatic.*
> *I want less than 80,000 miles on it*
> *and it must cost less than $1,500.*

When writing, remember to be general enough to include as much as you can. If you would consider buying a car that is ten years old, say so. Write down as much info as you can, but make it specific enough to help narrow down your search. Don't say, "I want a car with an engine and four tires," that's a waste of time.

When you are done writing, lay the piece of paper out on your altar. Pick up the candle that represents your old car and tilt it to the side, allowing a few drops of wax to pour onto the paper. Don't pour in just one spot; pour slowly and deliberately while moving the candle around to spread the drops out. As you do this, say:

> *My former car gives way for my new car,*
> *the old makes the new possible.*

Place the candle back on your altar. Pick up the green candle and also tilt this one to the side letting the green wax drip onto the paper. Move it around to allow the wax to drop in different locations. Say:

> *Let the funds I need for this car come forth.*

Take the orange candle and again allow it to drip on the paper. Say:

> *Allow the opportunities I seek to come forth.*
> *Place them before me.*

When finished, fold up the paper. It will be a little difficult but if you made sure to spread the drops evenly enough, it should work. Fold it in half three times and use the orange ribbon or yarn to tie it shut. Wrap it like a package, crossing the yarn, then flip it over and cross it again. Tie it off tightly. Close your circle and plant the paper in the location you have selected. Your funds and opportunities will soon begin to grow.

My ex-spouse stopped paying child support

To make a long story short, it took me ten years, getting my state to get a reciprocal agreement with a foreign country, and a $7 map of Switzerland (along with a bit of my own detective work) to finally be able to collect child support for my children.

Their father thought it would be appropriate to flee the country in order to avoid paying. He got away with it for quite a while, and still occasionally the checks stop showing up, but I immediately start making phone calls and throw a well-deserved fit, and within a couple of months the checks start coming in again.

I find it appalling that people don't pay child support. It's really quite simple: it is money to help support your child. How can anyone possibly want to deny their child that? Somehow, thousands and thousands of people do so every single day. For those of us who attempt to collect it, we know how badly it's needed, and we also know that it often doesn't make much of a dent in what it really costs to support a child, but every penny helps.

It's not a huge leap in logic to figure that a parent who isn't paying child support is often guilty of withholding other types of support as well. In my case, since my ex is in Switzerland, my children haven't seen him in years. He's had no contact with them, even when we have left messages about things like my son's hospitalization. All mental and emotional support is cut off, which results in hurting the child even more.

This spell is to help you get through the financial hardship of not receiving your child support payments. It will also help calm your nerves in this difficult time.

For this spell you will need:
- a green candle for finances
- lavender oil to help calm and relax

Set up your altar and cast your circle.

Take the lavender oil and lightly dress the green candle. Place the candle in a holder on your altar and light it. Say:

This candle represents the child support owed to me,
promised to me through the court system.
It is not coming now and I call upon the
Gods and Goddesses to take up my task and assist me
in recovering these lost funds.
I beseech the Lord and Lady to address
my needs and to bring
these funds back to my children.
I ask that the person responsible for paying the support
see the error in his/her ways and go about remedying the
situation immediately.
Let him/her know the distress he/she has caused.
Let him/her suffer as his/her children now do,
in order to exact justice.

Take a few deep, slow breaths before you continue, then say:

I also ask the Lord and the Lady to
help me in this difficult time.
Keep me calm and able to help my children
in the best way that I can.
Keep our family safe and cared for.
As is my will, so mote it be.

This is a short yet powerful spell. Back up your workings by doing what needs to be done through the legal system to get your child support coming in again.

I have to file bankruptcy

Sometimes in life we find the only answer is an unfavorable one. Bankruptcy has its pros and cons: it gets you out of debt, but at the same time your credit is messed up for many years. Granted, if you can't pay your bills, chances are your credit has been suffering for a while anyway. Bankruptcy can be the first step to a new start and a clean slate. Even though you are starting again with it in your credit history, you are starting off with a zero balance due—a life saver for many people.

Still, filing bankruptcy isn't all fun and games. You may be embarrassed, ashamed, or feel guilty that you weren't able to take care of your bills the way you wanted. Bankruptcies are often filed because of burdening medical bills, which isn't something you could even help and you shouldn't feel bad about. A smaller proportion file because of unwise spending, often with credit cards. Recently we've all learned how tricky credit card debt can be. The very nature of the credit card is to keep you in a long period of debt while the company or bank earns a nice chunk of interest. Whatever the cause, we all make mistakes sometimes. Bankruptcy is a way to get out of a financial one.

This spell is going to help you get over the stigma often attached to filing bankruptcy. It will help you deal with your feelings about what is going on and it will help open your mind to learning about better financial practices to keep you from making the same kind of mistakes in the future.

For this spell you will need:

- a small chalkboard and piece of chalk OR a small dry erase board with a dry erase marker (if you opt for the latter, try to use a red marker)
- a bowl of water (moon water if it's available, see page 4)
- a small black hand towel or wash cloth
- a green candle for neutralizing difficult situations, prosperity, finances, security, and calming

A note about the chalkboard: they are a bit difficult to find these days, but they works better for this spell as they are more natural, and we want to be able to erase extremely well.

Set up your altar and cast your circle. Begin by lighting the green candle. Say:

This candle represents what I need brought into my life:
better finances and prosperity to provide
my family and myself with security,
and the calmness to deal with the
situation I find myself in.

Take the chalk (or dry erase) board. Write BANKRUPTCY at the top. Along with this word, write any words that come to your mind when you think about that word. Some examples may include: debt, embarrassment, guilt, bad credit, bills, etc.

Take your time writing down as many words as you can, whether they be tangible objects or feelings you associate with the word "bankruptcy."

When you are done, take the washcloth and dip it into the water. You don't have to completely soak it, just get it wet enough to be able to thoroughly scrub the board.

As you scrub, washing away all of these words, say:

I cleanse the debt,
along with the feelings it has created inside of me.
I wash away the pain,
the bills,
the suffering,
to begin again with a new, fresh slate.

Wash the board off completely and close your circle.

Keep the board in an area of your home where you will be able to see it—a reminder of your fresh start.

My savings have been wiped out

Having your savings or nest egg wiped out is a scary experience. Whether it be from medical bills, getting laid off work, or losing your job all together, you really begin to worry when you find yourself going through that last little bit of what you had stashed for a rainy day. Where will the food come from? How will the bills get paid?

If you know you are in for a hard time, you must do everything you can to stretch your savings as far as you can. Use your local food banks, shut off things like cable and Internet. Truly, every little bit helps. Is it possible for you to rent out a room in your house to take in some extra money each month? Do you have anything of value you can sell? Is it possible to downsize your living situation to something less expensive?

But what about when you've gone through all of this already and the money has still run out? Your options become more and more limited. You need new opportunities to open up to you and fast.

This spell is to help get those opportunities opening for you and to get the money flowing once again. Don't wait until the last minute—when you see hard times coming, do whatever you can to head them off at the pass.

For this spell you will need:

- a green candle for finances, calming, and neutralizing difficult situations
- an orange candle for opportunities

Of course, if you are having a hard time financially, don't burden yourself with finding these items.

Set up your altar and cast your circle.

Light the green candle and say:

> *My income has subsided,*
> *my savings are trickling away,*
> *I find myself unable to support myself at this time.*
> *This candle represents the funds*

I need brought into my life,
the money I want to draw near,
and the calmness and patience I will need
while I wait for it to appear.

Take a moment to meditate on your situation. Think about what you have and what it is you need to be able to take care of yourself and your family.

Light the orange candle and say:

Opportunities abound around me,
but I am blind.
Open my eyes to help me see what is in front of me.
Open my eyes to find a way out of the
darkness that is surrounding me.

Visualize a veil of fog around you. The fog is very dense—you can't see through it but slowly it begins to dissipate. The fog becomes thinner and thinner, breaking apart, lifting, dispersing. Continue to visualize the fog burning away until the area around you is completely clear.

Extinguish your candles and close your circle. Using the new "clearness" you have, begin searching again for opportunities to help you out in your situation.

Someone owes me a lot of money but won't pay me back

My parents had loaned a man some money to get himself back on his feet. They had paperwork drawn up and everything to make sure everything was done legally and binding, but the man didn't pay them back. The money they had given him was wasted. My parents tried to get the money back from him but to no avail. When the man died a few years ago, he was deep in debt in addition to being penniless.

This spell is for helping you deal with the money not coming in. Because it may be money you were counting on, this spell will also help get that money in the direction it should be flowing—back to you. I only wish I hadn't waited so long to write this spell in the first place!

This spell will need to be repeated from time to time to refresh and strengthen the magic, especially if the money owed is a large sum or is a scheduled payment.

For this spell you will need:
- a piece of green paper and a writing utensil
- a green piece of yarn or ribbon

Set up your altar and cast your circle.

Take the paper and write:

(Name of person or business
who owes you the money)
Money owed from you to me,
keep it coming faithfully.
Make your payments,
regular and true,
this is what I ask of you.

Goddess great,
I ask of thee
grant this request.
So mote it be.

Roll up the paper into a scroll and bind it with the ribbon—wrap the ribbon around it three times, knotting it each time to help bind the spell.

Keep the scroll in a safe location where it won't get bumped around or messed with. If you have a spell box, store it in there for safe keeping.

I can't afford to go to college

There may be many reasons why a person can't afford to go to college. Sometimes younger people are unable to get grants because the government expects their parents to pay for school. Maybe someone has lost his or her job and can get a loan to cover tuition, but because of regulations and the person's income, the person can't get grants that pay for books, a considerable expense.

Maybe a person's family can come up with the money for tuition and books, but then wouldn't be able to work enough hours to support themselves and/or their family.

Whatever the reason, the fact remains that many people are simply unable to afford to go to school. Even if they can get loans, how wise is it to start a career and life thousands and thousands (sometimes even hundreds of thousands) of dollars in debt at such a young age? Having these kinds of bills over your head can be devastating.

While you should do everything you can to look for grants or scholarships, you can also do this spell to help new opportunities open to you. Because it deals with a lack of funds, you won't need many components.

This is a free-thinking kind of spell I really had a lot of fun with when I was looking for a way to pay for college.

For this spell you will need:

- a white piece of paper
- two crayons: one orange, one green

Set up your altar and cast your circle.
Take a seat somewhere with a hard surface for writing.
Say the following:

> *To better myself, to earn more money,*
> *I need to attend college.*
> *To attend college,*
> *I need money.*

As you say this, take the green crayon and begin drawing on the paper in whatever manner feels most comfortable to you. You aren't drawing a picture, just letting the crayon flow across the paper. You may find swirls or circles are comforting (most people do). Repeat the above chant three times slowly, and continue allowing the crayon to glide across the paper in a soothing manner.

After the third time, replace the green crayon with the orange crayon (again swirling and drawing however you see fit). Repeat the following three times:

Opportunities and good fortune
are what I need.
A chance to better myself,
a chance to succeed.

Finally, take both crayons (either one in each hand or both in the same hand) and again swirl away while finishing with:

Combine together to open to me,
the chances needed for me to be free.
Help me to find that which I need.
Dear Great Lady,
so mote it be.

Close your circle and keep the paper in a safe location.

Begin your search for new opportunities as soon as possible. This is a spell that should be repeated often. New opportunities pop up all the time, we just don't always see them.

My small business is going under

I've never owned my own business, but I know people who do and who have faced this problem. Sometimes people can anticipate it and are able to stop it from happening whether through a loan breathing new life into the business or other means (such as a competitor going under first—not that you should work a spell for this, but sometimes things like this happen). Other times, even if you see it coming, there might not be much you can do about it.

This spell will help you find a way to reinvigorate your business. It's a way to prevent it from going under and to turn things around.

As this spell deals with a lack of funds, supplies will be minimal.

For this spell you will need:

- two candles: one orange, one green
- a glass bowl filled with water (preferably moon water, see page 4)

Set up your altar with the bowl in the center and a candle on either side. Cast your circle.

Hold the bowl of water out in front of you. Say:

> *This water represents my business*
> (use the business name),
> *and right now my business is in great need.*

Set the bowl on the altar and take the green candle. Holding it in your hand, light it and say:

> *This candle represents the money that*
> *I need to infuse my business with.*

Tilt the candle over the bowl so the wax melts and drips into the water. Say:

> *Just as this wax is poured into the water,*
> *I need money to pour into my business.*

Don't cover the surface of the water entirely, but let about half of the water become covered in the wax.

Place the green candle on the altar and pick up the orange one. Light it and say:

> *This candle represents the opportunities*
> *out there to help resurrect my business.*

Tilt the candle over the bowl so the wax melts and drips into the water. Say:

> *Just as this wax is poured into the water,*
> *may the needed opportunities also flow in to my business.*

Place the candle back on the altar. Take a few moments to visualize your business doing well, recovering, and prospering. As you do this, stir the wax in the water with your hand in a clockwise motion.

When you are done, extinguish the candles and close the circle.

Begin looking for new opportunities or other changes you can make to save your business.

Our medical bills are wiping us out

Medical bills have created huge debts for many Americans. There is no doubt about it: when doctor visits are a couple hundred dollars a pop, things add up quickly. Even with insurance, between co-pays, deductibles, or percentage pays—plus the cost of the insurance in the first place—many of us are at our wit's end when it comes to medical bills. If you have a serious problem, or honestly, even a not-so-serious problem, the bills can become staggering.

The less people pay on these bills, the more expensive the medical services become. The more expensive they become, the harder it is for more and more people to pay. There isn't any easy way to get out from under medical bills, especially if you have an on-going condition. They just keep piling up and it's either pay them off or file bankruptcy. If the condition is chronic or ongoing, even bankruptcy might not help very much, and the solution isn't permanent by any means. Perhaps the changes in health care reform will make a difference, but for now, only time will tell.

While this spell won't necessarily get you out of debt (something very difficult depending on your situation), it will help you with budgeting and finding a way to pay your medical bills while still being able to take care of yourself and your family as well.

For this spell you will need:
- a fireproof container and lighter
- copies of your medical bills (make sure these are *copies*— not originals—alternatively, you can list your debts, including the debtor and how much is owed)
- a green candle for neutralizing difficult situations and for finances
- a place to bury ashes

Set up your altar and cast your circle.

Begin by lighting the green candle. Say:

> *This candle represents the funds needed*
> *to set my finances straight.*
> *I light it to bring me the money to pay my bills,*
> *and to support myself and my family.*

Place the candle back on the altar.

Hold the bills or listing of the bills in both hands and say:

> *These are the bills that are running my life.*
> *These are the bills that have taken over, and taken control.*
> *I need to retake control of my life,*
> *retake control of my finances.*

Lay the bills (or list) in the fireproof container. Hold your right hand out flat over the container. Circle it over the container and papers three times counterclockwise. As you do this, say:

> *You no longer hold power over me.*
> *You are no longer that which defines me.*

Using the candle, light the papers on fire in the container. As they burn, say:

> *As these bills go up in flames,*
> *my worries do the same,*
> *As these bills go up in smoke,*
> *their power over me,*
> *I do revoke.*
> *As these bills burn away,*
> *I start fresh,*
> *a brand new way.*

Continue this chant until everything is burned.

Close your circle and bury the ashes.

I can't get a job because my credit is bad, and my credit is bad because I can't get a job

Though many states have been enacting laws that make it illegal to require credit reports from job applicants, they are often required for certain types of jobs, especially those involving the handling of large sums of cash. These reports can prevent good, honest people from getting much-needed employment simply because they have fallen on hard times. In a typical marriage, the credit of one affects the credit of the other. So if only one person had been working and lost his or her job and the couple is unable to pay bills, not only does this make it more difficult for that person to find another job, it can affect whether or not the spouse is hireable as well. What a mess. Just when you need money the most, you can't get a job…because you have bills! You are stuck between a rock and a hard place, so this spell will help open up job opportunities.

This spell is best performed on a Thursday, so perform it each Thursday until you are able to find a job.

For this spell you will need:
- a copy of your credit report—if you can't get a copy of your report, take a piece of red paper and write "bad credit" on it
- a fireproof container
- an orange candle
- a place to bury ashes

Set up your altar and cast your circle.
Hold the credit report (or "bad credit" paper) in both hands. Say:

> *My bad credit is holding me back,*
> *it is preventing me from moving forward.*
> *I can't get a job because my credit is bad.*
> *My credit is bad because I cannot get a job.*
> *My past is holding me back,*
> *and preventing me from setting my future straight.*

Put the report into the fireproof container.
Light the orange candle and say:

> *This candle represents opportunities*
> *I need to draw near to me.*
> *As the opportunities open to me,*
> *the damage this report does is diminished.*

Using the candle, set the report on fire. As it burns, say:

> *As this report burns,*
> *its power weakens.*
> *As this report burns*
> *it loses its control over me.*
> *As this report burns,*
> *my opportunities grow.*

When the paper is completely burned, extinguish the candle and close the circle.

Bury the ashes either in the ground or in a flower pot. Remember to continue your job search.

I've maxed out all of my credit cards

Credit card debt is eating America alive. Most people who own credit cards owe on them. A lot of those people have at least one (or more!) of those credit cards maxed out to the credit limit.

As payments are set up, it can take many years to pay off credit card debt and the interest rates can cost you hundreds, if not thousands, of dollars above and beyond the original dollar amount charged in the first place.

This spell is going to help you control your credit card bills and get them paid off. It's also going to prevent you from charging.

For this spell you will need:
- a large plastic container
- a black candle
- enough moon water in a pitcher to fill the plastic container
  (see page 4 for details about moon water)
- your credit cards
- a freezer with room for the container
- a black towel

Set up your altar and cast your circle.

Take the credit cards and place them in the container. Say:

> *My spending with these cards has gotten out of control.*
> *These cards and my spending both need to be contained.*

Begin by taking the moon water and pouring it into the container over the cards. Say:

> *This water helps to wash away the debt.*
> *These cards will be cleansed and their balance paid down.*
> *No more will I use these cards.*
> *They will be contained.*

Light the black candle and say:

> *This candle absorbs the negativity these*
> *cards have brought into my life.*

Tilt the candle over the container and allow the wax to drip all over the water. As it does so, say:

The power of this candle
combines with the power of this water,
to strengthen this spell.

Cover the water so the top layer is a very thin layer of wax. Take the container and place it in the freezer. As you do this, say:

As I freeze this water,
I freeze my cards, I freeze my debt.

Go ahead and close your circle for now.

Because the cards may float, check on the container every half hour or so, stir the water as it freezes to get the cards to stay down closer to the middle of the container. The thin layer of wax that was on top will break up and be chunky in the water as it freezes. Once it is frozen all the way, take the container back to your altar. Lay out the black towel and dump the block of ice onto it. (You may have to run some hot water on the outside of the container in order to remove the block of ice inside.)

Wrap the block of ice up in the black towel and place it back into the freezer. As you do so, say:

Freeze my spending.
So mote it be.

Now with your cards frozen, obviously you can't use them. Continue to pay on your bills and watch your debt disappear.

I have an emergency and no funds to deal with it

Your car broke down, stove or refrigerator quit working, furnace went out in the middle of winter. Whatever it is, something has suddenly gone wrong and you don't have any cash or credit available to help you out. You need money right away, but you have no idea where to get it from.

This spell is to help make those funds materialize. Because this spell deals with a lack of funds, we won't use a large number of supplies.

You will need:

• a green piece of paper
• a writing utensil

Set up your altar and cast a circle. Say:

> *An emergency has come,*
> *and I am unprepared.*
> *I seek assistance in dealing with this problem.*

Take the piece of paper and write on it exactly how much you need and what for. For example, you might write down: "$350 for a new stove." Make sure you do some research first and find out exactly what you need.

After you write everything down, fold the paper in half, then in half again, and then in half a third time. Hold the paper close to your heart and say:

> *These funds are needed desperately.*
> *Help me to find a way,*
> *bring what I need*
> *close to me,*
> *to keep my problems at bay.*
> *From my lips to the Gods' own ears,*
> *so mote it be.*

Keep the paper in a safe place (like a spell box) until the money arrives. When you get the money you need, take the paper from the box and either burn it or bury it. This spell is for emergencies only, don't overuse it or it won't do you very much good.

My car was repossessed

Losing your car to a repossession screws up not only your credit, but your daily transportation, too. When the bank or lender takes your car from you, it can be very difficult to get another car unless you are able to pay cash for it, and if you had that kind of cash lying around, your car probably wouldn't have been repossessed in the first place.

Now you need a spell to help provide you with transportation.

For this spell you will need:
- a toy car (many stores have them for a dollar)
- a piece of orange paper
- orange yarn or string

Set up your altar and cast your circle.

Begin by saying:

> *My car is no longer my car—*
> *it is gone*
> *and I am without transportation.*
> *I need to find a way to get around.*
> *Whether it be good friends, family,*
> *or a different car,*
> *something needs to change.*

Lay the piece of orange paper on your altar and place the car on top of it. Crumple the paper around the car and use the yarn or string to tie it up like a package. As you do this, say:

> *This car represents the transportation I need,*
> *the paper represents the opportunities I crave.*
> *I ask for my needs to be smothered in opportunities.*
> *I come to the Goddess*
> *with this request,*
> *please grant it on my behalf.*

Keep the car wrapped up in the paper. Keep it in a safe place such as a spell box or on your altar until you have new, stable transportation.

My coworkers voted to strike—
even though I voted not to

Last summer my husband's union had to vote on a new contract. Economic times were pretty tough, so the union really didn't have a whole lot of power—power was all held by the company my husband works for.

As time and contract negotiations went on, the company gave a little. However, it wasn't enough for what the unions wanted and votes to strike were called for.

Most of the union members didn't seem to realize that a lot of what they get by being in the union in the first place is far more than what most "normal" non-union employees get. Some of the changes the company wanted to make were purely common sense that would hopefully save the company some money and keep them in business. But some people are selfish and don't seem to understand that what they believe may be best for them may not be best for the company at large. Put another way, if the employer ends up going out of business, people will end up unemployed.

There were arguments in the union halls that when it came down to the final vote, the situation literally almost came to blows. While several locals voted to strike, the overall majority voted to approve the contract by a narrow margin. Luckily, those people who voted not to strike saved our family and our home. Since my husband had been laid off the winter before, we were already behind on several bills, including our mortgage. A strike at that time would have cost us our home for sure—all because of a decision his coworkers wanted to make.

It was an extremely scary time for our family as there were other long-standing labor union strikes going on in the area. My husband was willing to work, and voted to approve the contract, but had only a few more people voted the other way, he would have been out of a job for who knows how long. To make matters worse, he would have been out of a job not because there wasn't work, or because his employer had laid him off or fired him, but because his own coworkers had decided he shouldn't be able to work to satisfy their *own* wants.

This spell will help minimize any effects a strike may have on you. It's important to note that this spell is only going to work if you yourself (or your spouse) did not vote for the strike. If you voted to strike, this spell will not help you. This spell is only for the victims of consequences brought on by others.

For this spell you will need:

- a brown candle for justice and stability
- a pot of moon water (see page 4)
- a wooden spoon
- your stove
- a hot pad
- agate for protection
- dragon's blood for potency
- bloodstone for business affairs
- amber for stability
- bayberry for money, good luck, harmony, and well-being
- blessed thistle for protection and breaking hexes (though it may not be an actual hex, it doesn't hurt to make sure)
- cedar for money, protection, breaking hexes, and self-control
- holly for protection from negative energy
- horehound for protection
- juniper berries for protection and banishing negativity
- marigold for protection and business matters
- nettle for protection and banishing negative energies

Begin at your stove with the pot of water. Say:

This water is the vessel to bring forth my wish.
To protect my family and me through this difficult time,
to bring us stability and stasis while we wait
for work to return.
This choice that was not mine to make
has been forced upon me.
Protect my family and me in our time of need
as if time stops until we are able to recover.

Turn on the burner. You will be adding the ingredients one by one. You will add them in the same order listed above. As you do so, you will say what each different stone or herb represents as follows:

I combine the following to protect us:
an agate stone for protection,
dragon's blood for potency,
bloodstone for business affairs,
amber for stability,
bayberry for money, good luck, harmony, and well-being;
blessed thistle for protection and breaking hexes,
cedar for money, protection,
breaking hexes, and self-control;
holly for protection from negative energy,
horehound for protection,
juniper berries for protection and banishing negativity,
marigold for protection
and business matters,
and nettle for protection and banishing negative energies.
These items combine together,
form together to create a powerful barrier.

Using the wooden spoon, stir the pot clockwise three times and say:

Oh Great Goddess with your guardian light,
empower this potion with your might.
Keep my family safe and sound,
until our lives
circle back around.

Allow the water to boil and give the herbs and stones a chance to release their essence into the water.

After the water boils, turn the stove off and, using the hot pad, remove the pot from the stove. Do a complete walk around your house, allowing the steam to vaporize into the air in front of you as you walk. Be sure to go through every area of your home with the potion.

As you walk, chant the following:

Protect this home
and all those inside,
while we wait
for cooler minds to prevail.

This spell will help keep finances and other aspects of your life from excessively deteriorating during the strike. It won't be able to stop the process entirely, but it will help slow things down in different ways. You may get money from an unexpected source or find a way around paying certain bills without penalty for a bit. Pay attention and watch for these opportunities so you can take advantage of them.

Perform this spell weekly until the strike is over and you are back at work.

Part Nine

★★★★

LEGAL
PROBLEMS

My child was arrested

We raise our kids as best we can. We teach them right from wrong and hope they will always make the right choices. When they don't, there isn't much we can do about it. We can try to protect them, but that can only be taken so far, and it's very hard to protect someone from him- or herself.

As parents, we have to learn that ultimately our children make their own decisions and have to face the consequences themselves. No matter how painful it may be to watch them suffer through some of those consequences, sometimes we simply do not have any sort of choice in the matter.

If your child is arrested, there isn't much you can do about it. You have to wait and allow the judicial system to go through its processes and handle the situation on its own terms—something that can be extremely difficult to swallow. As much as you may want to, you can't go and pick up your child when you want. He or she will stay at the police station, jail, or juvenile detention until officials say he or she can leave, which may end up being a couple of days.

Having a child spend the night in jail—no matter his or her age—is stressful for both parent and child. You have no idea what is going on, and people at the police station aren't going to be very forthcoming with information. No matter how much you hate it, this is one time where you will have absolutely no control over the situation.

Unfortunately, my son has had a few arrests in his short life, some of them requiring him to stay a few days while the judicial system decided exactly what to do with him because of his mental illnesses. The only information I was given was that they were keeping him out of the general population in the medical ward. It did help a little, but trying to sleep when you know your child is frightened isn't easy.

This spell is to help you deal with the stress and accept the fact that there is only so much you can do in this situation. Your hands are basically tied; you must deal with your child accepting his or her own consequences.

I don't generally recommend doing spells while feeling extremely upset. While there isn't anything you can do to help your child at this time, you can do something to help yourself. You need serenity when something like this happens, and time is of the essence.

For this spell you will need:

· lavender oil for peace, healing, and calmness
· lemon oil for mental clarity
· a fireproof container, charcoal tablet, and lighter

Set up your altar and cast your circle.
Begin by saying:

> *Right now I am filled with*
> *pain, anguish, and frustration.*
> *My child is in a place,*
> *physically, mentally, and emotionally,*
> *where I cannot help.*
> *My child has made*
> *his/her own choices which*
> *I cannot control.*
> *I cannot change what my child has done,*
> *nor can I suffer the consequences for him/her.*
> *I only have control over my own actions and*
> *the way I deal with this.*
> *I know that I must remain calm,*
> *and keep my mind open and ready*
> *to deal with what I will have to*
> *in the days, weeks, and months to come.*

Place a few drops of lavender oil on the lit charcoal and say:

> *May this lavender oil*
> *help to soothe my spirit and soul.*
> *May it bring me peace and calmness.*
> *May it help to heal my heart and soul.*

Do not inhale the lavender smoke directly, but smell it in the air. Let it soothe you. Let it calm you. Let yourself relax. Know that this situation isn't forever. Things will get better.

Place a few drops of lemon oil on the lit charcoal and say:

May this lemon oil
help to clear my mind.
May it help to uncloud my thoughts
and open them to all possibilities.
Help me to accept that I am unable
to help my child at this moment,
and that he/she will have to fend
for himself/herself—
it is the only way for him/her to learn.

Spend some time doing some deep breathing and let yourself unwind. It's very difficult to accept when we are helpless. Use this spell to help you accept that feeling and find a way to move on to what is next.

I'm going through a nasty divorce

As you read this title, you may be thinking "What other kind of divorce is there?" Fortunately, not all divorces get completely nasty and ugly. Some people actually realize when a relationship is over and want to go their separate ways instead of doing everything possible to hurt the other party involved. However, those kinds are often few and far between. There is a fine line between love and hate.

Regarding karma, it's important to remember that whatever you send out will come back to you. The same is true with the other party. Whatever your soon-to-be ex sends out to you will eventually return to him or her too.

As with all things, it's important to remember that while you cannot control the actions of your estranged spouse, you can control your own actions. If he or she wants to be petty, draw things out, and make the divorce as nasty and difficult as possible, you don't have to do the same thing. Take the high road. Judges can often tell when one party is being difficult on purpose, and they don't like it because it wastes their time. It also shows that a person doesn't have respect for the law, be it judicial laws of society or moral and ethical ones.

I've been divorced twice; my first one was quick and congenial. It was before waiting laws went into effect. The filing date to the final divorce decree date took a grand total of two weeks.

My second one was…not so quick or congenial. My ex kept delaying the proceedings. He knew that as soon as the divorce was final, he would have to start paying child support. During that *wonderful* six-month waiting period required by the courts, I wasn't able to collect any child support. He kept delaying his payment, making poor excuses one after another. I'm sure whoever came up with the idea of the waiting period in the first place had to be someone who had to pay a bit of child support himself and wanted to help others out by saving them some cash. After all, who cares about the kids who end up suffering when no support gets paid? Definitely not the people who refuse to pay it or do anything they can to avoid it! I came up with this spell, and soon after the divorce was final, his lawyer had his paralegal hand-deliver me a bottle of champagne to celebrate being rid of him!

When going through a divorce, keep your ducks in a row and perform this spell to hurry up the judicial process and give you an edge in the courtroom.

Because this spell is of an ending nature, it is best performed on a Saturday—and as many divorces take lots of time, you will have plenty of Saturdays for performing it.

For this spell you will need:

- a brown candle for integrity, justice, grace, and neutrality
- a piece of bloodstone for legal affairs
- cedar for protection and self-control
- columbine for courage and willpower
- frankincense for protection and banishment of negative energy
- holly for protection from negative forces
- mistletoe for good fortune
- a black glass or pottery bowl

Set up your altar and cast your circle. With both hands, hold the black bowl out in front of you and say:

> *The scales of justice*
> *must be balanced.*
> *Banish the negative energies from my life.*

Set the black bowl on your altar and say:

> *Help me to keep my composure*
> *during these proceedings.*
> *Help me to remain calm,*
> *and in control of my emotions*
> *and actions.*

Set the bloodstone in the bowl and say:

> *Bless this stone to help me through my legal battle.*

Place either cedar shavings or cedar oil on the bloodstone and say:

> *Bless this cedar,*
> *let it provide this stone with protection and self control.*

Pour/sprinkle columbine into the bowl on the stone and say:

Bless this columbine,
let it provide this stone with courage and willpower.

Pour/sprinkle frankincense into the bowl on the stone and say:

Bless this frankincense,
let it provide this stone with the power to
banish negative energy and to protect me.

Sprinkle some holly into the bowl on the stone and say:

Bless this holly,
let it provide this stone with the power
to repel negative forces.

Sprinkle some mistletoe into the bowl on top of the stone and say:

Bless this mistletoe,
let it provide this stone with the power to
bring me good fortune.

Again pick up the black bowl in both hands and hold it in front of you. Again say:

The scales of justice
must be balanced.
Banish the negative energies from my life.
Help me to keep my composure
during these proceedings.
Help me to remain calm,
and in control of my emotions
and actions.

Close your circle. Carry the bloodstone with you whenever you must deal with any of the details of your divorce: meetings with lawyers, mediators, or during court hearings.

Someone has stolen my identity

One of the fastest-growing crimes in the United States these days is identity theft. There are many different ways this can happen, and degrees to which damage can be done.

Though it is becoming a little easier to clean up after this sort of crime has been committed, there is still a long way to go in helping and protecting victims—not to mention in catching perpetrators.

Both my husband and I have been victims, as have a *lot* of people I know, whether it be a snagged debit or credit card number used for unauthorized transactions or the bank releasing information about their account. Luckily, our cases were relatively simple and required a few phone calls and faxes to clear everything up and start over, but not everyone is so lucky.

The person who stole your identity might never get caught—you have to accept this as a real possibility. (In the cases I'm familiar with, no one has ever been caught, much less convicted.) Sometimes the only justice that gets served is karmic justice.

This spell will ask karma to seek out the culprit and serve justice as deemed fit. It will also help with damage control and speed up the recovery process.

For this spell you will need:

- a green candle for the financial aspects of
  the identity theft
- a red candle to send karmic energy out into the universe
- a brown candle to send justice out into the universe

Set up your altar and cast your circle.

Begin by saying:

> *A wrong has been done to me:*
> *someone has decided to steal my identity,*
> *to steal my very name,*
> *and ruin my financial reputation.*
> *I come today seeking justice*
> *and assistance in righting this wrong.*

Light the green candle and say:

> *Help to restore my finances*
> *and my credit history*
> *to what it was before this*
> *person tried to steal my life.*

Light the brown candle and say:

> *May justice be served*
> *in this matter and all others*
> *in the universe.*
> *My offender may never be caught,*
> *might never be brought to justice legally—*
> *may the justice of the universe*
> *seek him/her out and*
> *penalize him/her for his/her crime.*
> *May justice be served.*

Light the red candle and say:

> *May karma seek out the offender*
> *and teach him/her the error of his/her ways.*
> *May karma help to restore balance to the universe,*
> *and hold this person accountable for his/her actions*
> *even if the law cannot.*

Close your circle.

It may take some time to get your credit restored—but it's very important you do not give up. These matters can take months to resolve. Keep on top of it, and keep repeating your spell.

My ex is suing me for full custody

Custody battles are never fun for anyone—except possibly the lawyers who make money off them given how expensive custody battles are.

The process is stress-filled, time consuming, and your life will feel like it's being put under a microscope. There are court hearings, appointments with lawyers, mediators, often times therapists, and anyone else the judge decides to pull in for an opinion.

My husband and his ex-wife went through a custody battle due to her mental instability in which she attempted to use the fact that I am Pagan to get sole custody. She even bought a copy of my first book to use as evidence against me. It didn't work too well; her lawyer had advised her to drop it before anything went before the judge but she refused. The judge was not happy that my beliefs were even brought up and let her know that. Not everyone is as lucky, though; in some parts of the country, being Pagan can influence a judge to side with the other party. I'd like to note here that if your religion is truly the only reason the judge sides with your ex, you need to contact the ACLU (aclu.org/affiliates).

You need a spell that will help give you a legal edge and at the same time take the stress off of you. Custody battles are one of the most stressful events anyone can ever go through. In addition, stress can cause problems in court and affect your physical and emotional well-being. Judges do not have high opinions of people who appear to be out of control.

For this spell you will need:
- a sky blue candle for peace, tranquility, patience, and calmness
- a small brown drawstring bag for stability, integrity, justice, decision making, family issues, and for grounding energies
- bloodstone for legal matters
- calcite for centering, grounding, peace, and calming fears
- cedar for courage, protection and self-control
- frankincense for protection and banishing negative energies

Set up your altar and cast your circle.

Begin by saying:

I am going through a most difficult time.
My former spouse is trying to take
our children away from me.
I come before the Lord and Lady to ask
for assistance in this matter.

Light the blue candle and say:

While fighting this battle,
help me to remain calm and composed,
peaceful and tranquil.
Ensure my patience while dealing with these matters.

Take the brown bag and hold it in both hands close to your heart. Say:

I pray for stability and justice,
I pray for integrity in the decisions I make.
Please keep me grounded while dealing
with these family issues.

Place the bloodstone into the bag and say:

Bless me in this custody case,
bring me a just ruling.

Place the calcite into the bag and say:

Bless me in this custody case,
keep me centered and grounded.
Keep me at peace and calm my fears.

Place the cedar into the bag and say:

> *Bless me in this custody case,*
> *keep me full of courage.*
> *Grant me self-control*
> *and protect me*
> *from the persecution of my ex*
> *and if necessary, from myself.*

Place the frankincense in the bag and say:

> *Bless me in this custody case,*
> *banish the negative energy that is being sent my way,*
> *and protect me from the persecution of my ex*
> *and if necessary, from myself.*

Tightly tie the bag closed and hold it to your heart. Say again

> *I am going through a most difficult time.*
> *My former spouse is trying to take*
> *our children away from me.*
> *I come before the Lord and Lady*
> *to ask for assistance in this matter.*

Then add:

> *Your blessings are greatly appreciated,*
> *and your love is forever returned.*

Close your circle.

Carry the bag with you whenever dealing with any matters involved in the custody battle.

My child has been placed into foster care

Children can be placed into foster care for many reasons—people assume that if a child is in foster care it is because the parent/s were abusive. This isn't true—sometimes a child is put into foster care because the parent is ill and there is no one to take the child. Other times a child is put into foster care because of how abusive the child is toward the parent. No one should ever assume they know the story behind why a child is in foster care unless they are intimately involved in the case.

My own adult son (he is nineteen) is a ward of the state and currently in the foster care system because of his mental illnesses and his violent history toward family members. No matter the reason the child is in foster care, much stress goes along with it. Just being separated from your child is a stressor, and you and your family may be under constant supervision. There are also therapy sessions, both individual and family, along with parenting classes and whatever else the court may deem necessary. If you weren't under enough stress before your child was put into foster care, you may find yourself in for a whole new load. While the classes are designed to help you deal with the stress and problems, they also create their own problems such as making time for sessions and for court appearances, which can lead to a loss of income among other things.

As I've learned from my son's caseworkers, for every set of parents who work with the system to help the child are another seventy-five parents who don't do anything at all. They don't attend classes, therapy sessions, and often not even court hearings and visitation. I'm told that most of the kids in foster care never have any contact with their parents because the parents don't show up. Granted, the system isn't perfect and it can be incredibly stressful, but there's no reason not to have any contact with your child.

Our family has a good relationship with our son and his caseworkers. When he had to be supervised for visits a year ago, his caseworker gave up Thanksgiving with her own family and came and spent it with us just so we could see my son. She has told us several times we are not the typical parents for children in foster care; too many parents give up and write the child off. The thought honestly and completely sickens me, so I want to tell you: do not give up on your child just because the system can sometimes suck really bad! Stick it out and use this spell to help you get through it.

This spell is designed to help minimize the negative impact this ordeal will have on you and magnify the positive instead.

For this spell you will need:
- a black candle to absorb negative energy
- an orange candle for positive energies

Set up your altar and cast your circle:
Begin by saying:

> *My child and I are both going through a difficult time.*
> *I come before the Lord and Lady*
> *to ask for help for both of us.*
> *I ask that you help us both*
> *to be patient and understanding and*
> *to learn to deal with our situation*
> *in the best ways we can.*
> *For my child, it will mean adjusting*
> *to his/her new surroundings.*
> *For me, it will mean adjusting*
> *to not having my child around.*

Light the black candle and get into a comfortable position. Say:

> *I project into this candle the negativity that*
> *surrounds and encompasses me,*
> *the negativity that eats away at me day by day.*
> *I project this negativity into this candle*
> *to burn away and disperse.*

Spend some time meditating, concentrating on sending negative emotions, feelings, and energies into the flame of the candle. Visualize that negativity burning away. When you feel clearer, take the orange candle and light it. Get into a comfortable position and say:

Bring into me positive energy—truth, honesty, love.
Positive feelings. Positive emotions. Positive energies.

Spend more time meditating, this time concentrate on receiving positive energies. Visualize positive feelings and energy emanating from the candle's flame. Continue this until you are feeling the positivity inside of you. When you are done, thank your deities and close your circle.

I was arrested for drunk driving

You may be wondering why I would include a spell for a topic such as this, so I want to explain right away—this spell is NOT designed to make your DUI disappear. It is also not designed to help you get out of any legal trouble you may be in for getting a DUI. Instead, it is designed to help you realize the severity of your crime and hopefully get through to you to *never* commit this offense again. Unfortunately many people who do get DUIs go right back to drinking and driving no matter the punishment.

Quite simply, drunk driving is not only stupid, it is downright murderous. Anyone who drinks alcohol or takes drugs and then gets behind the wheel of a car is putting the lives of everyone else on the roads into their own hands. It is simply wrong and there is no excuse for these actions. Ever.

This spell is to help you accept responsibility for your own actions. It is designed to bring justice to all—yourself included. This doesn't mean you will get off without any sort of punishment—not at all. In fact, it means you will get exactly what the universe deems you deserve.

It takes a brave and responsible person to perform this spell and accept the consequences of his or her actions.

For this spell you will need:

· a brown candle for integrity, justice, and grace

Set up your altar and cast your circle.

Light the candle and hold it in your hands. Say:

Lord and Lady,
I have made a bad and wrong decision,
a choice that could not only
have affected the lives of others,
it could have taken their lives as well.
Now I need to take responsibility for my actions.
I need to restore my integrity, which I have destroyed.
I need to deal with this situation with grace.

I need to accept the justice the universe
decides to assign to me.
I pledge to the Lord and Lady,
I pledge to the universe.
I pledge to myself,
to do what it is necessary to right this wrong.
I pledge to accept my fate.

Place the candle on the altar and get into a comfortable position. Do some meditation on your situation. Visualize yourself as being responsible for your actions. Visualize yourself being strong and regaining your integrity. When you are done, thank your deities and close your circle.

My house is in foreclosure

Financially, foreclosure may not be a bad thing for some people, believe it or not. It gives them a chance to start over, and most people going through a foreclosure are able to start saving money again. Once the foreclosure is final, people may have to rent for a couple of years, but afterwards can start over with a fresh house, fresh mortgage, new city, or even new state.

Obviously, it's a stressful time—losing your home isn't much fun no matter what the positives may be. It requires a move, which itself is a pretty big hassle. Having to sort everything, pack it, move it, store it, unpack it—and if you end up moving somewhere smaller, sorting and getting rid of stuff for which you have no room is a pain, and this doesn't even include finding a place to live!

Sometimes we simply don't have control over what is going on in our lives—not having enough money to make a mortgage payment generally takes away our control and gives it to the bank instead. Even if your house is in foreclosure, you still have some choices and decisions to make. You can try to save the house through different means. You can file bankruptcy, and attempt to reaffirm with the mortgage company. You could move in with friends or relatives or rent, for example. Make sure you speak with a financial advisor who can explain your legal choices and responsibilities. This spell is going to help you make any related decisions and help you follow through with those choices.

For this spell you will need:

- a green candle for finances, security, and to neutralize difficult situations
- a brown candle for stability and decision making
- paper and a writing utensil

Set up your altar and cast your circle. Say:

> *My life is in for a huge change,*
> *my house has gone into foreclosure.*
> *Though I know my options,*
> *I have not yet decided which path to take.*

I come before the God and Goddess
to help me make the decisions I have to make.
To help me discover which path I should follow.

Light the green candle and say:

My finances are a mess.
I ask for the ability to bring them under control,
to give myself and my family some security.
Though we may have to move,
I know this may be our chance for a new start.

Light the brown candle and say:

I ask for stability for myself and my family.
I ask for assistance in making
the decisions I need to make.

Write down your current options—and if known at this time, the pros and cons of each. When you are done, thank your deities and close your circle. Keep the list in a visible location—a location where you will see it often so you will have plenty of time to reflect on your choices.

After a week, repeat the spell and add to your list or, if necessary, remove some items. Continue to perform the spell weekly until your choice seems completely clear.

My past criminal actions are haunting me

We've all made mistakes in the past; unfortunately, some have made bigger mistakes than others, which can have longer lasting side effects.

I'm not going to tell you it isn't fair that what you did in the past is coming back to haunt you—that's karma for you. You've heard the saying, "You do the crime, you do the time," and what you are going through right now is part of that "time."

Perhaps you are trying to find a job and your crime isn't far enough in the past to be eliminated from your record. It can be very difficult to get a job when you have any kind of a criminal record. You will need to check with agencies designed to help out in situations such as yours to find places of employment that accept applications from people with a record.

Some crimes will follow you for the rest of your life, such as if you are required to register as a sex offender. You may also be court-ordered to never work in certain fields or occupations if the position is somehow related to your crime.

The important thing to remember is where the blame for this situation truly lies. After having missed several or even dozens of opportunities because of your history, people can often direct their anger to the wrong target. Is it the fault of some establishments if they don't want to hire someone with past criminal tendencies or is it the fault of that individual?

This is why it's important to think before you act. Perhaps you were living a completely different life when you committed your crimes—perhaps you didn't have any spirituality in your life at all. Perhaps you had an awakening afterwards or perhaps you awoke *because* of it. Even if you had no idea what karma is at the time, that doesn't excuse you from paying its price.

If you've grown and know better now, that's great. However, continued karmic retribution and restitution may continue for some time. You just have to accept it, and the sooner you fully accept the position you are in and why, the sooner things will start to get better. This spell will help you accept responsibility for your actions.

For this spell you will need:

- a black candle to absorb negative energies and define boundaries
- a silver candle for spiritual truth, intuition, stability, and relating to your inner self

Set up your altar and cast your circle.

Begin by saying:

> *In the past, I made some mistakes,*
> *and now they are affecting me in ways I hadn't imagined.*
> *I am learning that the consequences of my*
> *actions are far and long reaching.*

Light the black candle and say:

> *The negativity I caused in the past is now*
> *affecting me in my present.*
> *I know it is my own fault,*
> *though I am feeling the negativity grow exponentially.*
> *My negative behavior in the past*
> *is increasing my negative feelings now.*
> *I need help in controlling the negativity and*
> *keeping it from growing.*
> *I need to accept my fate and deal with it positively.*

Light the silver candle and say:

> *This situation brings to light my past transgressions.*
> *It also gives me the opportunity to look inside myself—*
> *to see myself for who I am,*
> *for who I was.*
> *I have the chance to reorder my life,*
> *to find the spiritual truth inside me.*
> *To use my own intuition to bring stability*
> *to my life as I reflect on my inner self.*
> *I must take responsibility for what I have done*
> *and deal with the consequences*
> *as long as they may last.*

Spend some time meditating if you like. When you are finished, go ahead and close your circle.

I have to go to court for a car accident

Whether you are the plaintiff, defendant, or a witness, court is never fun. People can get very nervous when they know they have to step foot into a courtroom. Though insurance companies often settle car accident disputes out of court, plenty of them still end up in front of a judge.

No matter what your role in the proceedings, it's important for you to relax and be 100 percent honest and forthcoming with information. Often when car accident cases make it before a judge, it's because it resulted in someone's serious injury or death. The severity of the situation dictates that you owe it to yourself, the others involved, and the universe itself to be completely honest so that justice may be truly served.

This spell will help you relax so you can be your best at court. It will also help to ensure that justice is served—just remember your idea of justice may differ from that of the judge or jury assigned to the case.

For this spell you will need:

- bloodstone for dealing with legal affairs
  and for courage
- black pepper for courage, mental alertness, and protection
- clove (ground works best) for protection, courage, and
  to enhance your memory
- columbine for courage
- costmary for stilling emotions
- fennel for courage
- a glass bowl

Set up your altar and cast your circle.

Hold the stone in both hands before you and say:

> *I come today to charge this stone,*
> *to instill it with the energies I need*
> *to help me at my court hearing.*
> *I will charge it with courage*
> *and the ability to remain calm—*
> *to still my emotions.*

To keep me calm through the court session
and allow me to be honest
and show my integrity.

Place the stone inside the bowl.
Take a pinch of black pepper and sprinkle over the bloodstone. Say:

Instill within this stone
the power to give me courage,
the power to keep me mentally alert,
the power to protect me.

Sprinkle clove over the bloodstone and say:

Instill within this stone,
the power to give me courage,
the power to protect me,
the power to enhance my memory.

Sprinkle some columbine over the bloodstone and say:

Instill within this stone
the power to give me courage.

Sprinkle some costmary over the bloodstone and say:

Instill within this stone
the power to still my emotions.

Sprinkle some fennel over the bloodstone and say:

Instill within this stone
the power to give me courage.

Hold the bowl in front of you with both hands. Say:

Lord and Lady,
bless this stone with your grace,
with your courage,
with your ability to calm emotions.
As I carry this stone with me,
I will carry your ever loving
embrace and grace with me too.

When you are finished, close your circle.
Carry the bloodstone with you when you go to court.

My constitutional rights have been violated

If you truly believe your constitutional rights have been violated, the very first thing you need to do is contact the American Civil Liberties Union. (www.aclu.org).

The next thing you need to do is document *everything*: anyone you have spoken to regarding your situation, names, dates, what was said—everything. Make sure you get it all written down.

Your next step will be this justice spell.

For this spell you will need:
- a brown candle for integrity, justice, endurance, strength, and grace
- dragon's blood incense to amplify the power

Set up your altar and cast your circle.

Light the dragon's blood incense and say:

> *This spell I work*
> *needs to be strong.*
> *Boost its strength*
> *protect me from wrong.*

Light the brown candle and say:

> *I have been violated,*
> *and want justice served.*
> *I will need strength, endurance, and grace*
> *to help me through this ordeal.*
> *Grant me this wish.*
> *Let my voice be heard.*
> *I was silenced,*
> *but I shall not be anymore.*
> *I was discriminated against,*
> *but I shall stand up tall.*

I was judged,
but I shall not be found lacking.
I have been harmed,
but will be compensated.
I have been oppressed,
but will demand my rights.
I have been persecuted,
but will demand what is fair.
My rights will be restored.
With the Lord and Lady
by my side, I shall prevail
and persevere.

Stand up for yourself and go after those who have violated your rights. When you stand up for yourself, you stand up for everyone who has ever had their rights violated. You also take giant steps toward preventing the same thing from ever happening to anyone else.

You must make sure, though, that the situation was truly a violation of your rights. The ACLU will help you determine that.

Several years ago a woman on the Internet sent emails to hundreds of groups claiming her civil rights had been violated after her child was taken away from her. She claimed it was religious discrimination. She even posted copies of the court papers. She claimed she contacted the ACLU, who refused to take her case. She began telling people the ACLU was also biased because she was Pagan. However, the court papers she herself posted clearly stated her child was being placed with another family because of the mother's self-admitted drug and alcohol abuse (for which she refused treatment) along with other criminal actions.

Of course the ACLU did not take her case. This woman was not being persecuted and harassed for being Pagan as she claimed—her being Pagan had nothing to do with anything. Her problems were because of her alcohol and illegal drug usage. This was not a case of civil rights violation even though the woman involved seemed convinced that it was.

If you are the only one who sees your situation as a violation, chances are it really wasn't. You simply aren't seeing the picture clearly. You need to take a step back and look at the situation with fresh eyes.

I've been accused of a crime I did not commit

Even though in our country we say someone is innocent until proven guilty, it often doesn't feel this way, especially to the accused. If you have been charged with a crime, it means you have already been arrested, fingerprinted, and probably spent at the very least a small amount of time in a cell. It doesn't sound like something done to innocent people, does it?

Often people assume that if there is enough evidence to arrest someone, it must mean the person is guilty. This couldn't be further from the truth. Not too long ago there was a case in the local news of a man who was released from jail where he had sat for five years waiting for his trial that still hadn't happened. (So much for the right to a quick and speedy trial!) He was released because the DNA evidence collected at the scene of the crime—the murder of his own child—proved that he had not been there. The DNA recovered actually belonged to another man, one who ended up in jail on a different charge not too long after the murder had taken place. Instead of being able to bury his own child, this man sat in a jail cell for five long years, waiting. I cannot imagine what this man must have gone through. Obviously his reputation was completely destroyed; his family moved away to start new lives. Everything he had known was basically gone. And the worst thing was that he had been innocent the entire time. Hopefully your case is not anywhere near this severe.

This spell is designed to bring you justice swiftly and to clear your name while minimizing any damage resulting from the accusation. Obviously, this spell must be done only once you have been released on bond. If you are unable to raise the bond, ask someone close to you to perform this spell for you.

For this spell you will need:
- a brown candle
- a brown piece of paper
- a writing utensil
- a fireproof container and charcoal tablet
- slippery elm

Set up your altar and cast your circle.

Light the candle and say:

> *I have been wrongly charged,*
> *the Gods and I know my innocence.*
> *I wish for everyone else to know as well.*
> *Let justice be served*
> *efficiently and quickly!*

Sprinkle the slippery elm onto the charcoal tablet and say:

> *Bind the tongues that speak of me,*
> *and act as if I have been convicted.*
> *Bind the tongues that speak lies of me,*
> *and allow my defense to be heard.*

Take the piece of paper, and write out your side of the story. Include as much information you can but make sure to keep it factual, not emotional.

When you are finished writing, place the paper into the fireproof container and set it on fire. Say:

> *I send the truth into the universe,*
> *may the truth prove my innocence and redeem me.*
> *May the Gods and Goddesses*
> *shine down on my innocence,*
> *and set me free.*
> *So mote it be.*

Extinguish the candle and close your circle. Allow the ashes to blow away in the wind, dispersing the truth with them as they scatter.

Part Ten

★ ★ ★ ★

WORLD

There has been serious
manmade damage to the environment

On April 20, 2010, an explosion on the Deepwater Horizon oil rig rocked the world. That explosion eventually allowed close to 206 million gallons of crude oil to seep into the Gulf of Mexico, and changed the way people looked at the oil industry. The damage done to the environment was astronomical, leaving a path of dead plant and animal life in its wake.

Throughout the world, witches, Pagans, and other magickal types gathered together in rituals, spells, and prayers to bring a solution to the gushing well, and to help heal the earth.

When these kinds of manmade catastrophes happen, people come together to do what they can to help the natural world recover and heal. Some people are able to go to the area in question and offer physical help or support, but for others, the best we can do is join in through healing spells or rituals to try to minimize the damage and set the world right once again. This is a spell designed to help do just that.

For this spell you will need:
- pictures of some of the damage done (these can easily be found on the Internet or newspapers—there is never a shortage of footage covering a disaster of some kind)
- a bowl of water
- a bowl of soil
- a green candle
- a place outside to do this spell
- some type of outdoor fire (use a charcoal grill if you have to)
- as many natural items as possible to decorate your altar—try to use items that represent the area where the disaster took place—for example, if the disaster took place in a tropical area, then add tropical plants or fruits to your altar (find the best representations you can)
- a small snack or something to eat for after the spell

Set up your altar outside and cast your circle.

Light the green candle and say:

Gaia, Mother Earth,
you have come to harm
at the hand of humankind.
You have been disrespected and unprotected.
I come to offer my hands, myself,
to aid in your healing.

Look at the pictures of the damage. Take it all in. Look past the pictures and really see into the actual damage. Recall reports of what you have heard. Let the full effect of the damage hit you even though it may hurt. Cry if you want. Feel that damage within you. See it with your mind's eye. Know there has been loss of life whether it was human, animal, or plant. Feel the damage as if it were coming out of the very ground around you. Feel the damage travel up from the ground through your body to your hands.

Take one hand and stick it into the bowl of water, and then place the other hand into the bowl of soil. Visualize the damage you feel leaving your body through your hands and going into the bowls of water and soil. You may see the water change colors, you may not. Continue to pour the damage into these two bowls. Feel your body ridding itself of the pain, the destruction, the debris.

When the energy runs clear, take a moment and sit on the ground, legs out in front of you, hands down at your sides, but firmly planted on the ground. Feel positive, clean, good energy coming into you from above and go out through you down below. You are recharging the earth. Take the good energy from above and send it down deep into the earth. Imagine where it needs to go, where it needs to travel to. Send it on its way to the place where the damage happened. Imagine it going through the earth until it arrives at its final destination where it swirls from the ground (or water) and begins repairing the environment around it.

Continue this energy flow until you start to feel tired. Stand up and close your circle.

Take the bowl of soil and pour it on the fire, slowly and carefully. You don't want it to extinguish the fire completely, so make sure you do it slowly. Next, do the same with the water, extinguishing the fire.

You are a conduit for this spell and it will probably tire you out quite a bit by the time you are done. Eat your small snack and take a short nap to refresh yourself.

This spell is best performed under a full moon, but don't let the moon phase stop you from performing it.

An extreme natural disaster has occurred

Uncontrollable flooding in California and Australia; mudslides; Hurricane Katrina; the eruption of the Icelandic volcano Eyjafjallajökull; earthquakes in Haiti, China, and Peru; tsunamis in Indonesia and Japan—all these traumatic events were the result of extreme natural disasters. In some of these events, the loss of life was astounding. In other events, while the loss of life was small, the damage to property, or loss of income was tantamount.

When these kinds of events occur, it can take years for things to return to how they once were. Hauling away rubble and debris, rebuilding—these things take time and money. Sometimes there may be plenty of time, but no money for rebuilding. Sometimes there just isn't the manpower. Sometimes, people don't want to start over. They pack up what few belongings are left behind and head off to look for a new future, a new home.

When something like this happens, the entire area where the disaster took place needs healing. The earth needs healing, the people who survived need healing, the souls of the people who did not survive need to be released and allowed to move on. With some of these disasters, such as the 2004 Indian Ocean tsunami, many bodies were never found. People were washed away, never to be heard from again.

These events are terrible tragedies and no matter what caused them (as some people like to argue that these things happen to punish people) the loss is profound.

This is a spell for helping heal the people and the earth after a natural disaster. This spell should be done outside under the full moon if you can; it can be done anytime.

For this spell you will need:

- a bonfire (or fire in an outdoor fireplace
  or similar container—a charcoal grill is fine)
- a small globe
- something to represent the disaster (if it was a flood a bowl
  of water, earthquake could be symbolized with sand and
  broken rocks, etc. Whatever you pick will go into the fire,
  so do not pick something you want to keep)
- a couple of handfuls of salt in a glass bowl

Set up your altar as close to the fire as you can. Include the fire in your circle.

Take the globe in your hands and say:

Mother Earth has been ravaged,
by Mother Nature.
Death and destruction result.
I come tonight under the moon
to give assistance in healing the earth,
and all those touched by this disaster.

Place the globe in the bowl with the salt and roll the globe around in it. Say:

The salt cleanses away the hurt, the pain,
the suffering, the debris.
The salt purifies to start anew.

Set the globe in a secure location on your altar where it won't be able to roll. Take a handful of the salt and toss it into the fire. Say:

The fire cleanses away the hurt, the pain,
the suffering, the debris.
The fire purifies to start anew.

Pick up your item that represents the disaster and say:

This (item name) represents (disaster name).
Though it is over and has passed,
the damage left in its path is incredible and intense.
Mighty fire,
burn away the past,
and forge a new future.

Carefully pour or toss the representation into the fire. If your representation happens to be water, pour it slowly and carefully enough that it will not extinguish your fire. You want the fire to consume as much of the representation as possible.

Take another handful of the salt and toss it into the fire. Say:

The fire cleanses away the hurt, the pain,
the suffering, the debris.
The fire purifies to start anew.

Visualize the healing process beginning. Because these events can take a long time to recover from, don't try to visualize the entire process at once. You can take several weeks to work on this spell, visualizing the healing process getting further along each time. Healing can't be rushed, but it can be helped along.

When you are done visualizing, say:

To all those gone,
your souls may move on.
To all those left behind,
your hearts may move on.
Mother Earth and Mother Nature,
join together and allow the healing to begin.

Close your circle.

These kinds of spells can be backed up in the mundane world in different ways such as donations to help disaster victims, volunteering your time, or even donating blood through organizations like the Red Cross. Just do whatever you can to help.

Spell for a country (or other area)
at war (or in other conflict)

I admit that while writing this book, this particular issue wasn't something I had originally thought to include. In fact, it wasn't until I was almost finished that the thought even crossed my mind. However, a friend of mine, Rebecca, had recently returned from Tunisia, and her husband was in the process of finishing his paperwork to come to America himself when turmoil struck his country.

Known as the Tunisian protests, Tunisian Revolution, or the 2010–2011 Tunisian Uprising, angry people took to the streets protesting and eventually ousting their president, Zine El Abidine Ben Ali. I don't want to get too far into the history of this event, but I would like to point out that during this revolution, many people were injured and killed. Right after this happened, we saw similar events in other countries taking place in a wave of revolutionary demonstrations now being called the "Arab Spring." While this was going on, Rebecca sat at home in northern Illinois worrying day in and day out about her husband and his family's safety.

We often think we have it tough, but to realize that someone you know and care for is in mortal danger simply because of where they live is astounding. Every day, Rebecca would wait for her husband to call to let her know they made it through another day. There were days he could glance out his window and see people with machine guns walking by.

Yes, the families of people in the military often have to worry about situations like this, but there is a difference. For starters, this was not an actual military action when it started. This was started by the people of Tunisia. No invading military force came in to try to conquer them and it wasn't a war with another country. This was a war within a country. Most of the people involved had no military experience whatsoever.

We have seen events such as this all around the world. People—often innocent people who happen to be in the wrong place at the wrong time—are killed left and right.

No matter the cause or reasons why, these kind of events are devastating. Each person injured or killed is a life that was tragically ended. Imagine the next time you are standing in line for a latte at a coffee shop what it would be like if all of a sudden an angry crowd with weapons came around the corner followed by tanks and soldiers with machine guns. At the other end of the street are people dressed in everyday clothes, t-shirts and blue jeans, yet they are armed with rifles, machetes, and machine guns themselves. And you? You are trapped in a store between these groups.

You can imagine the fear my friend had for her husband and his family. Any of us would feel the same. Any of us would be scared half to death.

This spell is to help anyone connected to a violent conflict on a large scale. It is a call for the violence to end. It is a call for the end of murder. It is a call for civility and for peace and rationalism. It is a tall order, no doubt. This is exactly the reason why when these types of events happen, we must pull together and send our voices and our energies out into the universe together to work for better days. Therefore, I highly suggest when working a spell of this magnitude to call together everyone you can for help. The more people sending their energies out into the universe, the more we can expect change to take place.

For this spell you will need:

- an outdoor area
- a large bowl of salt
- a map or picture of the affected area (it doesn't have to be detailed, just something that shows where it is and what it looks like—an outline of the country or state will do)
- at least three accounts of the violence (you can print articles from the Internet—these will be burned; if you are working with a group, make sure each person has at least one account)
- a small bonfire or other small fire (such as an outdoor fireplace)
- a drum and drummer (optional)
- food and drink for grounding afterwards

Set up your altar and cast the circle with the fire inside.

Have someone walk the circle three times while holding the picture or map of the area so everyone can see it. If you are doing the spell by yourself, walk the circle holding it so you can see the picture. While walking, everyone should chant:

> *Peace to this land,*
> *peace to this land,*
> *oh Great Goddess,*
> *bring peace to this land.*

Hand out the accounts of the violence so that each person has one. They should hold the account in their right hand and take a handful of salt in their left hand. Work going clockwise around the circle. Each person will step toward the fire, and first toss the account into the fire, followed by the handful of salt. As this is done, each person should say:

> *The violence must come to an end.*
> *Purify these people,*
> *purify their land.*

If you are doing this spell on your own, simply do the chant, accounts, and salt one at a time—one account burned with a handful of salt, followed by another account and another handful, until you have done at least three. Feel free to do more if you like.

Next, everyone should hold hands around the fire and chant:

> *Heal the people.*
> *Heal the land.*
> *Bring peace to the people.*
> *Bring peace to the land.*

Continue this chant over and over, feel the power build. If you have someone who can drum along with you as you chant, even better. Continue to build the power until you (or your group) feels ready to release it. Release the power into the universe.

This spell will probably take at least a half an hour to complete, depending on how many people participate and how long you can build the power before releasing it.

Make sure to take plenty of time to ground with your food and drink after this spell is finished.

Spell to help heal after a tragic national event

The difference between this spell and the previous one is largely the duration of the event. Though just as tragic, these are quick events and not drawn-out, longer-term battles. In America, these type of events include the Oklahoma City bombing and the Columbine High School shootings. In other countries were the Madrid subway bombings, the Mumbai attacks, and the Moscow Domodedovo Airport bombing.

These events happened quickly and were able to bring the people of their countries together to support the community and people involved in the tragedy.

Other events brought large portions of the world to their knees—all at the same time. The attacks on September 11th occurred in America, but hundreds of people from other countries were killed. News of the attack on America affected many parts of the world as well. Other tragic events that have garnered worldwide concern and mourning include the Chilean miner rescue (though this event did take a while to complete and had better than expected results—it drew the world's attention as people joined together in hope) and the shooting rampage in Norway. By the time we know about these events, they are usually already over. The event itself happens quickly, and the real suffering follows. Families and communities have to pick up the pieces and start over.

This is where this spell comes in: it is to help those recover and heal after a tragedy has occurred. This spell is ideal for a group, and it should be worked outside. The more people you can pull together to work this spell, the more energy you can charge for your purpose and send out into the universe.

For this spell you will need:

- an outdoor location with some type of contained fire
  (such as a bonfire or pit)
- wooden or glass bowls
- a drum and drummer (optional)
- food and drink for grounding afterwards

Any of the following herbs/plants/oils:

- allspice, angelica, balm of Gilead, bramble, buckthorn,
  burdock, carnation, cedar, coriander, cypress, elder,
  eucalyptus, gardenia, ginseng, honeysuckle, hops, horehound,
  hyacinth, lavender, lemon, lily, mistletoe, myrrh, nettle,
  pine, rue, sage, spearmint, vervain, violet, witch hazel,
  or yerba santa

Set up an altar. Use wooden or glass bowls to hold the herbs/plants/oils you will be using. The bowls may be placed in a circle around the fire on the ground. Put only one type of item in each bowl—do not mix them.

Cast a circle that encloses the fire.

Most of this spell will be chanting. If you are working it with a group, each person will pick up a bowl and take it closer to the fire where he or she can scoop out a handful and toss it into the fire. All the listed ingredients help with healing and coping with the sadness of loss.

You don't need to stop the chanting to throw a handful into the fire; keep the chanting going as each person takes a turn until all the bowls are empty. If you are doing this spell on your own, you will chant and toss each herb into the fire.

Once you are ready, begin with the following:

A great tragedy has taken place,
a sadness throughout the nation.
(take a moment now to briefly
describe the event)
We/I come tonight to join with others elsewhere,
to send healing energies to those who were injured,
and to the families and friends of those who were killed.
We/I come tonight to join with others elsewhere,
to send our strength, our compassion,
our prayers, our love
to those who tonight
are in need.

If you have someone who can drum, he or she should now start a slow beat for starting the chant.

Heal this land.
Heal this land.
Oh Great Goddess,
please heal this land.

Peace to this land.
Peace to this land.
Oh Great Goddess,
bring peace to this land.

As the power builds, both the drummer and the chanting should speed up to match the energy. Make sure everyone is taking turns throwing the healing herbs into the fire. When the herbs are all gone and when your group feels the energy is at its apex, hurl it out into the universe.

After releasing the energy, spend plenty of time grounding.

Part Eleven

★ ★ ★ ★

DEATH

*T*his section is going to deal with different aspects of death along with spells to help you deal with the grief you will suffer after losing a loved one.

You will notice some of these chapters are broken down according to the relationship you had with the deceased person. The reason for these different distinctions is because different relationships will bring about different feelings and types of pain when someone dies. No matter what the relationship, death hurts those of us who are left behind.

Generally speaking, most people will someday bury their own parents. Though it is not a pleasant thought, it is simply how the world works. It is often in the cards that we will indeed outlive the people who gave us life. We have lost the person who raised us and the person who helped to protect us. Parents taught us right from wrong among many other things. The loss of a parent is one type of pain.

Married people (or other romantically involved people) have a great chance of burying their partner. Everyone dies, and unless you and your partner die at the same time, one of you will outlive the other. Age and health (among other factors) may change the likelihood, but for the most part, people realize either they will bury their partner or their partner will be burying them.

Your partner is also just that—your partner. You have a completely different type of relationship with this person that what you had with your parents and so when you lose your partner, it is a whole different type of pain.

Losing a child has often been described as the most traumatic experience a person can have. It is at the top of the list of "most stressful life events." People do not expect to have to bury their own child. They expect to raise their children and protect them the best they can for their entire life. Parents expect their child will have to bury them someday—not the other way around. Parents often feel guilty for outliving a deceased child. They may feel they didn't do enough to protect their child or that they have failed. This type of death brings along several other types of pain with it.

Losing your best friend is another completely different type of pain. This person may have been your spouse or life partner, but for our purposes we will assume your best friend was someone with whom you shared a purely platonic relationship.

Not everyone has a spouse or other type of romantic partner, but almost everyone has that one friend who means more to them than all the others. This person may have been your confidant, your conscience, or even your partner in crime. When all of that is taken away, the pain you experience is unique.

Since an entire book could be written on this subject alone, I have included only a few spells that cover relationships with people you are probably closest to. Each of these spells will not only deal with the actual grieving process over the specific death, they will also deal with the particular types of loss often associated with each situation. After those, there will be a few more spells that deal with other problems that often surface following a loved one's death.

I want to point out that none of these spells is designed to stop you from grieving. The grieving process is extremely important—you work through the loss and any other issues that may arise. These spells won't stop your grieving, but they will help aid you in the grieving process. For each person this may be something different: for one it may mean the spell will help you get out of bed in the morning and go about your daily life as you used to, only now you are doing it alone instead of with someone by your side. For others it may simply give you a chance to cry and mourn in a private and safe location. Each person's needs are different, so you will get what you need from these spells to eventually be able to move on with your life.

Most importantly remember that there is no time limit on how long you have to grieve. If you believe your grieving process has been going on for a long time and you don't feel like you are doing any better, talk to a mental health professional or a professional grief counselor—they are there for you (but don't rush yourself through it because you think you "should"). Some people may go through the process faster than others; it's not a race. You will deal with your loss as it suits you. The important thing is that you do deal with it and don't try to shove it out of the way because you think you should be strong enough to deal with it. Take your time. Celebrate the life, cherish the love, and mourn the loss.

Finally, for anyone in need of the spells in this section, please allow me to say that I am truly sorry for your loss. I have buried many people in my lifetime (six alone in the time it took me to write this book). I am sympathetic to your loss and pain.

My spouse has passed away

I thank the Goddess frequently I have not had to deal with this type of death, though I know because my husband is seven years older than me, chances are I will bury him someday rather than the other way around. My husband and I have talked openly about what each of us wants when it comes to our funerals, which helps make the actual service part of our passing easier to deal with. That being said, getting through a funeral service and getting through life after that service are two completely different things.

I highly encourage you and your significant other to discuss what you each want done after you die while you both are still healthy and alive. Often a person wants to be able to provide the kind of farewell their spouse wanted, but doesn't know where to begin because the matter was never discussed. If these things are planned out ahead of time, it can help make the transition easier for those left behind. A funeral is the last chance you have to do something for your significant other, and so people strive to do the most perfect service they can. Knowing what the other person actually wants is a key factor. So go ahead, have the discussion while you still can.

Something else you may want to consider is leaving your spouse a letter to read after you have passed away. If you lay out plans now to follow after your death, you can write your significant other a letter to read while they are performing this spell to aid them in their time of grief. This may sound morbid, but if you really think about it, I believe you will see what a gift this can be for your survivors. Your last words are your last gift to those you loved. In a similar way, the service prepared is the last gift for the departed.

This spell can be performed whenever you feel you need it; it is for you, the survivor. It can be done before a funeral, after a funeral, every anniversary of your spouse's death, whenever you are feeling overwhelmed with grief and need the release, or feel the need to connect once again with the relationship you and your spouse once had.

For this spell you will need:
- a fireproof container, charcoal tablet and lighter
- frankincense resin for spirituality and meditation
- myrrh resin for spirituality and healing
- hyacinth oil to help you overcome grief (while grief is
  a necessary part of the healing process, you do not want
  to become completely consumed by it either)
- a picture of your spouse (if you like)

Set up your altar and cast your circle.

Light the charcoal tablet and sprinkle a bit of frankincense resin on it. Experience the scent of the frankincense as the smoke swirls into the air. Take a couple of deep breaths and relax your body and mind. Give yourself a moment or two to calm your mind. Say the following:

> (Spouse's name) *has gone on ahead,*
> *and left me here behind.*
> *Though he/she is gone from my sight*
> *he/she is forever in my mind.*
> *My days and nights are no longer the same,*
> *with my love gone away.*
> *The pain ebbs and flows,*
> *with some days worse than others.*
> *My strength comes and goes.*

Sprinkle some myrrh resin onto the charcoal tablet. Allow yourself to experience the scent of the myrrh. Say the following:

> *Today my strength is waning.*
> *Today my spirit is broken.*
> *Today my heart needs healing.*
> *Today I need help putting the pieces back together again.*

Take your time with this spell. Chances are you may become very emotional, which is fine and should be expected. You are mourning the loss of a great love, you aren't expected to not show any feelings. Take a moment now to say anything you want to say, anything you may have kept bottled up. Do you have something you want to say to your spouse? Maybe there was something left unsaid between the two of you. Maybe you just want to tell your spouse what has been going on in your life since his or her passing. Sometimes you will feel better just knowing you can still talk to your loved one. He/ She might not be able to answer back, but you can still talk to your spouse and unburden yourself, or simply know that he/she is listening to whatever it is you have to say.

After you say anything that you want to say, take the hyacinth oil and sprinkle a few drops onto the lit charcoal tablet. Say:

I ask for the Goddess to ease my pain,
to take some of my suffering away.
I have lost my partner,
my lover,
my other half.
Allow me to overcome my grief,
to be able to go on
at the end of each day.
Keep me safe through each night
and wake me with your guiding light.

Take a few more minutes to meditate and if you want, speak to your Goddess about the loss you feel. The situation you are in is very personal, so feel free to add whatever personal details you would like. This may be extremely difficult to do at first. It may be hard to know what you want to say. It may be difficult to put your feelings into words. This is fine. Take your time. If you can't say everything you want to say this time, that is okay. You can perform this spell again whenever you want to. Put into it whatever you need to and you'll be able to take out what you need as well.

When you are ready to move on, again say:

Allow me to overcome my grief,
to be able to go on
at the end of each day.
Keep me safe through each night
and wake me with your guiding light.

And add:

So mote it be.

It is okay to perform this spell frequently, as long as you aren't spending hours on it every day. If you find yourself spending more and more time instead of less as time goes on, you may be slipping into a clinical depression and will want to talk to a mental health professional to help you through this time. While there is no prescribed amount of time to mourn in a situation such as this, it is also important to remember that for the survivors, life does go on. We do have to carry on with our lives. While our pain may never completely go away, we do learn how to use it and look at it in different ways that can help us go on with our own lives.

My parent passed away

While this is something just about everyone will have to deal with at some point in their life, the knowledge doesn't necessarily make the pain any less difficult to deal with. Often it depends when and how your parent passes away.

My own mother died at the age of forty-eight when I was only eight years old. As a child, was I anywhere near prepared to say goodbye to my mother at that age? Of course not.

My father is still alive at eighty-three. We recently buried his sister, who was ninety-three at the time. While her children were of course upset that she had died, it was a peaceful death. She had children, grandchildren, and even a couple of great-grandchildren. She was no longer suffering and had lived a very long, happy life, for which her children were grateful. She had literally outlived all of her friends and much of her family. Her siblings and descendents were left, but her parents, uncles, aunts, cousins—all had already passed on.

Often for the survivors, knowing how the person lived makes a difference in the pain they experience. It is still a loss, but knowing someone lived a long, fulfilling life is often less tragic and painful than when a person dies at a young age—when, as I've heard some people put it, they still had a lot of life left to live.

We expect our parents to live to a ripe old age and while many of them do just that, some don't. This often does make their death harder to accept, but accept it we must. There is no changing death. It happens when it happens, and we must learn to adjust.

This spell will help you say goodbye when one of your parents has crossed over the great divide.

For this spell you will need:
- dried yew shavings for funeral rites
- frankincense resin for spirituality
- hyacinth oil for overcoming grief
- a chime size candle to represent your parent—
  the color choice is up to you
- a fireproof container, charcoal tablet, and lighter

Set up your altar and cast your circle. Light the charcoal tablet in the fireproof container.

Hold the candle in your hand and say:

> *This candle represents my mother/father.*
> *As the flame burns,*
> *it represents the life my mother/father lived.*

Light the candle and say:

> *As the flame burns longer,*
> *the life of the candle grows shorter,*
> *until eventually, it will burn completely away.*

Place the candle on the altar.
Sprinkle the yew shavings onto the lit charcoal and say:

> *I come today*
> *to ask for aid in helping to lay my mother/father to rest.*
> *He/she has departed from this world*
> *and gone on ahead.*
> *Though he/she is no longer with me,*
> *his/her memory will forever linger.*

Sprinkle some frankincense resin on to the lit charcoal and say:

> *I ask my Lord and my Lady,*
> *to take my mother/father*
> *into their loving embrace.*
> *Love him/her and guide him/her*
> *as he/she did for me for so very long.*
> *Connect with him/her,*
> *and bring him/her peace.*
> *Knowing my parent is in the*
> *care of the divine,*
> *my heart and mind may also rest at peace.*

Finally, sprinkle a few drops of hyacinth oil onto the charcoal and say:

My sadness will someday be curbed,
but for now I will let the tears flow.
I take this time to grieve my loss
so that I may eventually overcome the pain I feel.
I must first grieve in order to move on.
Let the sadness wash over and through me,
so that soon my heart can begin to mend.

Take some time to meditate or to send a message out to your parent. Was there something you always wanted to say but never got the chance? Go ahead and do it now. Take as much time as you need to meditate, speak with your parent, or even cry. Do not extinguish the candle yourself, allow the candle to burn out on its own. When it has, go ahead and close your circle.

Repeat this spell if you feel you need to.

My child passed away

I came very close to needing this spell myself this past year, and it was a huge eye-opener for me. While my parents have had to bury a son and a daughter, I was lucky as my child survived his ordeal. Unfortunately, friends of mine were not as lucky. A dear friend, Nancy, lost her son earlier this year; this spell was written with her in mind.

The death of a child is often described as the most stressful, most traumatic event that can happen in a person's life. I know how awful I felt when I received the phone call that my son was in the ICU and they didn't know if he was going to make it or not. I will not insult someone who has lost their child by claiming to know how he or she feels. I have a small taste of how bad it must be, but my child lived. I'm sure what I went through can't possibly compare to what it is like to have your child's life ripped from you.

Going through this difficult time in your life, you may not feel much like doing a spell at all. You may even be angry at your deities, wondering why they let this happen. You may blame them. This spell is for when you are ready. It's short and to the point with no preparation because, quite honestly, you have enough on your mind right already. You don't need to be worrying about whether or not you have the right color candles or the right type of incense. This spell isn't about *things*. It is about your child, you, and your loss.

To perform this spell, find a comfortable location and position, and cast your circle.

Begin by saying:

My son/daughter, (name),
has gone on ahead,
leaving me and our family behind.
Our loss is felt daily.
The pain cannot subside,
nor be numbed.
I must work through it,
in my own time,
in my own way.
The pain is mine,
to do with as I will.

This is your time to mourn. You probably wish right about now that the world would just stop spinning. That time could just stop so you can take the time you need to heal. While I can't make the world stop for you, I can help you take this time to mourn as you need. Perhaps you had to go back to work before you were really ready, not only to keep your job but also to prevent placing your family in jeopardy, making them suffer even more. Now you need to take advantage of the time you have available to mourn and just let it out. Meditate if you want. Cry if you want. Talk to your child if you want. Whatever it is you need at this point, go ahead now and do it. Are you angry with the Gods? Let them know. This moment in the spell has been set aside for you to do whatever it is *you* feel you need to do.

If you want, this is a spell you can also perform in the shower, as you may find it helpful to wash away some of the pain. You may want to hold on to the pain for a while; hold on to it and use it to do what you need to do in order to continue. Some parents use their pain to start scholarship foundations or to change laws—something that helps keep their child's death from being in vain.

Use the time given in this spell to think about your options, future, and what you are going to do next. Know deep down that someday it will be easier to deal with. Someday, it will be easier to accept that your child is gone. That day does not have to be today. It can be if you are ready, but you alone make that decision.

When you are done with your thoughts for the day, close your circle.

This spell can be performed as often as needed. It is a spell to allow you to feel how you need to feel. Each time you perform this spell, you will most likely focus on something different during your meditation time. Some days you will find you are rehashing ground you already covered. You may come up with a different solution this time. If you find yourself going over the same ground repeatedly with the same results, you will know it is time for you to move on to something new. Some things we will never be able to change; wisdom comes when we realize that.

My best friend passed away

When I originally wrote this spell, my best friend was still alive. A matter of days later, she wasn't. Her name was Charm and though she had lived here in America for just over twenty years, she was Jamaican. We met while we were in college together. Charm died suddenly from undiagnosed diabetes. Her only symptoms started two days before her death; she thought she had the flu. By the time her family called for an ambulance, it was too late—she died moments after arriving at the hospital.

I was devastated. This woman was the most giving, tolerant woman I have ever known, and suddenly she was ripped away from us all. Her two young daughters will now grow up without their wonderful mother. Her death set me into a shock that lasted for days, and I am sure I will never totally recover from this loss. She was my sister, my friend.

Your best friend may be your spouse, or it may be the kid from across the street you grew up with and have known since you were six years old. It may be someone who was in all of your high school classes and fate brought you together. Maybe you didn't meet your best friend until college or even later in life. But this person knows everything there is to know about you. Sometimes you feel like they know you better than you even know yourself. You've been through everything together, thick and thin. But now you have to go through his/her death alone. The one person you could always count on to help you get through the rough spots in life has gone from being your support network to being the rough spot.

Chances are you feel pretty alone right now. When suddenly that one person you've always counted on is gone, you can feel confused and unsure of where to turn. Now you have to learn to be strong on your own, while you say goodbye to this important part of your life.

This spell is going to help give you strength while you say goodbye to your dear friend.

For this spell you will need:
• a blue candle to represent honor and your friend
• an apple

Set up your altar and cast your circle.

Light the blue candle and say:

> *This candle represents (name),*
> *as I come today to pay respects,*
> *and honor his/her name.*

Take the apple in both hands and say:

> *Always by my side,*
> *I now feel the loss of you.*
> *This apple represents our strengths together.*
> *With you, I was always stronger.*
> *Now without you,*
> *I must go on alone and mourn you.*
> *The loss of the sound of your voice,*
> *your laughter,*
> *it is almost more than I can bear.*
> *Your passion, your strength, your friendship,*
> *have helped to make me who I am*
> *and for that I thank you.*
> *As I eat this apple,*
> *I eat of the life we shared,*
> *I take in your strength,*
> *and claim it as my own.*

Take your time and eat the apple. As you eat the apple, think of your friend and how you can help his or her memory live on by incorporating aspects of his/her memory, life, personality, into your own. As you say goodbye to your friend, take a part of them with you. Meditate for a while on the life of your friend. What did you admire most about him/her? Take this with you. Add this to your life as a way to honor your friend and to keep his or her spirit alive with you. Say goodbye for now, but know that you can always talk to your friend whenever you need to. All you need to do is listen a little deeper for an answer. When you are done, go ahead and close your circle.

Supplemental spell for suicidal deaths

Though the spell after this one deals specifically with a child's friend who committed suicide, this spell is designed to add to the previous spells in this section if your loved one who has passed on did so by his or her own hand.

Often in the case of suicide, those who are left behind experience a whole added range of emotions on top of those already felt when someone is lost. You may be extremely angry or guilty for not being able to help this person—to prevent him or her from taking their own life. You may have no explanation for why this person decided to end his or her life in the first place and may have many unanswerable questions. You want to know why, you want to know what you could have done to prevent this, you want to know if there *was* any way to prevent this. You are over-burdened with emotions and must reach a point where you can accept what has happened and that the situation was out of your control.

This spell can be added to any of the other spells in this section. You do not need any additional components, just add these words in where you feel it is the most comfortable for you—whether that is at the beginning of the spell or the end is up to you.

When you are ready, say the following:

My loved one (name),
has gone on ahead,
and left the rest of us behind.
He/she made this decision on his/her own,
and took his/her life on his/her own.
While I cannot condone
or understand this decision,
I ask the Lord and Lady
to help me accept what has been done.
Alleviate my anger, my guilt, my pain,
so that I may continue,
and (loved one's name) may rest in peace.

Take some time to meditate. Tell the person you have lost how you feel about the action he/she took. It is okay to be angry and hurt, or to feel guilty at this point. Recovery will take some time. Admitting your feelings to yourself and getting them out there where you can deal with them is the first step. Take all the time you need to complete this part of the spell. When you are done, finish with:

Lord and Lady,
I thank thee for your support,
your compassion,
and your love.
My heart will someday mend.
Thank you.

My child's friend committed suicide

If you have been paying attention to national news at all, you have probably noticed the extreme increase in publicized suicides of young people who have taken their own lives as a result of bullying in one form or another.

Though we live in a small rural community far away from large metro areas like Chicago, our town was struck by just such a tragedy.

The victim was a young man, just three months away from graduating high school. He simply couldn't take the abuse from his peers any more. Unlike some cases, the kids who taunted, teased, and physically abused this boy were never charged. They were never arrested or punished for their crimes. The school claimed no knowledge of any problem, though the boy's parents had called dozens of times. They were ignored while the bullies were protected. In the end, an innocent child lost his life.

This child was friends with some of my children. When the news story broke and a local affiliate station covered it, my daughter was one of the people interviewed about this tragic death.

I will be the first person to say that my daughter is probably stronger than a lot of kids her age. She stood up to the school and went on television saying that what had happened was wrong—that if the school had done the right thing and punished the perpetrators instead of letting them go time and time again, her friend would still be alive. The school's response again was simply, "We don't know what you're talking about." Somehow, they decided that feigning ignorance was the best way for an institution of learning to deal with the problem.

But what happens when something like this happens to your child? How can you help him or her cope when they burst into your room one night crying that someone their age is dead? Death is always tragic; death of a young person is worse. When a death occurs because the person felt there was no way to continue living, it is utterly unbearable.

You can do this spell with your child to help get him or her through this terrible time. While you can't take away the pain, you can let your child know you are there for them, and help lighten their load a bit.

For this spell you will need:
• a purple candle for spirituality and inner strength
• lavender incense to bring your child some peace

Set up your altar and cast your circle with your child.

Begin by lighting the candle. Say:

> *My child and I come today*
> *to share together his/her pain.*
> *We come together to*
> *ask for strength for* (child's name),
> *while he/she deals with the death of* (friend's name).

Light the incense and say:

> (Your child's name) *is in great pain*
> *over the loss of* (friend's name).
> *Help* (your child's name) *to understand*
> *the choice his/her friend made*
> *was their choice alone,*
> *No one else must ever suffer the same.*

At this time, encourage your child to say something if they would like. They may be having anger issues, denial issues, questions as to why; whatever it is they want to say allow them this time to say it. Let them get their feelings out into the open. Give them as much time as they need.

When your child is finished speaking, pick up the incense stick and waft it around you child's body. As you go, say:

> *Allow this lavender to purify you,*
> *to bring you peace*
> *and understanding.*
> *Allow your heart time to heal,*
> *to become whole once again.*

Chant this a minimum of three times; you may do it more if you want. When you are done, close your circle and give your child a big hug. Let him or her know you will be there in the coming days ahead.

I've been diagnosed with a terminal illness

The good news is that you are still alive. Being diagnosed with a terminal illness ... well, let's be completely honest—it would just downright suck. Fortunately, sometimes doctors are wrong. Unfortunately, they often aren't. There is one major important thing most people forget—we are all going to die someday. We just don't have any idea when so we often put it out of our minds. People who have been diagnosed with a terminal illness have their mortality brought before them in a profound way.

We say it's a terrible thing to be diagnosed with a terminal illness, we feel sorry for ourselves knowing that the end is coming near and that we may end up having many bad days ahead. Why on earth does it take a doctor telling us we have a disease that will kill us to realize this is true of everyone already? The only difference being diagnosed with an illness is that it gives us a somewhat shorter timeline. We all really are going to die someday; no one lives forever.

The fact that we are each going to die generally doesn't hit us until that mortality jumps up and down in front of us, waving its arms around screaming "Look at me! I'm here! Right here!"

By many different means, any one of us could literally die tomorrow, but we don't think about that. We go through each day thinking our lives will go on for decades. We put off doing things today we could do tomorrow, but what happens if tomorrow never comes?

If you've been diagnosed with a terminal illness, you've been given a new kind of sight. The sight that sees tomorrow isn't always the answer because tomorrow isn't always there. We need to stop putting things off until tomorrow. We need to look through the eyes of someone who already knows that tomorrow may never arrive.

So what exactly is the point of this spell? This spell is to ask for healing for you, and it will also help give you strength—not just the physical kind, but strength and ambition to live each day to the fullest, and as if it is your last. You may have had many things you wanted to do in life—a bucket list. Now is the time to go through that list, revise it, and start completing as many items as you possibly can.

People in this situation often give up the will to live. They don't fight the illness, they don't get treatments, and they don't attempt to achieve any of their life's goals. Don't let this happen to you. Embrace the time you have left. Make the most of every moment. Be glad that you have been given the warning that time may soon be at an end, but also take that time to fully live your life.

This spell is best performed on a Sunday for strength—you might want to use it as a way to start your week, but by all means if you feel you need it more often, don't wait a full week before performing it again.

For this spell you will need:
- an agate stone for strength, protection, and courage
- a cauldron or other large pot
- a fire source (a stove or another open flame)
- water (moon water if you have it, see p. 4)

One each of the following candles:
- black for absorbing negative energy
- green for healing
- blue for protection and healing
- brown for strength, endurance, and grace

The following herbs:
- allspice for healing
- bay leaves for healing
- bergamot for physical energy
- black pepper for physical energy, protection, and courage
- blessed thistle for protection
- bluebell for strength
- bramble for healing
- burdock for healing and protection
- carnation for protection, strength, healing, and physical energy
- cedar for healing, protection, and courage
- clove for protection, healing, and courage
- dragon's blood for protection and to amplify the spell's power
- garlic for protection, physical energy, and healing
- ginseng for healing, vitality, and protection
- horehound for protection, healing, and banishing negative energies

- mistletoe for protection and healing
- nettle for protection, healing, and banishing negative energies
- sweet pea for courage and strength

Combine as many as these ingredients together as possible; the more you use, the stronger your potion will be. I recommend combining a large batch of this together at once and then use a little each time you perform the spell.

Cast your circle wherever your heat source is—for example, if you are going to use a stove in this spell, cast your circle in the kitchen.

Place the pot or cauldron on the heat source. Add a cup of water to the cauldron. Next add a heaping tablespoon of the mixture you made to the water. While the water begins to heat and the herbs steep, light the candles and begin a chant.

Light the black candle. Say:

> *This candle I light to banish the negativity from my life.*
> *So easy would it be now to let the negativity*
> *take over and consume me.*
> *I light this candle to burn it away and keep*
> *brightness and light in my life.*

Next light the blue candle. Say:

> *I ask my Lord and my Lady to wrap*
> *me in your protective arms,*
> *keep me safe until my days come to an end.*
> *Allow me the chance to live each day to the fullest.*
> *Heal my body, mind, and soul.*
> *My existence is in your hands.*

Light the green candle and say:

> *Lord and Lady, bless me with your healing grace.*

Light the brown candle and say:

> *Lord and Lady, grant me strength and endurance,*
> *and when my time does come, allow me to*
> *accept my end with grace.*

After all the candles are lit, stir the mixture in your cauldron. You don't need the water to actually boil, but you do want it to steep a lot of the plant essence into the water. Make sure you give it at least a few minutes once the water starts heating and steaming. As you wait, chant the following:

> *These herbs I combine together*
> *to make a potion strong;*
> *to give me strength and courage,*
> *and protect me all along.*
> *This fight I fight is difficult*
> *as my days draw near an end;*
> *the Lord and Lady comfort me*
> *and I pray my soul to mend.*

When the water is dark and hot, carefully remove the cauldron/pot from the heat. Take the agate stone and say:

> *I charge this stone with power*
> *to keep me through my days;*
> *to heal and protect me*
> *through the Goddess*
> *and her ways.*

Drop the stone into the herb and water mixture. While the water cools, take time to meditate. Think about plans you need to make in order to accomplish what it is you want to do with the time you have left. Visualize yourself feeling well enough to be able do the things you want to do. Visualize your illness getting better or simply going away. Continue your meditation and visualization until the water has cooled.

Remove the agate from the water and allow it to dry. Extinguish your candles and close your circle. Carry the agate with you at all times. When you feel you need a boost of healing energy or courage, hold it close to your heart in your hands and take a moment to meditate.

Repeat this spell whenever you feel you need it or if you feel your agate needs to be cleansed and recharged.

I had a miscarriage

Shortly after I started writing this book, I was expecting six new babies to come into my life among family and friends. Unfortunately, by the time I got to this chapter, that number dwindled to just two. The others were all lost (including a set of twins) due to miscarriage. As the news kept coming in that a baby had been lost one after another, I felt devastated. I cried for the lives that wouldn't be. I cried for my family and friends who had lost the child or children they were so hoping and waiting for.

A miscarriage is a terrible, terrible ordeal. My own took place twenty years ago now, as I lost a child due to an ectopic pregnancy. It is something you wonder about for years. What happened? Why me? Why now? The depression a woman (and oftentimes her partner) feel afterwards can infiltrate every area of life. You see a child walking down the street and your mind immediately thinks of the child you won't be walking next to.

Even though you had not yet given birth, when a child is planned and wanted and desired more than anything, from the moment you confirm you are pregnant, the child has existed for you. You have thought of names, you may have planned his or her room, you have already probably wondered what he or she will look and sound like, and what kinds of things they will do when they grow up. In just a short amount of time, you have made plans, become attached, and fallen in love. You would give your life for your child, and then suddenly, without having any say or being able to do anything to stop it, your child is gone, and you are left alone wondering why. You believe you were unable to protect your baby and save your child.

Many women feel it is their own fault when they have a miscarriage, and though it's true that sometimes actions such as smoking and drinking may have been a contributing factor, in the long run, something just wasn't right. This child just wasn't ready to be born yet for one reason or another—reasons that will probably never be known. In this situation, placing blame doesn't do a whole lot of good. Hard lessons can be learned, but even people in perfect health who have no risk factors whatsoever have still miscarried.

No matter what or why, the outcome is the same, and you have to learn how to put this behind you and go on with your life—easier said than done, I know. This spell will help you deal with your grief, pick up the pieces of your life and move on.

For this spell you will need:
- a red candle for willpower, courage, and strength
- a hematite stone for grounding, calming, physical strength, and healing (you can also use a hematite ring, bracelet, or necklace)
- cypress for comfort, healing, and for easing feelings of loss
- hyacinth oil for overcoming grief
- a fireproof container, charcoal tablet, and lighter

Set up your altar and cast your circle.

Dress the candle in the hyacinth oil. As you do so say:

> *I have experienced a profound lost,*
> *one that has broken my heart*
> *and torn my life to pieces.*
> *Guide me, Goddess,*
> *help me overcome my grief,*
> *reclaim my strength,*
> *find my courage to move on,*
> *and give me the will to live and love life again.*

Place the candle on the altar and light it.

Light the charcoal tablet in the fireproof container. Sprinkle some cypress on the tablet, and sit back and relax for a few moments. Take some deep breaths. Allow the feelings that have built up inside you to purge themselves from your system. The guilt, anger, sadness, all of it. Let it go. Let it lift from your soul and wrap itself in the cypress smoke. Visualize this happening. Watch the anger float away from you; watch the smoke encircle and carry it away from you, and dissipate into the air. Watch as each negative emotion is carried up and away from you. Cry if you want to. Let all the negative go. If you feel the need to scream and yell, go ahead and do it now. Purge all of the negativity, the sadness, the pain, the grief from your body, mind, and soul. This may take a while and that's fine. Add more cypress to the charcoal if needed. Spend as much time as you need. When you begin to feel lighter, more at ease, or simply exhausted, stop for the time being. Extinguish your candle and close your circle.

This is a spell you can repeat whenever you would like. Though you may feel better for a while, negativity has a way of sneaking up on us and you never know what might set it off again. You might see an adorable baby on television or a cute little infant outfit in a store; even a bunny rabbit can trigger these feelings. Pay attention to your feelings and mind your thoughts. When you feel the depression and pain closing in on you again, repeat the spell.

As always, with any type of traumatic situation, it is quite all right to find a mental health professional to talk to about your loss. If you need to seek therapy—do it! Use this spell to back up any work you do with your therapist.

There was a death in my family, and now everyone is fighting about the service and the will

My will is extremely specific for a good reason. Many years ago, I went with a friend, John, back to his family home after his mother unexpectedly passed away in her sleep. It was very difficult for the family—one day she was fine and the next, she simply didn't wake up. She didn't have a will and the family was unsure of her wishes about a service and burial. John's family was quite large; each member felt he or she felt they knew what she would have wanted, and of course they clashed. It made an already difficult situation even worse. There was arguing, fighting, and name calling. It left a bad taste in my mouth as an outsider. I can barely imagine how the actual family members felt. It didn't end there, unfortunately.

At the end of the funeral, family and friends all went to one of the daughters' houses to eat, and while we were there, we noticed several of the family members had disappeared. Their cars were gone and they had left without so much as a goodbye. John and I headed back to his parents' home, where we were staying. When we arrived, we were shocked to discover several of his sisters inside the house arguing with one another while carrying things out of the house—their mother's possessions. They hadn't even waited for the dirt to be piled on her coffin before they were back at her house grabbing everything they could get their hands on. The real kicker was that their father was still alive and still living in the house! These siblings didn't seem to care at all. They were taking everything of value or use. Jewelry, a television, a stereo, even the food out of the refrigerator. It was the most despicable display I had ever seen. Angrily, John grabbed the items from his sisters and threw them out of the house. Later that day he changed all of the locks on the house as well. Needless to say, he was disgusted and embarrassed—this was on top of the pain and shock he was already dealing with.

While this was (I hope) an extreme example, I'm sure similar arguments have happened in other families. I hope that having a detailed will helps eliminate any of these kinds of problems after I'm gone. I also hope my kids will be far more respectful and won't act like a bunch of greedy, insane people!

Unfortunately, you may find yourself in a situation where your siblings, cousins, or some other relatives are fighting because there wasn't a will, or they may contest a will that does exist. This spell is for those of you who aren't embroiled in the mess, and want to try to calm the rough seas around you. Death is difficult enough, how people act afterwards can make the loss significantly easier or harder to deal with. Use this spell to make it easier on everyone.

For this spell you will need:

- a brown candle for integrity, justice, neutrality, strength, grace, and family issues
- a brown piece of paper for the same attributes as above
- writing utensil
- fireproof container and lighter

Set up your altar and cast your circle.

Hold the brown candle in prayer hands. Say:

> *Life has gone awry and gotten out of hand.*
> *I light this candle so it will help bring me*
> *neutrality, strength, and grace*
> *while dealing with these family issues.*
> *Help to restore integrity and bring justice to this situation.*

Place the candle on your altar and light it.

Take a few moments to meditate on what has been going on with your family. Think about the way people have acted and how it has made you feel. Think about how you wish it was different. Think about how you would feel if things were different.

Take out the piece of paper and on the front side write down all the negative aspects you have just gone over in your mind—the way people are acting, the things they are fighting over, how bad it makes you feel. Try to be as specific as you can. When you are done with the negatives, turn the paper over and write down how you want things to change. Write about how this situation could be better and how would it make you feel if everything goes the way you want. Write down what you would like to see happen instead of what is actually happening. Fill this side of the page with positives. Once you are done, roll the paper up. Light the roll of paper with the candle and let it burn in the fireproof container. As the smoke swirls in the air, watch the negativity dissipate into the air. The positives are sent out into the universe to reach out to the people who have been involved in all of the fighting. Visualize the negativity dispersing into the air, and the positives reaching out to those family members who need it. When the paper is consumed and the smoke all gone, extinguish your candle and close your circle.

To deal with this problem in the mundane world, let your family members know how you feel about their behavior. Let them know you are disappointed in them, offer alternatives, but don't get pulled into the drama. Walk away when necessary.

Bibliography

Connor, Kerri. *The Pocket Spell Creator: Magickal References at Your Fingertips.* Franklin Lakes, NJ: New Page Books, 2003.

Conway, D. J. *Moon Magick: Myth & Magic, Crafts and Recipes, Rituals & Spells.* St. Paul, MN: Llewellyn, 2002.

Cunningham, Scott. *Cunningham's Encyclopedia of Crystal, Gem & Metal Magic.* St. Paul, MN: Llewellyn, 1992.

———. *Magical Aromatherapy: The Power of Scent.* St. Paul, MN: Llewellyn, 2000.

Dugan, Ellen. *Garden Witchery: Magick from the Ground Up.* Woodbury, MN: Llewellyn, 2006.

———. *Garden Witch's Herbal: Green Magick, Herbalism and Spirituality.* Woodbury, MN: Llewellyn, 2009.